INTERNATIONAL
AND
REGIONAL
CONFLICT

The Peace Science Studies Series
edited by Walter Isard

INTERNATIONAL AND REGIONAL CONFLICT
Analytic Approaches

Edited by

WALTER ISARD

Cornell University

and

YOSHIMI NAGAO

Kyoto University

International Standard Book Number: 0-88410-030-8

Library of Congress Catalog Card Number: 82-22692

Printed in the United States of America

Library of Congress Cataloging in Publication Data
Main entry under title:

International and regional conflict.

Includes index.
1. International relations — Research — Congresses.
I. Isard, Walter.   II. Nagao, Yoshimi, 1922—   .
JX1291.I425 1983   327.1'6'072   82-22692
ISBN 0-88410-030-8

Contents

List of Figures

List of Tables

Preface

Conflicts between individuals, groups, and nations often become manifest when one of these units makes a decision to take action in furtherance of one of its goals. These conflicts result from the fact that each has differing and mutually exclusive interests.

At a corporate or governmental level, conflicts over policy may arise both within and between the respective units. Controversies over the construction of such public facilities as highways, airports, or nuclear power plants are examples of such conflicts. These conflicts arise because benefits from a proposed facility are not necessarily distributed impartially.

At the international level, it may be said that all relationships among nations contain issues over which conflicts may occur. These controversies and conflicts often prevent the achievement of the original goals and result in disputes or exacerbate continuing ones. War, of course, is an extreme example of the result of such conflicts.

In order to avoid these kinds of outcomes, a decisionmaking process that leads to consensus and cooperation is needed. A necessary step in establishing such a process is to find and develop methods for analyzing the structural characteristics of conflicts, for removing or mitigating points of conflicts, and for arriving at a consensus.

Below the international level, analytical tools of conflict analysis—ranging from those that permit the identification of Pareto-optimal solutions to such modern techniques as multicriteria analysis—have been developed by economists, management scientists, civil engineers, planners, and regional scientists. At the international level, contributions to conflict analysis and resolution have been made by political scientists, economists, and peace scientists, using such approaches as game theory, Delphi, ISM, DEMATEL, and so on.

The wider use of such analytical tools and theories in conflict-laden situations could contribute to the development of scientific and, possibly, universal approaches to problems of conflict resolution. In recognition of this possibility, Professor Walter Isard, in October 1980, wrote and suggested to Professors Tatsuhiko Kawashima, Noboru Sakashita, Hiroyuki Yamada, and me that it would be useful to hold a conference on conflict management to foster contributions to conflict analysis. We considered the suggestion of Professor Isard and decided to hold an international symposium in Kyoto, Japan, in August 1981. This symposium was supported by the World University of the World Academy of Arts and Science, the Kansai Branch of Japan Association for Planning Administration, and the Japan Section of the Peace Science Society, International.

Even though the symposium followed a simple format, I believe that the participants were quite satisfied with the high quality of the contributed papers and the intensive discussions. Topics included axiomatic theories of conflict management, multicriteria analysis and decisionmaking, applied studies of actual international conflicts, and welfare criteria analysis. We felt the symposium was much more successful than we had anticipated.

Given its outcome, I decided that it would be useful to publish the major papers presented in order that the results could be distributed to as wide an audience as possible. I hoped that these papers would make a small contribution to the development of the field of peace science.

The chapters of this book were carefully selected from the larger number of outstanding contributions that were submitted. Unfortunately, limited space prevented the inclusion of all the worthy papers.

It should be noted that the success of the symposium was largely due to the efforts of Professor Walter Isard. I also express my sincere gratitude to those scholars worldwide whose contributions promoted the successful and fruitful outcome of the symposium. In addition, I am very grateful to the members of the Japan orgainizing committee for their efforts and would like to extend special thanks to Professors Masahisa Fujita, Tatsuhiko Kawashima, Katsuhiko Kuroda, and Hisayoshi Morisugi for their cooperations in editing the papers.

Yoshimi Nagao
Kyoto University

1 Introduction

Walter Isard and Bruce Burton

As Professor Nagao indicated in the preface, these papers were presented at a conference designed to foster contributions to conflict analysis and conflict management. The emphasis was on the dissemination and stimulation of creative approaches and ideas, rather than on the discussion of specific topics. Predictably then, the papers deal with a variety of topics, with each, however, making some contribution at the frontiers of our knowledge on conflict. In this short summary paper, we wish to identify these various contributions.

The papers that comprise the chapters of this book can be put roughly into three categories. The first, covering papers by W. Isard and C. Smith, and by J.H.P. Paelinck and P.H. Vossen, advances our abstract thinking on conflict, particularly that relating to the dynamics of learning in conflict situations and to the definition of a proper theory of conflict. The second set of papers, covering those by Y. Leung; Y. Nagao, K. Kuroda, and I. Wakai; R. Funck and U. Blum; P. Nijkamp; and by N. Sakashita, deal with more practical analysis. They relate to value-based decision rules in conflicts involving multiple objectives and decisionmaking units, especially under uncertainty; conflicts among several interest groups with regard to a particular project; conflict among parties with respect to infrastructure development and between regional growth and environmental objectives; conflict in the international system because of dissimilarities of nations; and, finally, conflict among countries induced by an embargo threat.

The third set of papers, covering those by H. Eto and K. Makino; by H. Morisugi; and by M. Fujita, bring to the fore welfare aspects involved in the management of conflict. They relate to the very important problem of the technology gap among developing and developed regions; the welfare implications of cost-benefit analysis; and at a more specific level, the omnipresent conflict between efficiency and equity as objectives in regional development.

We now attempt to state briefly the main contributions of each paper.

CONTRIBUTIONS AT THE ABSTRACT LEVEL

It is generally recognized that most of our tools, theories, conceptual frameworks, and models fail to capture in any significant way the dynamics of reality. A basic aspect of this dynamic is the learning that occurs when debate, discussion, negotiations, and other inter-action takes place among participants in a conflict situation. Isard and Smith attempt a small contribution here, utilizing a dynamical systems approach to replicate an oversimplified learning process.

Initially, the authors present a static-type model to define the labor-allocation problem involved. Each participant must decide how much labor to provide as an input in the assembling, processing, and production of information (data) and how much to consume in leisure and other uses. This is a utility-maximization question.

A second model stipulates the situation where two participants are passive and therefore do not learn from interaction, but where the mediator does. A dynamical system learning model is developed for the leader. The third model, a further dynamical systems model, allows one participant to learn instead of the mediator.

To maintain simplicity, Isard and Smith have not considered the more complex cases where more than one participant can learn. While their models greatly detract from reality, their effort clearly begins to define and account for knowledge accumulation and decumulation processes in workshop and other interaction situations.

J.H.P. Paelinck and P.H. Vossen probe into the problem of extending the theoretical base of conflict study. Their aim is to reduce the global issue of conflict to its simplest state (its fundamental elements), and thereby reduce the confusion that the concept produces.

Initially, the authors present a basic conflict model which, given a set of axioms, is in general a representation of a conflict situation. In the second part of the chapter they test the model with certain conflict situations illustrating that different types of conflict can be clearly distinguished in a very exact and logical manner. The purpose of their research is not to present a method for resolving conflict nor to attempt to define every type of conflict that does or can exist; it is to convince the reader of the usefulness of the axiomatic approach to conflict theory. If one conceives and defines conflict as a concept common to diverse conflict situations and therefore concludes that there should and can be one basic conflict model with many applications, much of the misunderstanding about conflict can be reduced.

CONTRIBUTIONS AT THE APPLIED LEVEL

Along with abstract theoretical research, it is important to conduct studies that focus on applied issues, whether at the level of the individual decisionmaker, a region, or a nation. One of the fundamental problems in this area has been the inability of researchers to formulate models which describe real-world, conflict-resolution processes in such a way that solutions can be logically and mathematically derived. In recognizing this problem, Leung presents a value-based decision approach to conflict management, consisting of multiple objectives and multiple decisionmaking units.

The notions of local ideal and local compromise solutions are formulated as a basis for the resolution within the decisionmaking unit. The proximity between these two measures is often characterized by linguistic terms, such as "close to" or "very close to." These linguistic variables can be described by varying mathematical functions which Leung incorporates into the model. Interaction is therefore allowed to occur between the decision analysts and the decisionmaking units so as to enable adjustment of objectives and alternatives throughout the resolution process.

In his first model, a central coordinating committee is present and has the role of identifying a global ideal. This committee is removed in a second model, and therefore the decisionmaking units' alternative preferences may not be completely revealed. Consequently, a global ideal for all units cannot be derived. Without being able to refer to a global ideal as a reference point, compromise solutions must be proposed among the decisionmaking units.

To account for the inexactness of the analysis, Leung has introduced fuzzy set concepts into the extended framework. This is an important notion, with Leung illustrating how fuzzy set theory is a viable framework for decision analysis in general and more particularly for conflict analysis.

One area of decisionmaking throughout the world that is particularly prone to conflict concerns the evaluation of projects. Nagao, Kuroda, and Wakai propose two methods to assist the decisionmaker in selecting the "best" public project (such as the site for a new road) from a set of alternatives, taking into consideration conflicts that exist among interest groups.

One of the methods pertains to the case where all the alternatives are available for consideration by the public, with the decision process formulated as an n-person, non-zero sum game. Equal weights are given to all representatives with the Majority Power Rule used to define payoffs. The best solution to the game is defined by Schmeilder's concept of "nucleolus," in which the choice of the best alternative is one that minimizes the maximum dissatisfaction a coalition has.

The second case that the authors consider occurs when all of the alternatives are not made available to the public. The decisionmaker is given the option of selecting only one alternative to be presented to the public for its evaluation. The assumptions made are that all criteria for evaluating the alternatives and the utility functions are common to each interest group, and that the only difference among the groups is the scaling constants with which each group weights these criteria. Consequently, the decisionmaking of the executive organization is based on the least favorable of the scaling constants, as the decisionmaker is uncertain as to which one of the scaling constants will produce a consensus.

Of importance is that the authors have recognized that whatever alternative is selected there will exist some group or individual who will not agree with the final decision. Consequently, they have presented a procedure for providing compensation or other adjustment to help reduce this problem.

The evaluation of a region's potential for development and investment is another source of considerable conflict for decisionmakers, especially when there is concern for both growth and environmental objectives. To address this issue, Funck and Blum develop a concept for relating a region's production to its infrastructure. The level of production in a region depends greatly upon the composition of its infrastructure as well as the extent to which these facilities are utilized. It follows that a regional production function can be defined which describes the importance of the various infrastructural categories for assessing a region's income potential. Moreover, the knowledge obtained from these relationships can be used to define regional growth strategies which in turn can be balanced against other interests, such as in the environmental field. If transformation functions for these other conflicting interests can be found, it is then possible to include them in a decision model.

Following a definition of infrastructure and a brief description of the level of infrastructure investments in West Germany, Funck and Blum describe the productive and environmental regional impacts of infrastructure investments. The authors present their decision model to balance productive and environmental interests in the planning and implementation of infrastructural investments. Next they define a model which measures the regional effects of infrastructure investments with respect to the conflicting production and land use goals. Funck and Blum selected data from West Germany to illustrate the applicability of the models.

At the international level, conflict analysis has the objective of identifying the discrepancies and differences in characteristics that exist among nations, or groups of nations, to provide some understanding of the economic or political conflicts which arise. International consensus is considered by Nijkamp as beyond the possibilities of the present international system; hence it is important to determine structural differences among nations. Moreover, due to the highly interdependent structure of the international system, any change in the state of one nation will either directly or indirectly affect the states of other nations because of their interdependencies as trading partners, as members in different international institutions (for example, The United Nations), or in political alliances.

Recognizing that conflict arises from discrepancies among nations, Nijkamp uses multidimensional scaling analysis to identify these discrepancies. In particular he focuses on issues and attributes, and employs differences on these items to explain the differences in behavior among nations and to provide a more rational basis for interpreting international strategy. In turn, this leads to identifying potential conflict and makes more transparent compromise strategies.

A very elusive area of conflict analysis pertains to the impact on power of *threats*. All kinds of notions have been put forth on how threats condition the perception, manner of negotiation, and probability of resolution (or management) of a conflict. Sakashita's chapter on the specific topic of the effect that a threat of an embargo has (in an international system) develops an approach that digs down more deeply than ever into this elusive area of analysis.

The counteraction by resource-importing countries to an embargo threat which has been implemented by resource-exporting countries usually takes the form of a precautionary cutback in the quantity of imports. The level of this cutback is usually in accord with some semi-optimizing scheme, which has the effect of destabilizing the world trade market in that particular resource. This also has harmful consequences on the trading position of exporting countries, who react by adopting a monopolistic approach, which results in a further shrinkage of the world trade market.

The purpose of Sakashita's chapter is first to evaluate the mutual loss effect that an embargo threat produces and then to use these results to identify measures which may resolve the conflict. The conclusions that follow from the analysis stress that both parties should analyze the outcome of all policy options that they have available and start the process of negotiation before the adoption of any retaliatory action. Otherwise, it is likely that everyone will lose out by an embargo, including the exporting nation.

CONTRIBUTIONS TO CONFLICT ANALYSIS AND SOCIAL WELFARE

No one who has studied the international system, no matter how cursorily, is unaware of perhaps the most pervasive and protracted social conflict—namely, that between developed and developing nations. There are many important dimensions of the conflict and many "causes" set forth by experts on it. One basic factor on which there appears to be unanimous agreement is the technology gap between developed and developing nations. Here, Eto and Makino make a general contribution. They identify technology as the most scarce of the development resources. The distribution of technology among nations is considered more skewed than capital or science, as very little transfer of technology occurs between nations. This uneven distribution leads to basic conflict.

The purpose of Eto and Makino's chapter is to present a mathematical model of the technology gap, and hence to provide a tool for analyzing the distribution of technology in the world. They provide empirical verification of the model, obtaining a better fit to the data than for other models based on existing statistical distributions.

To avoid data problems from inadequate time series, Eto and Makino adopt a method of inferring dynamics from static (that is, nontime series) data by applying a stochastic process to their conceptual model to yield a statistical distribution. The Yule distribution is shown to fit better than other skewed distributions, while the Bradford distribution is shown to express effectively the variation and "clusterization" of technology throughout the world.

Welfare disparities are another major source of conflicts; and the problem of conflict resolution is often how to guarantee increase in the welfare of all participants, hopefully in an equitable manner. While Morisugi is not able to address this problem directly and the related problem of equitable social change, he takes a step forward by developing a new and more embrasive framework for cost-benefit analysis. He shows that if social costs and benefits are measured in terms of an equivalent variation index ΣEV, then any proposed social change which satisfies the resulting cost-benefit criterion is guaranteed to improve social welfare in both the Kaldor and Hicksian compensation tests whenever these welfare concepts are well-defined. From this welfare viewpoint he argues that the equivalent variation is more appropriate for measuring social costs and benefits than the compensating variation ΣCV. Emphasized is the fact that all the indices are subject to the same limitation; they can guarantee only the potential Pareto superiority of accepted social changes.

One of the most pressing and widespread sources of conflict arises from the inconsistent objectives of maximizing aggregate efficiency and minimizing interregional discrepancies; no part of the world is free of this problem. In making a specific attack on this critical problem, Fujita employs a simple aggregate model of a two-region economy to assess how agglomeration economies and diseconomies precipitate the conflict between efficiency and equity and also to investigate conflict resolution. By assuming that both regions possess the same production function, it is possible for the analysis to concentrate on the pure effects of agglomeration economies and diseconomies.

Fujita considers the efficient allocation of capital between the two-region economy so as to maximize aggregate income. His first model is static, with the total amount of capital fixed and only its allocation considered. He shows that when the total amount of capital is not excessively abundant, efficient development requires a polarized allocation of capital between the regions. Consequently, if the interregional income transfer is politically infeasible, then the trade-off between aggregate efficiency and interregional equity must be explicitly considered. To this end, he derives transformation curves between regional incomes from which efficiency—equity trade-off curves are obtained.

Fujita recognizes that a definitive account of the problem requires a dynamic approach. Hence he reconsiders the problem within a dynamic framework. The primary concern is the specification of the switching function which regulates investment allocation between regions; generally this is a question of when to start investing in the less developed region, since the more developed region is usually favored at first. The efficient growth process always takes the form of polarized development in the initial stages. Given the efficiency of polarized development, the issue of equity is evident. Consequently Fujita equips his model with a political constraint on income transfer so as to be able to study the efficiency—equity trade-off problem in a dynamic context.

The results Fujita obtains are useful. However, as he is well aware, they are based on a number of simplifying assumptions. Consequently it is recognized that to deepen the theory and make it more comprehensive, a number of extensions of his model are needed.

This concludes our summary of the 1981 Kyoto Conflict Management Conference papers published here. To reiterate, this book does not purport to present a comprehensive or systematic survey of knowledge on conflict analysis. Rather it consists of a series of papers aimed at pushing back the frontiers of knowledge at a number of important places. We believe this aim has been achieved.

I Contributions at the Abstract Level

2 A Dynamical Systems Approach to Learning Processes in Conflict Mediation and Interaction*

Walter Isard and Christine Smith

In workshops and brainstorming sessions concerned with conflict management, models can emerge of the learning process that scholars from various social science disciplines can study and find effective. In approaching these models here, we are also concerned with the learning process that goes on in many of the recursive interaction procedures (often including multi-objective problems) that regional scientists have been discussing in their writings.[1]

The question we ask is: to what extent can we fruitfully adapt dynamical systems models for replicating or simulating workshops or brainstorming sessions? Furthermore, to what extent can we use these models to select among conflict-management procedures and identify new, superior procedures? Clearly the state of dynamical systems analysis is too primitive to deal with the dynamics of reality, and yet it is worthwhile to see what we can learn from its use. In the following presentation we shall concentrate upon the stock of information as the basic state variable which is undergoing change over time—a variable which many would agree is key in

---

*The valuable assistance of Kai Michaelis in presenting the mathematics is gratefully acknowledged; however, the authors alone are responsible for any errors.

1. See Isard and C. Smith (1983: Ch. 10) for a general discussion of the workshop as a tool for conflict management and the learning process that goes on therein. This chapter follows the notation and definition of concepts presented there.

workshop and interactive sessions. Because of the difficulties of dynamical systems analysis we shall not consider changes in any other key variable.

In our dynamical systems analysis, we posit that at the start each behaving unit (participant, mediator, and others) possesses a stock of knowledge. Each then utilizes this stock plus the labor and other stocks and resources that the person commands to maximize satisfaction (utility, pay-off, profit) over a time period perceived as relevant. This time period may be considered a planning horizon. In allocating resources among diverse activities to maximize satisfaction, the individual considers the utility from use of resources for: (1) current consumption; (2) the production of other goods for current and possibly future consumption; and (3) the production of new information to serve as capital, thereby to make the future use of resources in production much more effective.

To keep things simple we shall assume only two participants, J and L, and a mediator, Z. Our first model is constructed for pedagogical purposes alone. It is a static-type model designed to familiarize the reader with the notation and to present the problem more sharply. A second model posits a situation wherein both the participants J and L are passive, that is, do not learn from interaction; the mediator, however, does. A third model posits a situation wherein one participant, say, J, does learn; the mediator and L are passive and do not learn.

A BACKGROUND STATIC-TYPE MODEL

For the first model we employ Figure 2–1. We associate with each participant J and L a box C^J and C^L, respectively, which covers the cognitive decisionmaking activities of that participant. The contents of this box as well as the I box to be mentioned immediately below are fully described in Isard (1979, 1980). Associated with the mediator Z is the I box, which corresponds to the political arena in which debate, discussion, and interaction take place. For our purposes here, however, we may also view the upper part of this box as the C^Z box. The M box corresponds to system information, and again its contents and relationships to the other boxes are fully presented in Isard (1979, 1980).

Associated with each participant and the mediator is a "two-goods"

Figure 2–1.   Static Model of Workshop-Type Interactions

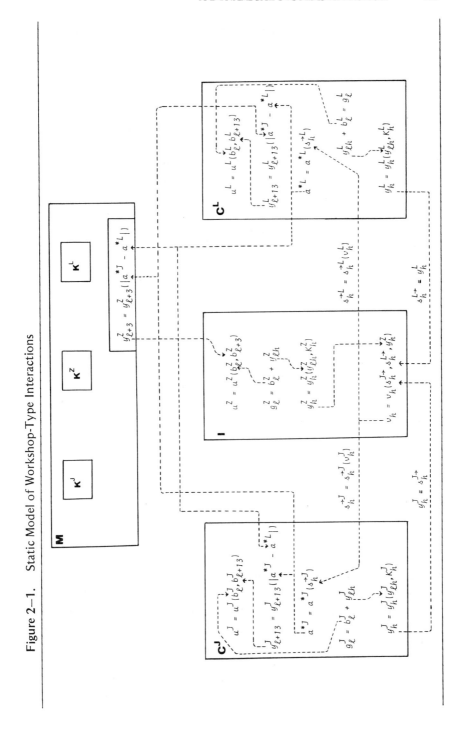

utility function as indicated at the top of the relevant box. For example, for J, the utility function is

$$u^J = u^J(b_l^J, b_{l+13}^J).$$

Here b_l stands for the consumption of leisure (non-use of labor), and all other goods obtainable through exchange for labor or from production generated by the direct use of labor. Also, b_{l+13} is taken to be consumption of the good c-security although the reader may wish to view it as some composite of noneconomic goods. In equation (2–1), u^L (the utility of participant L) is not included as a relevant variable, although Burton and other workshop analysts would include it (see Isard and C. Smith 1983: Ch. 10).

We take J to be male and a self-interested participant. He is motivated to maximize his utility, subject to his labor constraint:

$$g_l^J = b_l^J + y_{lh}^J$$

(2–2)

where g_l^J is his currently available amount (say, twenty-four hours) of labor; y_{lh}^J is the amount of his currently available labor which he explicitly decides to use in the production of information; and b_l^J is the amount of this labor devoted to normal economic pursuits and leisure, and may be viewed as a residual once the amount y_{lh}^J is determined.

The production function for J is, in its simplest form:

$$y_h^J = y_h^J(y_{lh}^J, K_h^J)$$

(2–3)

which is depicted in the lower part of the C^J box. J's stock of knowledge, K_h^J, is assumed constant in this version of the model.

The second good b_{l+13}^J entering J's utility function is the amount of c-security he comes to possess and currently consume. (C-security is a good which cannot be diminished by consumption (see Isard and C. Smith 1983: Ch. 10)). The amount of c-security y_{l+13}^J produced, which, as we have already noted, becomes available for immediate consumption, is a function of (inversely related to) the absolute difference ($|a^{*J} - a^{*L}|$) between the most preferred joint actions of the two participants. That is, as indicated in the C^J box:[2]

$$y_{l+13}^J = y_{l+13}^J (|a^{*J} - a^{*L}|) \qquad (2\text{-}4)$$

The most preferred proposal of a participant, say, J, is dependent upon the information $s_h^{\rightarrow J}$ he obtains from debate, discussion, and interaction within the political arena. That is, as indicated in the C^J box:

$$a^{*J} = a^{*J}(s_h^{\rightarrow J}) \qquad (2\text{-}7)$$

and symmetrically for L, we have

$$a^{*L} = a^{*L}(s_h^{\rightarrow L}). \qquad (2\text{-}8)$$

The information $s_h^{\rightarrow J}$ and $s_h^{\rightarrow L}$ received by J and L, respectively, is a function of the total interaction v_h in the political arena. That is, as indicated between the I and C^J, and the I and C^L boxes, respectively:[3]

2. Our measure of difference, which is here a distance, requires that if there are two or more dimensions relevant for defining a joint action, then there exists a constant with appropriate units which transforms (equates) one unit of distance on any one dimension to a unit on any other second dimension. Although a general Minkowski metric could be employed to measure $|a^{*J} - a^{*L}|$, the reader may find it more convenient to think in terms of the more familiar Euclidian metric. An alternative, $(a^{*J} - a^{*L})^2$, would result in a relation which has nicer mathematical properties.

Note that when there are more than two participants, we need to specify differently equations (2–4) and (2–24) which show how the noneconomic commodities c-security and c-respect, respectively, are produced. For example, when we refer to L and c-security, among possible specifications are

$$y_{l+13}^L = y_{l+13}^L \left(\max_{Q,Q'} |a^{*Q} - a^{*Q'}| \right) \qquad Q, Q' = L, J, J', J'' \ldots \qquad (2\text{-}5)$$

and

$$y_{l+13}^L = y_{l+13}^L \left(\sum_{Q,Q'} |a^{*Q} - a^{*Q'}| \right) \qquad Q, Q' = L, J, J', J'' \ldots \qquad (2\text{-}6)$$

The former focuses on the range, paying no attention to the differences between proposal pairs within that range. The latter focuses on a simple summation of differences, without paying attention to the size distribution of these differences. Still other specifications might associate weights with the proposals of each pair of participants, and so forth.

3. We make the strong assumption that all information produced by any mediator or participant is "good" information in that it leads to more good debate, discussion, and interaction which in turn enables participants to narrow down their differences. Thus the partial derivatives in equations (2–9), (2–10), and (2–11) are all positive, and we assume that other partials to be noted below have the sign implied by this assumption. When this is not the case, interaction may lead to escalation rather than resolution of the conflict.

$$s_h^{\rightarrow J} = s_h^{\rightarrow J}(v_h) \tag{2-9}$$

$$s_h^{\rightarrow L} = s_h^{\rightarrow L}(v_h). \tag{2-10}$$

In turn this interaction, as indicated in the I box, is a function of information $s_h^{J\rightarrow}$, $s_h^{L\rightarrow}$, and y_h^Z provided (transmitted) by participants J, L, and the mediator Z, respectively, namely[4]

$$v_h = v_h(s_h^{J\rightarrow}, s_h^{L\rightarrow}, y_h^Z) \tag{2-11}$$

Note that as indicated in Figure 2–1 we are assuming that all the information y_h^J and y_h^L produced, respectively, by J and L is transmitted to the political arena. That is,

$$s_h^{J\rightarrow} \equiv y_h^J \tag{2-12}$$

$$s_h^{L\rightarrow} \equiv y_h^L. \tag{2-13}$$

The y_h^J and y_h^L, as we have already noted, are produced in the C^J and C^L boxes, respectively, and we have taken them to be a function of the inputs of labor y_{lh}^J and y_{lh}^L, respectively. This then brings us back to the basic decision which the individual J must face: given his labor constraint, how much labor should be put into current production in order indirectly to produce and consume c-security, namely, b_{i+13}^J, and thus how much to consume in leisure, and other uses, namely, b_i^J? Formally speaking, the answer to this question when all functions are well behaved is given by the first-order condition for maximization of his utility associated with his single control variable y_{lh}^J (or b_i^J). To derive it (bearing in mind that the amount b_{i+13}^J of c-security realized depends not only on J's input of labor for producing information, but also the inputs of L and Z,

---

4. We assume here and subsequently that there is no transmission (transport) cost in or resistance (lack of receptivity) to the flow of information. Also here as well as later we must reiterate that what is important for J is not an actual magnitude (state) of a variable (whether quantitative or qualitative) but rather his perception of that magnitude. To conduct a dynamical systems analysis, however, it is necessary to ignore the perception factor, or where possible, embody it in a mathematical function.

Additionally, with regard to equations (2–9) and (2–10) we could make explicit a process whereby J inputs labor to filter out relevant information v_h generated by the interaction. Such filtering or similar processes like scanning may also occur elsewhere within the system to which we will henceforth not refer.

and using the constraint (2–2)), assuming an interior maximum,[5] our problem is:

$$\max u^J = u^J[(g_l^J - y_{lh}^J), b_{l+13}^J(y_{lh}^J, y_{lh}^L, y_{lh}^Z)] \qquad (2\text{–}14)$$

for which, given y_{lh}^L, y_{lh}^Z, we set

$$\frac{du^J}{dy_{lh}^L} = 0$$

which implies

$$\frac{\delta u^J}{\delta(g_l^J - y_{lh}^J)}\frac{\delta(g_l^J - y_{lh}^J)}{\delta y_{lh}^J} + \frac{\delta u^J}{\delta b_{l+13}^J}\frac{\delta b_{l+13}^J}{\delta y_{lh}^J} = 0. \qquad (2\text{–}15)$$

Since

$$\frac{\delta u^J}{\delta b_l^J} = \frac{\delta u^J}{\delta(g_l^J - y_{lh}^J)}$$

and

$$\frac{\delta(g_l^J - y_{lh}^J)}{\delta y_{lh}^J} = -1,$$

5. When this assumption is relaxed, we set up the Lagrangian

$$L^J = u^J[(g_l^J - y_{lh}^J), b_{l+13}^J(y_{lh}^J, y_{lh}^L, y_{lh}^Z)] - \lambda^J(g_l^J - y_{lh}^J) - \mu_l^J(-y_{lh}^J)$$

$$(2\text{–}16)$$

which leads to the following first-order conditions:

$$\frac{dL^J}{dy_{lh}^J} = 0 = -\frac{\delta u^J}{\delta(g_l^J - y_{lh}^J)}\delta(g_l^J - y_{lh}^J) + \frac{\delta u^J}{\delta b_{l+13}^J}\frac{\delta b_{l+13}^J}{\delta y_{lh}^J} + \lambda^J + \mu^J \quad (2\text{–}17)$$

$$\lambda^J(g_l^J - y_{lh}^J) = 0; \qquad g_l^J - y_{lh}^J \geqslant 0; \qquad \lambda^J \geqslant 0 \qquad (2\text{–}18)$$

$$\mu^J(-y_{lh}^J) = 0; \qquad y_{lh}^J \geqslant 0; \qquad \mu^J \geqslant 0. \qquad (2\text{–}19)$$

Note that it is not possible for *both* λ^J and μ^J to be greater than zero; λ^J can be greater than zero only if $g_l^J - y_{lh}^J = 0$; and μ^J can be greater than zero only if $y_{lh}^J = 0$. In equation (2–16), λ^J represents the welfare (shadow price) to J were he to have another unit in his initial stock of labor; and μ^J represents the welfare (shadow price) to J *were* he able to go into debt for one unit of labor input.

we obtain[6]

$$\frac{\delta u^J}{\delta b_l^J} = \frac{\delta u^J}{\delta b_{l+13}^J} \, \frac{\delta b_{l+13}^J}{\delta y_{lh}^J}. \tag{2-20}$$

From equation (2–20) we see that to maximize his utility, J should allocate his labor between leisure and production of c-security in such a way that the marginal utility of labor in leisure and other uses (that is, $\partial u^J / \partial b_l^J$) comes to equal the utility of that c-security derivable from his marginal unit of labor engaged in the production

of information $\left(\text{that is, } \dfrac{\partial u^J}{\partial b_{l+13}^J} \, \dfrac{\partial b_{l+13}^J}{\partial y_{lh}^J}\right)$.[7]

Note that in this model, the variable K_h^J, J's stock of information does not enter since this stock as well as L's and the mediator's does not change. This is a basic assumption of our static model which must be relaxed when we proceed to the next models involving dynamic elements.

For the second participant, L, the exact same type of analysis pertains. For the mediator Z (whom we take to be female), however, we have a slightly different problem. Z's utility function is related not to the consumption of c-security but to the consumption of

6. In longhand form, the righthand side of the equation may be written:

$$\frac{\delta u^J}{\delta b_{l+13}^J} \, \frac{\delta b_{l+13}^J}{\delta y_{l+13}^J} \, \frac{\delta y_{l+13}^J}{\delta (|a^{J*} - a^{L*}|)}$$

$$\left[\frac{\delta (|a^{J*} - a^{L*}|)}{\delta a^{J*}} \, \frac{\delta a^{J*}}{\delta s_h^{\rightarrow J}} \, \frac{\delta s_h^{\rightarrow J}}{\delta v_h} \, \frac{\delta v_h}{\delta s_h^{J \rightarrow}} \, \frac{\delta s_h^{J \rightarrow}}{\delta y_h^J} \, \frac{\delta y_h^J}{\delta y_{lh}^J} \right.$$

$$\left. + \frac{\delta (|a^{J*} - a^{L*}|)}{\delta a^{L*}} \, \frac{\delta a^{L*}}{\delta s_h^{\rightarrow L}} \, \frac{\delta s_h^{\rightarrow L}}{\delta v_h} \, \frac{\delta v_h}{\delta s_h^{J \rightarrow}} \, \frac{\delta s_h^{J \rightarrow}}{\delta y_h^J} \, \frac{\delta y_h^J}{\delta y_{lh}^J} \right] \tag{2-21}$$

7. It does not necessarily follow that at all points of time the individual does input his labor to produce information. At some if not many or all points of time, the marginal utility of labor in leisure and other uses may exceed whatever utility may result for J from the information he may produce with any labor.

c-respect, namely, b^Z_{l+3}. That is, as noted in the upper part of the I box,

$$u^Z = u^Z(b^Z_l, b^Z_{l+3}) \qquad (2\text{–}22)$$

Z, too, is subject to a labor constraint, namely,

$$g^Z_l = b^Z_l + y^Z_{lh}. \qquad (2\text{–}23)$$

She faces the problem of how to allocate her current available amount g^Z_l of labor for consumption b^Z_l in leisure and other uses and as an input y^Z_{lh} in the production of information which ultimately will yield her c-respect for current consumption.

The production of this c-respect is a function of the differences between the most preferred joint actions of J and L, that is:[8]

$$y^Z_{l+3} = y^Z_{l+3}(|a^{*J} - a^{*L}|). \qquad (2\text{–}24)$$

The production of this c-respect represents the bestowal by the world community of c-respect upon Z according to the degree of success she achieves in reducing the difference between these most preferred joint actions. Therefore, the production of c-respect is indicated in Figure 2–1 as taking place within the M box, and c-respect flows from this box to the mediator's utility function. As already noted, a^{*J} and a^{*L} are given by equations (2–7) and (2–8) which are related to $\vec{s}_h^{\,J}$ and $\vec{s}_h^{\,L}$, respectively. These information flows in turn derive from the debate, discussion, and interaction, namely v_h, which is given by equation (2–11). Note that in that equation the information y^Z_h produced by Z enters as a basic input which thus comes to influence the difference $(|a^{*J} - a^{*L}|)$. The amount of y^Z_h produced, however, is a function

---

8. Whereas in equation (2–4) we visualize J and L each obtaining more and more c-security for current consumption as the difference $|a^{*J} - a^{*L}|$ becomes smaller and smaller, the reader may hesitate to accept the notion that Z obtains more and more c-respect as that same distance becomes smaller and smaller. She may hesitate to do so because in certain real conflict situations only a negligible amount of c-respect is accorded the mediator until a compromise solution is actually achieved—for example, until a treaty is signed. Analytically this would cause problems with our formulation involving well-behaved, continuous functions. We can avoid the problem, however by, employing a function such as

$$y^Z_{l+3} = 1 - (|a^{*J} - a^{*L}|)^{1/10,000} + c \qquad (2\text{–}25)$$

where c is a constant depending upon the maximum distance. Specifically we set

$$c = \max(|a^{*J} - a^{*L}|)^{1/10,000} - 1$$

of the labor input y_{lh}^Z that Z makes and the fixed capital stock K_h^Z of information. As indicated in the I box:

$$y_h^Z = y_h^Z(y_{lh}^Z, K_h^Z). \qquad (2-26)$$

Hence, to repeat, the mediator, like each participant, faces the labor-allocation problem—namely, how much labor to provide as an input to produce information (which ultimately determines in part how much c-respect she consumes) and how much residually to consume in leisure and other uses. Formally speaking, the answer to this question when all functions are well behaved is given by the first-order conditions for maximization of her utility associated with her single control variable y_{lh}^Z (or b_l^Z). To derive it (bearing in mind that the amount b_{l+3}^Z of c-respect to be realized depends not only on her input of labor for producing information but also those of J and L, and using the constraint (2–23)), assuming an interior maximum,[9] our problem is:

$$\max u^Z = u^Z[(g_l^Z - y_{lh}^Z), b_{l+3}^Z(y_{lh}^J, y_{lh}^L, y_{lh}^Z)] \qquad (2-27)$$

for which, given y_{lh}^J, y_{lh}^L we set

$$\frac{du^Z}{dy_{lh}^Z} = 0$$

which implies

$$\frac{\delta u^Z}{\delta(g_l^Z - y_{lh}^Z)} \frac{\delta(g_l^Z - y_{lh}^Z)}{\delta y_{lh}^Z} + \frac{\delta u^Z}{\delta b_{l+3}^Z} \frac{\delta b_{l+3}^Z}{\delta y_{lh}^Z} = 0. \qquad (2-28)$$

Since

$$\frac{\delta u^Z}{\delta b_l^Z} = \frac{\delta u^Z}{\delta(g_l^Z - y_{lh}^Z)}$$

and

$$\frac{\delta(g_l^Z - y_{lh}^Z)}{\delta y_{lh}^Z} = -1,$$

---

9. When this assumption is relaxed, we must set up a Lagrangian, and first-order conditions must be stated in a fashion parallel to that indicated in footnote 5.

we obtain[10]

$$\frac{\delta u^Z}{\delta b_l^Z} = \frac{\delta u^Z}{\delta b_{l+3}^Z} \frac{\delta b_{l+3}^Z}{\delta y_{lh}^Z}.$$ (2-29)

From equation (2-29) we see that to maximize utility, Z should allocate her labor between production of c-respect and consumption in leisure and other uses in such a way that marginal utility of leisure (that is, $\delta u^Z/\delta b_l^Z$) comes to equal her utility of that c-respect derivable from her marginal unit of labor engaged in the production

of information $\left(\text{that is, } \dfrac{\delta u^Z}{\delta b_{l+3}^Z} \dfrac{\delta b_{l+3}^Z}{\delta y_{lh}^Z}\right).$[11]

The above model does not guarantee the compatibility of the necessary conditions for equilibrium of the three participants J, L, and Z. To ensure compatibility certain very strong assumptions must be made about the utility functions on the participants. These restrictions are formally stated in Lemma 1 of Appendix A which contains the proof of compatibility under these restrictions.

A DYNAMICAL SYSTEMS LEARNING MODEL FOR THE MEDIATOR

Having now presented the framework of a static model, we take up a first dynamic model for which Figure 2-2 on p. 30 pertains. In this figure we only indicate those aspects which are different than in

10. In longhand form the righthand side of the equation may be written

$$\frac{\delta u^Z}{\delta b_{l+3}^Z} \frac{\delta b_{l+3}^Z}{\delta y_{l+3}^Z} \frac{\delta y_{l+3}^Z}{\delta(|a^{*J} - a^{*L}|)}$$

$$\left[\frac{\delta(|a^{*J} - a^{*L}|)}{\delta a^{*J}} \frac{\delta a^{*J}}{\delta s_h^{\rightarrow J}} \frac{\delta s_h^{\rightarrow J}}{\delta v_h} \frac{\delta v_h}{\delta y_h^Z} \frac{\delta y_h^Z}{\delta y_{lh}^Z}\right.$$

$$+ \left.\frac{\delta(|a^{*J} - a^{*L}|)}{\delta a^{*L}} \frac{\delta a^{*L}}{\delta s_h^{\rightarrow L}} \frac{\delta s_h^{\rightarrow L}}{\delta v_h} \frac{\delta v_h}{\delta y_h^Z} \frac{\delta y_h^Z}{\delta y_{lh}^Z}\right]$$ (2-30)

11. Note that this formulation of the problem does not imply that complete resolution of the conflict is always achieved. In many situations, particularly when $|a^{*J} - a^{*L}| \to 0$, the marginal utility of leisure and other uses foregone because more labor is required by J and L to reduce this difference any further, comes to exceed the utility gains from additional c-security that may be generated.

Figure 2–1. In the first model only the mediator learns. She learns in the sense that she builds up a stock of relevant knowledge so as to be able to take "more informed" actions, make "more informed" suggestions, and reach "more informed" decisions. Participants J and L do not learn. Hence at any point of time t, when the latter make a decision as to how to allocate their labor, they have comletely forgotten about the knowledge both (1) produced in all previous time periods (whether they or others produced the knowledge); and (2) acquired: for example, regarding the a^{*J} and a^{*L}, during the debate, discussion, and interaction in previous time periods.

Only Z does not forget. While this assumption is extremely strong, it does permit us to chip away at the problem.

Since J and L do not learn, both their situation and behavior are as depicted in the static model. The equation (2–20) is the first-order condition for J's maximization of his utility; and when L replaces J in these equations and J replaces L, it is the first-order condition for L's maximization of utility.

As already indicated, we consider Z's learning as equivalent to building up her stock K_h^Z of information. One of the simplest ways to treat such learning then is to assume that of the information $v_h(t')$ produced at time t' (see equation (2–11)), only a fraction of it comes to be added to the mediator's stock of knowledge—stock of knowledge at the initial point of time t_o being K_{ho}^Z. That is, setting

$$s_h^{\to Z}(t') = v_h(t') \qquad (2\text{–}31)$$

we have the highly simplified "learning" equation[12]

---

12. A more realistic learning equation would include a decay factor in order to preclude unlimited exponential growth in the stock of knowledge. Thus equation (2–32) might be replaced by:

$$\dot{K}_h^Z(t') = s_h^{\to Z}(t') - \alpha(K_h^Z(t'))^\beta \quad \text{with} \quad \alpha > 0 \quad \text{and} \quad \beta > 1$$

where the term $\alpha(K_h^Z(t'))^\beta$ represents "forgetting" and other factors leading to a decrease in Z's stock of knowledge at time t'.

To illustrate, let $s_h^{\to Z} = aK_h^Z$ with $a > 0$, a term which leads to exponential growth of K_h^Z. We then have:

$$\frac{\delta \dot{K}_h^Z}{\delta \overline{K}_h^Z} = a - \alpha\beta(K_h^Z)^{\beta-1} \qquad (2\text{–}33)$$

For $K_h^Z < 1$, we have steadily increasing $\dot{K}_h^Z$ when $a > \alpha\beta$. Also, when $a = \alpha\beta$, $\dot{K}_h^Z$ reaches a maximum when $K_h^Z = 1$ and then starts decreasing, reaching a value of zero (a steady state) for large enough values of K_h^Z. More generally, when $a > \alpha\beta$, $\dot{K}_h^Z$ reaches a maximum for some $K_h^Z > 1$; and when $a < \alpha\beta$, $\dot{K}_h^Z$ reaches a maximum for some $K_h^Z < 1$.

$$\dot{K}_h^Z = \zeta^Z(s_h^{\to Z}(t')) \qquad \text{where} \qquad \frac{\delta \dot{K}_h^Z}{\delta s_h^{\to Z}} < 1. \qquad (2\text{--}32)$$

See Figure 2–2, which shows how the $s_h^{\to Z}(t)$ enters at time $t + 1$ into Z's production function (2–26). The subsequent increase in v_h yields $s_h^{\to Z}(t + 1)$.

Since the increase in the mediator's stock of knowledge at t' makes it possible for her to produce knowledge at later points of time still more effectively than possible without such an increase, the mediator now associates with an increase in a unit of her labor in producing knowledge at t', not only the value of that knowledge at t'. But also, the mediator considers its value as an addition to her capital stock of knowledge in making more productive her labor at producing knowledge at all subsequent points of time, which in turn leads to still greater additions to the stock of knowledge. This enhanced value is then to be compared with the utility from the consumption of leisure and other goods foregone at the current point of time.

Note, however, that because the mediator must now consider the value of currently produced information for use in generating additional information at succeeding points of time, the mediator must necessarily be concerned with the stream of utility flows over all these points of time and with the maximization of this stream and no longer with the maximization of her utility at the current point of time.[13]

In brief, leaving out the time argument t, the problem is to select a time path for $y_{lh}^Z \equiv g_l^Z - b_l^Z$ so as to

$$\max \int_{t_0}^{t_1} u^Z \left[(g_l^Z - y_{lh}^Z), b_{l+3}^Z(y_{lh}^Z, y_{lh}^J, y_{lh}^L)\right] dt' + G^Z(K_h^Z(t_1))$$

$$(2\text{--}34)$$

for the relevant time-horizon or planning period t_0 to t_1, where t_1 may in some cases correspond to the time when the mediation process ends, and where $G^Z(K_h^Z(t_1))$ corresponds to the value, often designated scrap value, of the stock of knowledge at the end

---

13. In the usual problem, utility at a future point of time is appropriately discounted (upcounted). However, here we avoid such complication and the associated additional notation by assuming a zero discount rate.

of planning period t_1. At every point of time t' the mediator is subject to the learning equation (2—32).[14]

To obtain first-order conditions for the mediator to maximize her utility in this new, learning situation, we set up the current Hamiltonian[15]

$$H^Z = u^Z [(g_l^Z - y_{lh}^Z), b_{l+3}^Z (y_{lh}^Z, y_{lh}^J, y_{lh}^L)] + \beta_h^Z [\zeta^Z (s_h^{\to Z})].$$

$$(2—35)$$

Assuming that the above function attains an interior maximum,[16] the maximum principle with respect to the control variable y_{lh}^Z, given y_{lh}^J and y_{lh}^L, is $dH^Z/dy_{lh}^Z = 0$ which, in accord with the discussion associated with equations (2—15) through (2—20) and (2—28) and (2—29), yields[17]

$$\frac{du^Z}{db_l^Z} = \frac{\delta u^Z}{\delta b_{l+3}^Z} \frac{\delta b_{l+3}^Z}{\delta y_{lh}^Z} + \beta_h^Z \left[\frac{\delta \zeta^Z}{\delta s_h^{\to Z}} \frac{\delta s_h^{\to Z}}{\delta v_h} \frac{\delta v_h}{\delta y_h^Z} \frac{\delta y_h^Z}{\delta y_{lh}^Z} \right]; \qquad (2—36)$$

and the canonical equation

$$\frac{\delta H^Z}{\delta K_h^Z} = -\dot{\beta}_h^Z$$

14. And, of course, an initial condition where $K_h^Z(t_o) = K_{ho}^Z$ where K_{ho}^Z is Z's initial stock of knowledge at the initial point of time t_o.

15. Strictly speaking the utility function u^Z should include K_h^Z as an argument. Following conventional practice, however, we assume that Z derives no utility directly from holding a capital stock.

16. When this assumption is relaxed, we need to maximize the Hamiltonian using a Lagrangrian formulation similar to that discussed in footnote 5.

17. The longhand expression for $\dfrac{\delta u^Z}{\delta b_{l+3}^Z} \dfrac{\delta b_{l+3}^Z}{\delta y_{lh}^Z}$ is given in equation (2—30).

yields[18]

$$\dot{\beta}_h^Z = -\frac{\delta u^Z}{\delta b_{l+3}^Z}\frac{\delta b_{l+3}^Z}{\delta K_h^Z} - \beta_h^Z\left[\frac{\delta \zeta^Z}{\delta s_h^{\to Z}}\frac{\delta s_h^{\to Z}}{\delta v_h}\frac{\delta v_h}{\delta y_h^Z}\frac{\delta y_h^Z}{\delta K_h^Z}\right].$$

$$(2-37)$$

We know from equation $(2-37)$ that β_h^Z is the value generated by an additional unit of capital stock of information.[19] This value

18. The longhand expression for $\dfrac{\delta u^Z}{\delta b_{l+3}^Z}\dfrac{\delta b_{l+3}^Z}{\delta K_h^Z}$ is

$$\frac{\delta u^Z}{\delta b_{l+3}^Z}\frac{\delta b_{l+3}^Z}{\delta y_{l+3}^Z}\frac{\delta y_{l+3}^Z}{\delta (|a^{*J}-a^{*L}|)}$$

$$\left[\frac{\delta (|a^{*J}-a^{*L}|)}{\delta a^{*J}}\frac{\delta a^{*J}}{\delta s_h^{\to J}}\frac{\delta s_h^{\to J}}{\delta v_h}\frac{\delta v_h}{\delta y_h^Z}\frac{\delta y_h^Z}{\delta y_{lh}^Z}\right.$$

$$\left.+\frac{\delta (|a^{*J}-a^{*L}|)}{\delta a^{*L}}\frac{\delta a^{*L}}{\delta s_h^L}\frac{\delta s_h^{\to L}}{\delta v_h}\frac{\delta v_h}{\delta y_h^Z}\frac{\delta y_h^Z}{\delta y_{lh}^Z}\right]. \qquad (2-38)$$

Strictly speaking, we should add to the two conditions in the text the following:

$$\frac{\delta H^Z}{\delta \beta_h^Z} = \dot{K}_h^Z = \zeta^Z(s_h^{\to Z}) \qquad (2-39)$$

$$K_h^Z(t_o) = K_{ho}^Z \qquad (2-40)$$

and

$$\beta_h^Z(t_1) = \frac{\delta G^Z(K_h^Z(t_1))}{\delta K_h^Z}. \qquad (2-41)$$

19. For any t, this is seen by multiplying both sides by dt' and integrating to obtain

$$\int_t^{t_1}\dot{\beta}_h^Z(t')dt' = -\int_t^{t_1}\left(\frac{\delta u^Z}{\delta b_{l+3}^Z}\frac{\delta b_{l+3}^Z}{\delta K_h^Z}\right)dt'$$

$$-\int_t^{t_1}\beta_h^Z\left(\frac{\delta \zeta^Z}{\delta s_h^{\to Z}}\frac{\delta s_h^{\to Z}}{\delta v_h}\frac{\delta v_h}{\delta y_h^Z}\frac{\delta y_h^Z}{\delta K_h^Z}\right)dt' \qquad (2-42)$$

so that performing the integration of the RHS and other operations we get

$$\beta_h^Z(t) = \int_t^{t_1}\left(\frac{\delta u^Z}{\delta b_{l+3}^Z}\frac{\delta b_{l+3}^Z}{\delta K_h^Z}\right)dt' + \int_t^{t_1}\beta_h^Z\left(\frac{\delta \zeta^Z}{\delta s_h^{\to Z}}\frac{\delta s_h^{\to Z}}{\delta v_h}\frac{\delta v_h}{\delta y_h^Z}\frac{\delta y_h^Z}{\delta K_h^Z}\right)dt' + \beta_h^Z(t_1).$$

$$(2-43)$$

is the sum of three parts. The first two parts represent values stemming from the presence of that additional unit of capital stock in the production function of equation (2–26). As a result, the output of information (y_h^Z) is increased currently and at each subsequent point of time, and leads to increased utility from the resulting greater output of c-respect (b_{l+3}^Z) currently and at each subsequent point of time. This is indicated in the first term of equation (2–37) and constitutes the first part of the value of β_h^Z. The second part results from the fact that the above increase in output of information (y_h^Z) currently and at each subsequent point of time leads to increase in $s_h^{\to Z}$ and thus Z's stock of knowledge currently and at each subsequent point of time. Each unit of this additional stock has a value $\beta_h^Z(t')$. The third part constitutes the scrap value of a unit of K_h^Z at time t_1.

Thus, as anticipated, equation (2–36) equates the marginal utility of leisure with the utility from c-respect directly derived from the value of the marginal unit of labor in producing c-respect (the first term on the RHS of equation (2–36) plus the value β_h^Z of a unit of capital (stock of information) times the number of units of capital (that is, $s_h^{\to Z}$ or v_h) produced by the marginal unit of labor, a fraction of which by equations (2–31) and (2–32) is automatically added to Z's capital stock).

A DYNAMICAL SYSTEMS LEARNING
MODEL FOR A PARTICIPANT

A third model, again a dynamical systems model, but one which is as simplified as the previous one, allows only one participant, say, L, and not the mediator Z, to learn. It is easily seen that the format and conditions of the model are exactly the same as the previous model except that L's stock of knowledge, K_h^L, changes while Z's stock, K_h^Z, does not.[20]

Again, however, we must be explicit about our assumptions. We are assuming that J and Z do not learn, a very strong assumption, as we already noted.

In this third model, both J's and Z's situation and behavior is as

20. A figure very similar to Figure 2–2 can be constructed to depict the changes in the stock of knowledge of L.

depicted in the static model. Equation (2–20) is the first-order condition for J's maximization of his utility, and equation (2–29) is the same for Z's maximization of her utility. For L, the problem is different than in the static model since now L must associate with any increase in a unit of labor in producing knowledge at t' not only the value of that knowledge at t' but also its value as addition to the stock of knowledge (capital) in making labor more productive at all subsequent points of time. This enhanced value is then to be compared with the utility from the unit of leisure foregone at the current point of time.

In brief, L must consider the stream of utility flows over all points of time from t' to t_1 and with the maximization of this stream. The problem is then to

$$\max \int_t^{t_1} u^L \left[(g_l^L - y_{lh}^L), b_{l+13}^L (y_{lh}^J, y_{lh}^L, y_{lh}^Z) \right] dt' + G^L (K_h^L (t_1))$$

$$t < t' < t_1 \qquad\qquad (2-44)$$

and where in our simplified fashion we postulate

$$\dot{K}_h^L (t') = \zeta^L (s_h^{\rightarrow L} (t')) \qquad \text{where} \qquad \frac{\delta \dot{K}^L}{\delta s_h^{\rightarrow L}} < 1. \qquad (2-45)$$

That is, L's increase in the stock of knowledge at t' is equal to flow of information received from debate, discussion, and interaction in the workshop.

Paralleling equation (2–35) we set up the current Hamiltonian

$$H^L = u^L \left[(g_l^L - y_{lh}^L), b_{l+13}^L (y_{lh}^J, y_{lh}^L, y_{lh}^Z) \right] + \beta_h^L \left[\zeta^L (s_h^{\rightarrow L}) \right].$$

$$(2-46)$$

Assuming that the above function attains an interior maximum,[21] the maximum principle with respect to the control variable y_{lh}^L yields[22]

---

21. When this assumption is relaxed, we need to maximize the Hamiltonian using a Lagrangian formulation similar to that discussed in footnote 5.

22. The longhand expression for $\dfrac{\delta u^L}{\delta b_{l+13}^L} \dfrac{\delta b_{l+13}^L}{\delta y_{lh}^L}$ is as given in equation (2–21) once the symbol L replaces J and vice versa.

$$\frac{du^L}{db_l^L} = \frac{\delta u^L}{\delta b_{l+13}^L} \frac{\delta b_{l+13}^L}{\delta y_{lh}^L} + \beta_h^L \left[\frac{\delta \zeta^L}{\delta s_h^{\to L}} \frac{\delta s_h^{\to L}}{\delta v_h} \frac{\delta v_h}{\delta s_h^{L \to}} \frac{\delta s_h^{L \to}}{\delta y_h^L} \frac{\delta y_h^L}{\delta y_{lh}^L} \right]$$

$$(2-47)$$

The canonical equation yields[23]

$$\dot{\beta}_h^L = - \frac{\delta u^L}{\delta b_{l+13}^L} \frac{\delta b_{l+13}^L}{\delta K_h^L} - \beta_h^L \left[\frac{\delta \zeta^L}{\delta s_h^{\to L}} \frac{\delta s_h^{\to L}}{\delta v_h} \frac{\delta v_h}{\delta s_h^{L \to}} \frac{\delta s_h^{L \to}}{\delta y_h^L} \frac{\delta y_h^L}{\delta y_{lh}^L} \right].$$

$$(2-48)$$

The interpretations of these two equations are similar to those of equations (2–36) and (2–37) in the previous model.

CONCLUDING REMARKS

This chapter has made a start at employing dynamical systems analysis to replicate the learning process, particularly as it goes

23. The longhand expression for $\dfrac{\delta u^L}{\delta b_{l+13}^L} \dfrac{\delta b_{l+13}^L}{\delta K_h^L}$ is:

$$\frac{\delta u^L}{\delta b_{l+13}^L} \frac{\delta b_{l+13}^L}{\delta y_{l+13}^L} \frac{\delta y_{l+13}^L}{\delta (|a^{*J} - a^{*L}|)}$$

$$\left[\frac{\delta (|a^{*J} - a^{*L}|)}{\delta a^{*L}} \frac{\delta a^{*L}}{\delta s_h^{\to L}} \frac{\delta s_h^{\to L}}{\delta v_h} \right.$$

$$\left. + \frac{\delta (|a^{*J} - a^{*L}|)}{\delta a^{*J}} \frac{\delta a^{*J}}{\delta s_h^{\to J}} \frac{\delta s_h^{\to J}}{\delta v_h} \right] \frac{\delta v_h}{\delta s_h^{L \to}} \frac{\delta s_h^{L \to}}{\delta y_h^L} \frac{\delta y_h^L}{\delta K_h^L} \qquad (2-49)$$

Strictly speaking, we should add the following to the two conditions in the text:

$$\frac{\delta H^L}{\delta \beta_h^L} = \dot{K}_h^L = \zeta^L(s_h^{\to L}) \qquad (2-50)$$

$$K_h^L(t_o) = K_{ho}^L \qquad (2-51)$$

$$\beta_h^L(t_1) = \frac{\delta G^L(K_h^L(t_1))}{\delta K_h^L}. \qquad (2-52)$$

on in workshops and brainstorming sessions concerned with conflict management. From a practical standpoint, little is gained from this exercise. Moreover, to avoid excessively extended mathematical statements, we have allowed only one participant or mediator to learn. Where more than one learn, their interactions over time involve many effects of different orders of indirectness.

Despite this lack of reality, the effort clearly reveals the need to account for knowledge accumulation and decumulation processes in workshops and other negotiation-type situations. Unfortunately it is also extremely difficult to model these processes since the participants involved: (1) have limited stocks of information and capacity to learn; (2) frequently misperceive outcomes, actions of others, the state of the environment, and so on; and (3) usually possess rather fixed (inflexible) belief patterns. Also the production of information typically is by discrete units, and at times new information may have negative as well as positive effects on the outcome of the conflict-resolution process. Nevertheless this chapter gives some inklings of how to proceed to do more realistic dynamic modeling of these, even though much more work needs to be done: for example, the group equilibrium solution of a Nash-type must be replaced by an interaction mechanism over time which allows for a more accurate specification of conditions under which participants will achieve mutually acceptable and stable outcomes.

APPENDIX A: CONDITIONS FOR AND PROOF OF EXISTENCE (COMPATIBILITY) OF A NASH EQUILIBRIUM FOR J, L, AND Z

Define

$$Y_{lh}^K = [0, g_l^K] \qquad K = L, J, Z$$

$$Y_{lh} = Y_{lh}^J \times Y_{lh}^L \times Y_{lh}^Z$$

$$\bar{y}_{lh}^K = (y_{lh}^J, y_{lh}^L) \quad \left.\begin{matrix} \\ \\ \end{matrix}\right\}$$

$$\bar{Y}_{lh}^K = Y_{lh}^J \times Y_{lh}^L \quad \text{where, for example, } K = Z$$

and let

$$\Psi^K(\bar{y}_{lh}^K) = \max_{y_{lh}^K \in Y_{lh}^K} u^K(y_{lh}^K, \bar{y}_{lh}^K)$$

Figure 2–2. Dynamical systems learning model for a mediator Z

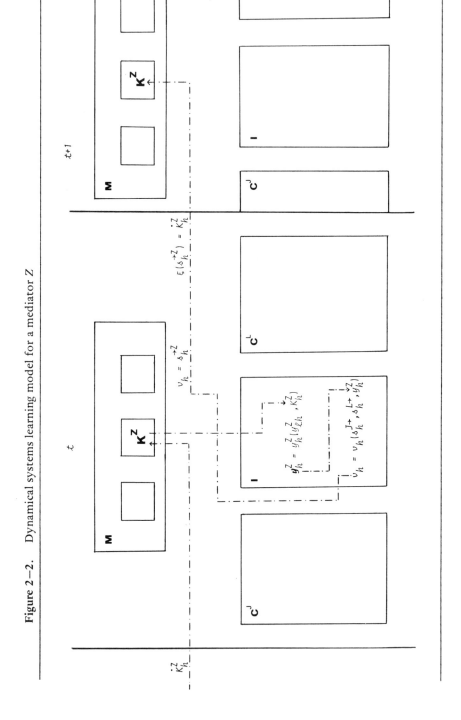

and

$$\Upsilon_{lh}^{K}(\bar{y}_{lh}^{K}) = \{y_{lh}^{K} \in Y_{lh}^{K} | u^{K}(y_{lh}^{K}, \bar{y}_{lh}^{K}) = \Psi^{K}(\bar{y}_{lh}^{K})\}.$$

Lemma 1. If $u^{K}(y_{lh}^{K}, \bar{y}_{lh}^{K})$ is continuous and bounded on Y_{lh} and quasi-concave in y_{lh}^{K} for every $\bar{y}_{lh}^{K}$, then $\Upsilon_{lh}^{K}(\bar{y}_{lh}^{K})$ is nonempty, convex, and compact valued.

Proof. u^{K} is continuous and bounded; Y_{lh}^{K} is compact. Hence u^{K} attains its maximum over Y_{lh}^{K}, and consequently $\Upsilon_{lh}^{K}(\bar{y}_{lh}^{K})$ is nonempty. To show convexity, assume $y^{1}, y^{2} \in \Upsilon_{lh}^{K}(\bar{y}_{lh}^{K}), y^{1} \neq y^{2}$. Then $u^{K}(y^{1}, \bar{y}_{lh}^{K}) = u^{K}(y^{2}, \bar{y}_{lh}^{K})$. Since u^{K} is quasi-concave, $u^{K}(\lambda y^{1} + (1 - \lambda)y^{2}, \bar{y}_{lh}^{K}) \geqslant u^{K}(y^{i}, \bar{y}_{lh}^{K})$, for $0 \leqslant \lambda \leqslant 1$, $i = 1, 2$. But y^{i} maximizes u^{K}, $i = 1, 2$. Hence $u^{K}(y^{i}, \bar{y}_{lh}^{K}) = u^{K}(\lambda y^{1} + (1 - \lambda)y^{2}, \bar{y}_{lh}^{K})$, $i = 1, 2$. So $\lambda y^{1} + (1 - \lambda)y^{2}$ $(0 \leqslant \lambda \leqslant 1)$ also maximizes u^{K}. Then $\lambda y^{1} + (1 - \lambda)y^{2} \in \Upsilon_{lh}^{K}(\bar{y}_{lh}^{K})$ for $0 \leqslant \lambda \leqslant 1$ and hence $\Upsilon_{lh}^{K}(\bar{y}_{lh}^{K})$ is convex. By continuity of u^{K}, $\Upsilon_{lh}^{K}(\bar{y}_{lh}^{K})$ is clearly closed. As subset of the bounded set Y_{lh}^{K}, it is bounded, hence compact.

By the Remark and Theorem in Debreu (1952), *there exists an equilibrium point*, that is, there exists $\tilde{y} \in Y_{lh}, \tilde{y} = (\tilde{y}^{K}, \tilde{\bar{y}}^{K})$ such that for all $K = J, L, Z, u^{K}(\tilde{y}) = \max\limits_{y_{lh}^{K} \in Y_{lh}^{K}} u^{K}(y_{lh}^{K}, \tilde{\bar{y}}^{K})$.

REFERENCES

Debreu, G. 1952. "A Social Equilibrium Existence Theorem." *Proceedings of the National Academy of Sciences* 38:886–893.

Isard, W. 1979. "A Definition of Peace Science, the Queen of the Social Sciences, Part I." *Journal of Peace Science* 4, no. 1:1–47.

———. 1980. "A Definition of Peace Science, the Queen of the Social Sciences, Part II." *Journal of Peace Science* 4, no. 2:97–132.

Isard, W., and P. Liossatos. 1979. *Spatial Dynamics and Optimal Space-Time Development*. Amsterdam: North Holland.

Isard, W., and C. Smith. 1983. *Conflict Analysis and Practical Conflict Management Procedures*. Cambridge, Mass.: Ballinger Publishing Company.

Isard, W.; T. Smith; and others. 1969. *General Theory: Social, Political, Economic and Regional*. Cambridge, Mass.: MIT Press.

3 Axiomatics of Conflict Analysis*

J.H.P. Paelinck and P.H. Vossen

Conflict has been a subject for scientific investigation for quite a long time already (Fink 1968; Patchen 1970; Plasmans and de Zeeuw 1980; Rapoport 1969), and has been approached with empirical as well as logical problems in mind. In this chapter, conflict will be mainly studied as a logical problem; our intention is to contribute to the abstract theory of conflict rather than to concrete empirical matters concerning conflict. The importance of the latter is not to be denied; rather, the fact is emphasized that an adequate general theory of conflict has still to be worked out.

In the first part of this chapter we shall introduce a basic conflict *model* and define the underlying elementary notion of conflict. In the second part we look at certain conflict *situations* to test the basic model; from our analysis it will be clear that different types of conflict can be reduced to specification distinctions between conflict situations which can be made very exact and logical. It is in this sense that our study is interdisciplinary, crossing a number of disciplines and specialities said to belong to the complex of the social and behavioral sciences.

The purpose of this research is not to provide agents in a conflict

*The authors would like to thank J. Prins for his valuable assistance in an extensive literature search during the revision stage of this chapter.

situation with ready-made answers to a (threatening) conflict: agents in a conflict situation are as much components of the problem as designers of a solution to the problem. Just as there are different types of conflict, there are different ways of preventing or resolving conflicts. Furthermore, we will not go into details and technicalities concerning every conflict model that agents could think of; we will, however, be satisfied when we have convinced the reader of the fruitfulness of an axiomatic approach to conflict theory. Much of the confusion in discussions about the concept of conflict can be taken away by acknowledging that there is one common concept and one basic conflict model with many applications to it.

A BASIC CONFLICT MODEL

Axioms and Propositions

To have a clear, logical definition of the concept of conflict it suffices to make use of the elementary mathematical notions of sets and mappings.

Consider the following structure: $\Sigma \triangleq \{A, B, C, S; P\}$. Here A represents a set of agents (or, more generally, a set of points of view), and B represents a set of (behavioral) options (or, more generally, a set of objects for choice). Furthermore, P symbolizes a mapping (called pay-off function) from the product set $A \times B$ to the set C of pay-off values. Finally, S is some subset of C containing all those pay-offs which are considered satisfying.

We call this structure a representation of a conflict situation, if the following axioms are fulfilled:

Axiom 1

A contains at least two different agents:

$$|A| \geqslant 2. \qquad (3-1)$$

Axiom 2

B contains at least two (behavioral) options or objects for choice:

$$|B| \geqslant 2. \qquad (3-2)$$

Axiom 3

C contains at least two different pay-off values and is at least (partially) preordered:

$$\langle C, \geqslant \rangle \quad \text{with} \quad |C| \geqslant 2. \tag{3-3}$$

Axiom 4

S is a non-empty proper subset of C:

$$\phi \subset S \subset C, \quad \bar{S} \cup S = C, \quad \bar{S} \cap S = \phi. \tag{3-4}$$

Axiom 5

The following statements concerning P are true:

1. For all a in A there is some b in B such that $P(a, b)$ is not an element of S: every agent does effectively constrain the space of behavioral options;

$$\forall a \; \exists \; b / P(a, b) \in \bar{S}. \tag{3-5}$$

2. For all b in B there is some a in A such that $P(a, b)$ is an element of S: every behavioral option is, in fact, a satisfactory option for at least one agent;

$$\forall b \; \exists \; a / P(a, b) \in S. \tag{3-6}$$

3. For all a in A there is some b in B such that $P(a, b)$ is an element of S: every agent finds at least one behavioral option satisfactory for him or her;

$$\forall a \; \exists \; b / P(a, b) \in S. \tag{3-7}$$

4. For all b in B there is some a in A such that $P(a, b)$ is not an element of S: every behavioral option is, in fact, disliked by at least one agent;

$$\forall b \; \exists \; a / P(a, b) \in \bar{S}. \tag{3-8}$$

As usual, these axioms are intended to eliminate trival ("non-interesting") and extreme ("pathological") cases from the discussion. However, one can never be sure that these trivial or extreme cases will not—some day—appear really interesting and nonpathological when viewed from a completely different point of view. Axiom 1 excludes the case in which there is no agent at all or no agent to be in conflict with; axiom 2 likewise excludes the case in which there is nothing to choose from. Axiom 3 ensures that different options can be expressed and that these options can at least be ordered on some scale; by axiom 4 two extremes cases can be settled: the one in which all pay-offs are considered unsatisfactory, and the one in which all pay-offs are considered satisfactory. Finally, according to axiom 5, only relevant agents and options should be taken into account; no agent should be unreasonable in the sense of disliking every option; and the conflict should really be about the current options.

The crucial condition is, of course, equation (3–8), that is, no option is satisfactory for all the agents at once. We like to state here two simple but noteworthy conclusions following from these axioms.

Proposition 1

If a structure Σ is in conflict, then any structure Σ' obtained from Σ by including new agents will also be in conflict; only cutting down the set of agents may lead to conflict resolution.

Proof.   Indeed, if $A \subset A'$, then whatever $P \subset P'$, equation (3–8) still holds; conversely, if $A \supset A'$, there may be cases in which (3–8) ceases to hold.

Proposition 2

If a structure Σ is in conflict, then any structure Σ' obtained from Σ by excluding some options from B will also be in conflict; only enlarging the set of options may lead to resolution of the conflict.

Proof.   For, if $B \supset B'$, equation (3–8) continues to hold taking into account the axiom represented by equation (3–5); if $B \subset B'$, this may invalidate (3–8).

It will be clear from these propositions that even for these minimal axioms it is possible to formulate exactly conditions under which conflicts might be resolved; in other words, conflict analysis can proceed along mathematical lines of reasoning.

Finally a word of interpretation: what does it mean to say that there is no conflict in a given situation? Essentially, there are two distinct cases. In the first place, it could happen that there is exactly one behavioral option satisfying all agents; this may seem to be an ideal situation: not only is there no (reason for) conflict but there is also no doubt whatsoever about what to do. In the second place, it could happen that there are several options, all satisfying all the agents; this seems a more common situation: it is possible to avoid a conflict, but there still remains a problem of choosing among several alternatives: on which ground should one pick out one satisfying option rather than another one? Or should one choose on no ground at all (such as by a random process)? Interesting as these questions are, they are not relevant in a discussion about conflict as defined here: they belong to another domain of problemsolving to be discussed later.

Examples

A clear example of a conflict situation is the following. Let $A = \{A1, A2\}$, $B = \{B1, B2\}$, $C = \{0, 1\}$, $S = \{1\}$, and let P be as stated in the following bimatrix:

$A1, A2$	$B1$	$B2$
$B1$	1, 0	0, 0
$B2$	0, 0	0, 1

The off-diagonal entries in this matrix are all set at 0 because it is impossible for some agent to behave simultaneously in two different ways. There is a conflict here because the only behavioral option satisfying the first agent $(A1 \rightarrow B1)$ does not satisfy the second agent $(A2 \rightarrow B2)$.

In terms of the standard model, we arrive at the following interpretation. Value 0 represents a nonsatisfying pay-off, while value 1 represents a satisfying pay-off. According to the last statement of axiom 5, the agents are in conflict if for all behavioral options b there is an agent l such that $P(a, b) = 0$. Using the binary operations MIN and MAX defined on $\{0, 1\}$, this condition of conflict amounts to: $MAX\{MIN\{P(a, b)/a\}/b\} = 0$. Typically, this standard model of conflict proceeds from the assumption that agents appreciate options as simply good or bad; it leaves no room for ambiguity of opinion or errors in the statement of opinions, nor for negotiating the threshold between nonsatisfactory and satisfactory pay-offs. In the next two variants of the basic model, however, this room for negotiation exists.

Let us then take as a second example basic models for which C is $[0, m]$, that is, the interval between 0 and 1, and S is $S(m) = [m, 1]$ for some $m > 0$. These models allow for a continuous scale of pay-offs, called degrees of satisfaction, ranging from completely unsatisfactory (0) to completely satisfactory (1). Besides that, there is in principle a whole spectrum of criteria differentiating between unsatisfactory and satisfactory pay-offs: one for each value of m. The condition of conflict is read now as follows: for every option b there is at least one agent a for whom $P(a, b) < m$; again, this condition can be concisely formulated by $MAX\{MIN\{P(a, b)/a\}/b\} < m$. Now, depending on the result of negotiations about the value of m, there will be conflict, and it will remain. Mappings like $P: A \times B \to [0, 1]$ are sometimes called "fuzzy relations on the product set $A \times B$." In this case we may speak of fuzzy pay-off functions, meaning that the pay-offs of some options for some agents cannot be stated in a clear-cut manner; furthermore, in the same context, the criterion sets $S(m)$ are called satisfaction-level sets.

As a last example we take $C = Z$ (the set of all integers) and $S = N$ (the set of all natural numbers including 0). Clearly then, we assume here, too, that agents have more precise information about and opinions on the pay-offs of behavioral options than could be modeled using a binary scale. Conflict, in the case of this model, means that $MAX\{MIN\{P(a, b)/a\}/b\} < 0$. Of course, a threshold other than 0 could be agreed upon so that there is room for negotiation in this case, too; yet whether this freedom can be used effectively or not depends on further qualities of C. If C is only an ordinal scale, then it will always be possible (without loss of valid information or addition of invalid information) to transform the threshold back to 0.

It is important at this point in our discussion to realize that the well-known problem of incomparability of individual pay-off functions does not arise here because we make use of a rather robust condition of conflict. The detailed information about the agents' pay-offs can and will still be used in searching for solutions of a (threatening) conflict.

We would like to conclude this first section with a yet more specialized example for conflict analysis; as a matter of fact, this example is well studied and allows us once again to distinguish between a conflict-theoretical and a decision-theoretical approach. Let $P: A \times B \to Z$ be any integer-valued pay-off function which defines, for each agent a in A, an order on B (a permutation of the elements of B); the question arises whether there exists any order on B which can be said to be a good representation of all of the individual orders, such that a collective choice can be based on this single order. One of the possible aggregation procedures (see Arkhipoff 1979, 1980) is multicriteria analysis of which an example is QUALIFLEX, a method developed by one of the authors (see Mastenbroek and Paelinck 1976; Paelinck 1976, 1977, 1978 for technical details). This method allows of aggregating individual preferences into a single transitive preference ordering on a relative-difference scale; also, it yields a transitivity or consistency index t as a measure of how well this collective preference ordering reflects the individual preference orderings. The method is relatively easy to explain. First, we have only to assume that the preferences are directly expressed for each pair of options (for example, by the method of paired comparisons); this information will be summarized in the mapping $P^*: A \times B \times B \to \{0, 1\}$, where $P^*(a, b, b') = 1$ *iff* $P(a, b) > P(a, b')$. Second, these preferences have to be aggregated over individuals by calculating the absolute or relative frequency of each pair of options: $Q(b, b')$. Finally, find that mapping $R: [Q(B \times B)] \to [Q^*(B \times B)]$ for which some $f(Q, Q^*)$ is maximal; for instance Q^* is the set of permutations of a Q-matrix, with a value $f(Q, Q^*)$ attached to each permutation.

Take, for instance, the following situation:

.	B1	B2	B3
B1	—	0.8	0.4
B2	0.2	—	0.3
B3	0.6	0.7	—

Here, it has been observed that 80 percent of the agents would choose A over B, 40 percent would choose A over C, and so on; from these data QUALIFLEX computes the following order, relative distances, and consistency:

$$B3 \overset{0.125}{\rule{1.5cm}{0.4pt}} B1 \overset{0.875}{\rule{2.5cm}{0.4pt}} B2 \;(t = 0.70).$$

Now, decision analysis would suggest taking option $B3$, in view of the fact that this option is collectively preferred to all other options. There exists conflict in this situation, however, because the first best option $B3$ in the collective orderings is not the first best option for all agents taken individually; it is known since the works of Arrow that generally no unanimous preference orderings can be constructed from this kind of data. *Decision analysis* aids in constructing procedures by which a solution can nevertheless be computed and justified; *conflict analysis*, on the other hand, aims at finding the reasons and causes of the apparent conflict and thereby aids in preventing or resolving the conflict. In this example, conflict analysts would point out that the distance between the first-best option and the second-best option is only small and that the transitivity index is not high; therefore, information should be gathered to separate them better and to raise the transitivity index above, say, 0.80.

General validity of the model

Our basic conflict model on $\Sigma = \{A, B, C, S; P\}$ can be tested by applying it to different situations described in the current literature, out of which we have selected the following ones:

Situation 1.   Cooperative versus noncooperative conflicts; the agents are or are not dependent on certain others in choosing satisfactory options.

Situation 2.   Deterministic versus stochastic conflicts; the behavioral options considered for selection by the agents are clear-cut executable actions, the outcomes of which may or may not depend on some random process.

Situation 3.   Single- or multiple-criteria conflicts; agents can compare and select options on one and only one aspect, attribute, or dimension, but options could also happen to be considered more satisfying by one, and less satisfying by another aspect.

Situation 4.   Static versus dynamic conflicts; the conflict situation is evaluated once and only once as it is, or a conflict is considered in a long-term perspective, that is, as a part or stage of some ongoing social process.

Many real-world conflict situations are difficult to tackle precisely because they lack the clarity of noncooperative, deterministic, single-criterion, static conflicts; in fact, too, much of current research on conflicts is precisely devoted to conflict situations that belong to the more difficult part of these situations. Classical game theory, for example, starts from the noncooperative two-player zero-sum games, and from there proceeds to general non-deterministic solutions for situations evolving in time; mathematical analysis on a multiple-criteria basis also require considerable mathematical sophistication.

Remarkably, in many studies so far the problem formulation has favored a decisionmaking approach rather than a conflict-resolution approach (White 1979; Yo and Olsder 1981); by that conclusion we want to point again at the important distinction between "choosing the best from the given" and "choosing so as to satisfy everybody," to put it as simply as possible. Of course, there may be situations in which the two approaches lead to the same answer, but that must not distract us from the fact that the underlying premises are different.

In this section we shall discuss in more detail each of the four dichotomous situations; we shall also explain what kind of conflict model specification is necessary to accommodate conflict situations of more complex types. As we will show, these types of conflict models are subsumed under our prototype model; while they imply additional structure in the conflict situations they also offer more opportunities for realistic conflict resolution. Put otherwise: to aid conflict resolution it might be a good idea to extract more information from the conflict situation and to integrate it in a more elaborate model.

Cooperative and noncooperative conflict situations

In our basic model each option is considered to result, possibly and eventually, into a final collective action; the implicit assumption is that in the absence of conflict all agents agree with each other on this collective action and that they will all participate in its execution. What if the set of agents breaks up into two or more subsets of agents, called coalitions (in the extreme, each coalition consisting of one and only one agent so that there are as many coalitions as there are agents)? Each coalition acts for its own, and among coalitions there is only regular consultation or communication insofar as it serves the interest of one or more of them inside the conflict situation.

What does such a conflict model look like? In other words, in what way does this type of conflict respect our prototype?

It can in fact easily be integrated within the framework of the first section.

Take the *initial* existence of coalitions; then the model is a two-stage or hierarchical one, conflicts *within* coalitions existing or not, and having possibly to be resolved. Take two coalitions of economic agents that exert duopoly power on a market: there can be *internal* conflicts about joining or not joining each other in forming a monopoly. Once the internal conflict has been solved, an *external* conflict can arise between the two groups, and this has to be solved again. Let us mention that a third type of conflict may arise after the internal conflict has been solved, to wit how to divide the possible extra results of the external decision (for example, how to divide monopoly rents).

A second aspect of coalitions falls outside the scope of this chapter, namely, coalitions as conflict-restricting devices; the case just mentioned of duopoly-monopoly transformation is an example of how a market war can be terminated. It falls under the general applicability of proposition 1 as a reduction of the set of agents.

Stochastic conflict models

Our basic model is based on the assumption that agents have perfect knowledge and complete control of all behavioral options open to them. There are certainly situations, however, in which it would be wise to put this assumption aside; for instance, "nature" is often accused of interfering with the execution of an action. It is not generally assumed, however, that nature is doing this on purpose, that is, because of fixed preferences with regard to actions. That constitutes one possible source of randomness in conflict situations, but there is also another possibility. In cases where we know that the results of our actions depend partly on acts of other people whom we do not regard as true co-actors or whom we do not know much about, we should be glad to have at our disposal conflict models allowing us to express our uncertainty about the results of our own actions.

The apt modification would be to replace the set of elementary options B with an appropriate set $F(B)$ of cumulative probability distribution functions over B (on the assumption that B has all the properties necessary to allow one to speak about such functions defined over it). The new options we will consider hereafter integrate these cumulative probability distributions; the pay-off functions would look like:

$$P: A \times F(B) \to C. \qquad (3-1)$$

According to this model, our preferences with respect to actions will depend not only on their intrinsic value for us but also on their probability of occurrence. The manner in which these intrinsic values and probabilities of occurrence are evaluated may or may not correspond to standard methods of statistics.

Our point at this moment is that such an evaluation does not impair the application of our basic conflict model. By taking only probability distributions, for example, for which all probability is condensed at one point, we are back with our basic model.

In fact, given the possible use of subjective probabilities, the individual choice sets (or the sets of individually satisfactory options) are bound to be more "varied" than under the certainty assumption, as they finally result from taking expectations with possible degrees of risk aversion or risk liking. Anyhow, there will eventually result a set of individual choice sets, and the nature of their intersection will determine the existence or absence of a conflict.

Multiple-criteria conflict models

Our basic model seems single-criterion because C is assumed to be a one-dimensional, at least ordinal, scale; the actions of the agents, we believed, were of such a simple nature that their evaluation in terms of pay-offs could be reduced to one single scale. But what if that belief proves false? Suppose, for example, that the agents have to choose between projects the value of which can be adequately described only by an n-tuple of pay-off; then our basic model should be extended in the following way:

$$P: A \times B \to X \{C_1, C_2, \ldots, C_n\} \qquad (3-2)$$

where $n \geqslant 2$.

If we set n equal to 1, then we would be back with our basic model: hence the qualification "extension of the basic conflict model." Take $n > 1$; at the one extreme we have the conjunctive rule which dictates us to call an option overall satisfactory iff its pay-off on each dimension is satisfactory; at the other extreme we have the disjunctive rule which dictates us to call it satisfactory iff its pay-off on at least one dimension is satisfactory. In between, we can imagine many variants; except for the conjunctive case, there could typically arise some new kind of conflict in this model, not between agents but between dimensions on which agents scale their options.

In fact, the return to the basic model can again be effected in a hierarchical way, this time by combining a multicriteria decision-making process at the agents' level and a conflict model on the resulting choice sets. In other words, the product set $X \{C_1, C_2, \ldots, C_n\}$ collapses in the original C-set, for each individual along the lines of the graph of the section on "Examples," on which an m-cut would decide the acceptable values of a payoff.

Dynamic conflict models

The situation treated up to now is that we have merely faced a single conflict at a single moment and that all will be well again as soon as that conflict has been resolved; but this very conflict could very well be one in a series of threatening conflicts, started in the distant past and continuing in the near future. Is that not a more plausible assumption than the reverse? For the current conflict might well be the result of (successful or unsuccessful) conflict management in the past, while the way we handle it now might largely determine whether future conflicts can be prevented or resolved. That amounts to a dynamic or diachronic view of conflict situations and suggests us to think of them as processes of conflict rather than states of conflict.

To model these situations we need to replace the pay-off mapping P with a time-dependent pay-off function

$$P(t): A \times B \rightarrow C \quad \text{with } t \text{ in } T \tag{3-3}$$

where we assume that the sets A, B, and C do not change during the time interval T; our basic model is now seen to represent only one instant of a conflict process: $t = t_o$.

Analogous questions arise here as in the previous section: should we adopt a very strict conflict criterion for this extended model or a weaker criterion? Taking a strong criterion, we should consider the process "in conflict" only if after a certain lapse of time there were still conflicts. In the weakest sense, conflict would mean that even at the end of the time interval the conflict has not been resolved. Whichever the criterion, it will be clear that in this model the term conflict has a second meaning: it denotes not only a certain relationship among agents but also the dynamics of that relationship. Differential game theory, among others, is devoted to the study of changing relationships among agents.

In fact, equation $(3-3)$ is again easy to accommodate: the time-multidimensionality of C has to be reduced by some process (discounting over a dynamic decision tree, for example) so that we are back in the realm of the basic model. Again, this situation has to be distinguished from conflict management or sequential decision-making within this process; as will be said in the following section, this part of conflict analysis will possibly be submitted to some axiomatics in a later stage of the research.

CONCLUSIONS

Further specification of the axioms

The axiom system for conflicts presented in the previous section should now be specified; let us briefly mention here some of our ideas on this matter.

First of all it would be interesting to have a fresh look at relations which determine the individual choice sets; a detailed classification of binary relations (to which preference or pre-order relations belong) and associated calculi could help in formulating new propositions about the (non)existence of conflicts.

Related to this, there appears to be some interesting work to be done on the topology of the set of options as well as the set of agents; this may lead to a completely different way of representing agents, namely, not as sources of preference relations but as sources of preference topologies on the set of options. Fixed points as well as fuzzy subset theory may come into play; the notion of distance between agents can also be introduced in order to render conflict measurement possible.

Finally, the significance of dynamic systems theory for studying conflict processes should be stressed here. Given the notion of trajectory, it is possible to model the evolution of a conflict towards or away from a solution region; catastrophe or, more generally, bifurcation theory could be illuminating of the way that conflicts can gradually arise from nonconflicting initial states, and of conditions under which these conflicts could again be resolved.

From the foregoing, it will be clear that there still remains a lot of technical work to be done before one will be able to present a comprehensive system for conflict analysis.

We are aware that we skipped over some issues concerning conflict and the scientific study of it which really deserve more attention. In particular, we feel a need to say something about the embedding of conflict theory in a much more broadly conceived theory of society, the empirical approach to conflict, and the practical use of a conflict theory.

Context of conflict

Conflict as defined in this chapter has been reduced to a state or a sequence of states of a social system (any society); it could well be argued, however, that real conflicts are embedded in or are phases of conflicts. We admit frankly that there is this danger of too much this leads to a rather colorless and myopic vision on the very essence of conflicts; we admit frankly that there is this danger of too much abstraction and overgeneralization in an axiomatic approach, but we think also that the search for a more systematic and integrated theory of conflict justifies taking this risk. Integration of knowledge about conflict will be much more a question of conceptual analyses than of collecting more data about related issues; a relevant recent example in favor of this standpoint is the curious merging of classical control theory and game theory into differential game theory (see, for example, Ho and Olsder 1981; Koehler 1978; Krassovski and Soubbotine 1979).

Research on conflicts

The study of conflict embraces more, one might say, than its mathematical reconstruction and logical axiomatization; especially, it would seem desirable to have more or better empirical data about certain kinds of conflict situations. It is, however, futile and premature in our opinion to try and start research (for instance, empirical research) on this topic without clear conceptual foundations for it; these conceptual foundations would consist of specified models of conflict together with testable research hypotheses emanating from them. Such a framework has yet to be built, although much work has been done on certain specialized models. Moreover, if one would like to study actual conflict situations from the past or in the present, there is no other way than to focus on certain aspects and fields of conflict separately. For instance, historical or sociological studies of conflict often turn out to be concentrated on only certain types of conflict situations; by definition, then, these would not constitute genuine interdisciplinary studies of the concept of conflict. While such empirical inquiries might well throw more light on the pecularities of these particular conflicts, they do not bring us much further on the way to a comprehensive view on conflict and conflict resolution.

Conflict management

Let us finally discuss methods of conflict management. We will make a clear distinction between proper and improper conflict management.

By the term "improper conflict management" we refer to social processes in which the possibility of conflict is simply ignored or tolerated; for instance, if axiom 5 is completely dropped, then there will be no criterion on which to base the statement, "The system is in conflict." On the contrary, there are plenty of ways of (rationally or nonrationally) selecting from among the given ones one option that will become the collective behavior. It may well be the case, however, that no agent will be really satisfied with this option, even if he or she concedes for the moment. This approach underlies much of decision analysis insofar as its goal is to reach a decision given certain alternatives and preferences, not to prevent or resolve a conflict inherent in these alternatives and preferences. In this sense, decisionmaking and conflict resolution are opposite approaches to the same social problems; however, practitioners of decision analysis will presumably answer that the conflict is prevented or resolved on a higher level because apparently the agents agree on a procedure to arrive at a collective choice rather than on the choices themselves.

Another attitude toward conflicts is based on the belief that they are more the rule than the exception, and that it is therefore practical to accept them and to try only to mitigate them somewhat. The advice, then, would be not to take into account any agent who is not at all satisfied with the current set of options and not to hesitate to choose an option which is satisfactory for most agents. Of course, what constitutes the subset of "most agents" has to be made more precise in a particular situation: for example, it may be any subset of at least half of the agents who agree on a particular option as being satisfying; following this line of reasoning, it does not matter that some agents would not be satisfied as long as many others are. Clearly, such an attitude can not be justified within a framework of conflict prevention or resolution.

By the term "proper conflict management" we refer to social processes in which the threat or fact of conflict is taken seriously and an attempt is made to prevent it from arising or—if it has already arisen—to confine and resolve it. Logically, there are several ways in which this can be done. All of them require that one or more of the components of the basic model are changed without modification of the overall structure itself. First, the set of agents A could be redefined by having some agents withdrawing themselves; this seems a rather brute solution, but logically speaking it is one, so why not mention it? Secondly, adding new behavioral options to B (possibly by some mathematical closure operation like convex or linear combination) might also result in a nonconflicting situation; this is like saying that the former B was merely a sample from a much larger domain. Thirdly, refining the set of pay-off values or enlarging the subset of satisfying pay-offs can conceivably solve the problem. The justification for this procedure is, of course, that the original pay-off scale C or the original range of satisfactory pay-offs were rather coarse approximations of the actual ones. Fourth and finally, there is the possibility of modifying the pay-off function, whether or not the other components remain the same; in this last case one presupposes that preferences of people are changeable or that errors could have been made in their communication. These procedures may be followed separately or in combination, but it may be argued that the first three procedures logically imply the fourth procedure (although the converse is clearly not true).

This is as far as we can go in analyzing what we have called the prototype model of conflict and conflict resolution. Does this mean, however, that the study of basic conflict situations has to stop here? Certainly not; one can easily imagine many special studies based on particular choices of the sets A, B, C, S, and the mapping P. For example, it makes a difference whether the set A is small or large, whether C is just an ordinal scale or a metric scale, whether S is fixed or variable, and whether P is continuous in B or not. The difference may be relevant from a mathematical point of view, from a computational point of view, or from a methodological point of view. It is neither possible nor necessary to give here an overview of all those specialized studies: they can be found in many textbooks, monographs, and articles, some of which are included among the list of references.

A final word as to the applicability of these analyses. In science, there is always the fruitful tension between the search for pure or theoretical knowledge and that for applied or practical wisdom; this tension is also present in the study of and research on conflict. Eventually the question will arise as to whether the results of the axiomatic analysis of the concept of conflict would be of any value to real agents in a real conflict situation. Although, as mentioned at the chapter's opening, this is not the primary purpose of such an analysis, it certainly is one of the long-term goals. Of course, this contribution to conflict resolution will be mainly in the form of improved methods for the cognitive structuring and restructuring of the conflict situation by the agents themselves; but whether or not this potential value of conflict theory will be exploited, will depend on the willingness and ability of agents to learn and practice these improved methods. And that—unfortunately—is something lying outside the sphere of influence of social science.

REFERENCES

Arkhipoff, O. 1979. "Introduction à l'Axiomatique des Procedures d'Aggrégation." Paris. Mimeo.

———. 1980. "An Introduction to the Axiomatics of Procedures of Aggregation." *Mathematical Social Sciences*: 69–83.

Banks, M. 1981. *Resolution of Conflict: A Manual and Theoretical Framework*. London: Frances Pinter.

Bacharach, M. 1972. *Economics and the Theory of Games*. London: Macmillan.

Bell, D.; R.L. Keeney; and H. Raiffa. 1977. *Conflicting Objectives in Decision*. New York: Wiley.

Bennett, P.G. 1980. "Hypergames: Developing a Model of Conflict." *Futures* 12:489–507.

Case, J.H. 1979. *Economy and the Competitive Process*. New York: New York University Press.

Debreu, G. 1968. "Neighboring Economic Agents." *La Décision:* CNRS, Paris, 85–90.

Fink, C.F. 1968. "Some Conceptual Difficulties in the Theory of Social Conflicts." *Journal of Conflict Resolution* 12, no. 4:412–460.

Fishburn, P.C. 1964. *Decision and Value Theory*. New York–London: Wiley.

———. 1970. *Utility Theory for Decision Making*, New York–London: Wiley.

———. 1972. *Mathematics of Decision Theory*. The Hague–Paris: Mouton.

Grote, J.P. (ed.) 1974. *The Theory and Application of Differential Games*. Dordrecht: Reidel.

Henn, R., and O. Moeschlin (eds.) 1977. *Mathematical Economics and Game Theory*. Berlin–Heidelberg–Yew York: Springer Verlag.

Ho, Y.C., and G.T. Olsder, 1981. "Differential Games: Concepts and Applications." Harvard University. Mimeo.

Isaacs, R. 1972. *Jeux Différentiels*. Paris: Dunod.

Jones, A.J. 1980. *Game Theory: Mathematical Models of Conflict*. Chichester: Ellis Harwood.

Klaassen, L.H., and J.H.P. Paelinck, 1976. "Energie, Grondstoffen en Groei: Enkele Theoretische Beschouwingen (Energy, Raw Materials, and Growth: Some Theoretical Considerations). In *Praeadviezen Voor de Vereniging voor Staathuishoudkunde* (Introductory report for the Dutch Economic Association), pp. 56–60. 's-Gravenhage: Martinus Nijhoff.

Koehler, M. 1978. *Differentialspiele mit Ökonomischen Anwendungen*. Zürich: Juris.

Krassovski, N.H., and A. Soubbotine. 1979. *Jeux Différentiels*. Paris: Mir.

Leonardy, R.; W. Rothengatter; and K.H. Woll. 1975. "Ein Verfahren zur Unterstützung kommunaler Entscheidungsprozesse unter Partizipation von Interessengruppen." *Karlsruher Beiträge zur Wirtschaftsforschung*, Universität Karlsruhe/Institute für Wirtschaftspolitik und Wirtschaftsforschung 3:49–71.

Lindley, D.V. 1971. *Making Decisions*. Chichester: Wiley.

Mastenbroek, P., and J.H.P. Paelinck. 1976. "Multicriteria Decisionmaking: Non-linearities and Uncertainty." *International Journal of Transport Economics* 3, no. 3:43–62.

Menges, G. (ed.) 1974. *Information, Inference and Decision*. Dordrecht: Reidel.

Paelinck, J.H.P. 1976. "Qualitative Multi-criteria Analysis: Environmental Protection and Multiregional Development." *Papers of the Regional Science Association* 36:59–79.

——. 1977. "Qualitative Multi-criteria Analysis: An Application to Airport Planning." *Environment and Planning* A-9:883–895.

——. 1978. 'QUALIFLEX: A Flexible Multicriteria Method." *Economics Letters* 13:143–197.

Patchen, M. 1970. "Models of Cooperation and Conflict: A Critical Review." *Journal of Conflict Resolution* 14, no. 3:389–407.

Plasmans, J.E.J. 1979. "Linked Econometric Models as a Differential Game: Mark-Optimality-I." Tilburg University, Department of Econometrics. Research Memorandum.

Plasmans, J.E.J., and A.J. de Zeeuw. 1980a. "Incentives To Cooperate in Linear Quadratic Difference Games." *International Journal of System Science:* 11, no. 5:607–619.

——. 1980b. "Mark Pareto and Stackelberg Solutions for Interplay: A Model for the Common Market." Tilburg University, Department of Econometrics. Research Memorandum.

——. 1980c. "Pareto optimality and incentives to cooperate in linear quadratic differences games." Tilburg University, Department of Econometrics. Research Memorandum.

Raiffa, H. 1968. *Decision Analysis*. London: Addison-Wesley.

Rapoport, A. 1969. *Fights, Games and Debates*. Ann Arbor: Michigan University Press.

Roth, A.E. 1979. *Axiomatic Models of Bargaining*. Berlin: Springer Verlag.

Schelling, T.C. 1960. *The Strategy of Conflict*. London: Oxford University Press.

Thomas, K. 1976. "Conflict and conflict management." In *Handbook of Industrial and Organisational Psychology* edited by M. Dunnette. Chicago: Rand Monaux.

Vincke, P. 1976. "Modélisation des Préférences et Théorie de l'utilité: Résultats Existants et Voies de Recherche." *Revue Belge de Statistique, d'Information et de Recherche Opérationelle* 16, no. 4:1–15.

White, D.J. 1974. *Decision Methodology*. Chichester: Wiley.

Zeeuw, A.J. de. "Stackelberg Solutions in Macro-economic Policy Models with Decentralised Decision Structure, I and II." Tilburg University, Department of Econometrics. Research Memorandum.

II Contributions at the Applied Level

4 A Value-Based Approach to Conflict Resolution Involving Multiple Objectives and Multiple Decision-making Units*

Yee Leung

Policy analysis and decisionmaking in socioeconomic planning, environmental management, and international disarmament, to name but a few areas, often involve the selection of a mutually agreeable course of action in an environment characterized by multiple conflicting objectives and multiple decisionmaking units with noncommensurable internal and external interests. Though the problem is centuries old, development of rigorous mathematical procedures for conflict resolution has only recently become a major area of research. A fundamental problem is the formulation of models which best describe real-world conflict-resolution processes in such a way that solutions can be logically and mathematically derived.

Over the years, various mathematical methods such as the game theoretical models (summarized in Rapoport 1974), dominated structures and nondominated solutions (Yu 1973, 1974), a concept of a displaced ideal (systematized by Zeleny 1976), and various optimization methods (evaluated by Nijkamp 1979) have been

* This is the revised version of a paper presented at the International Symposium on Conflict Management held in Kyoto, Japan, Aug. 8–9, 1981. The revision was completed while the author was a Visiting Senior Fellow of the Center for Metropolitan Planning and Research and a Visiting Associate Professor of the Department of Geography and Environmental Engineering at the Johns Hopkins University in the spring semester, 1982.

55

proposed. Among these methods, the interactive approach based on a concept of a displaced ideal (Zeleny 1976) seems to be a viable method for realistic conflict resolution. The model permits dynamic interaction between decision analysts and decisionmaking units (henceforth referred to as DM units) to adjust, whenever necessary, objectives and alternatives throughout the resolution process. The concept has been employed to analyze conflicts within a collective entity which can pool DM units' resources and information together to select a compromise solution (Nijkamp 1978). However, such a powerful central committee usually does not exist in real-life conflict resolution involving multiple conflicting objectives and multiple interest groups (see, for example, Isard and Smith 1966). Instead, a central coordinating committee which has limited institutional power is ordinarily encountered.

In general, individual DM units resolve their own internal conflicts prior to the resolution of intergroup conflicts. Compromise solutions obtained within individual DM units are then pulled together by a central coordinating committee to derive a compromise solution for all DM units. For example, the oil-exporting and -importing countries may try to resolve their internal conflicts over the embargo and counter-embargo policies before negotiation is attempted to search for a mutually agreeable policy. In some instances, however, conflict among DM units may even need to be resolved without a central coordinating committee. Individual DM units still need to resolve their own internal conflicts and obtain their own compromise solutions. In place of a central coordinating committee, the overall compromise solution is derived through direct negotiation among the DM units.

Thus, a mathematical model should be formulated to analyze these types of two-stage conflict-resolution processes involving multiple objectives and multiple DM units.

Due to the complexity of our decisionmaking environment, the inexactness of information, and the vagueness of our cognitive and decisionmaking processes, value-based rules (oriented to natural language) are ordinarily employed in problemsolving and decision-making. Conflict resolution is no exception.

In this paper, fuzzy sets concepts are incorporated in an extended framework of a displaced ideal to analyze conflict resolution involving multiple objectives and multiple decisionmaking units (1) with a central coordinating committee, and (2) without a central coordinating committee.

In what follows, conflict resolution with a central coordinating committee is analyzed first. Conflict resolution without such a committee is then examined. The chapter concludes with a discussion of the appropriateness of applying fuzzy sets theory to conflict analysis.

CONFLICT RESOLUTION WITH A COMMITTEE

Assume that there is a group of DM units, which can be individuals, interest groups, regions, or nations, who try to select a mutually agreeable alternative in a joint venture. Suppose that the DM units are completely independent in making their own decisions with the exception that their decisions may be influenced by the information on other DM units' decisions. Let there be a central coordinating committee which has only an institutional power to provide necessary information, such as the possible actions of other DM units, and to coordinate the conflict-resolution process by proposing ideal and compromise solutions for the group.

In this situation, the decisionmaking process consists basically of two stages. The first stage is the conflict resolution within the DM units, while the second stage occurs among the DM units. Let us assume that the concept of a displaced ideal is employed to resolve the internal conflict of a DM unit in the first stage. In this stage, individual DM units will formulate their own "local ideals" and determine their "local compromise solutions" (to be discussed later). Displacements of the initial local ideals and compromise solutions may happen as a result of additional information gathered or change of perspectives on the importance of the objectives or the adequacy of the alternatives. The derivation of the compromise solution essentially follows the displaced ideal method (Zeleny 1976).

In the second stage, all DM units' local compromise solutions are turned in to the central coordinating committee for evaluation. Depending on the compatibility of the local compromise solutions, the central coordinating committee may provide additional information, such as the initial proposed course of action of other DM units or the commensurability of objectives or alternatives. Such information may change DM units' evaluations of objectives and alternatives and thus may possibly displace the initial local ideals and the corresponding local compromise solutions within the DM

Figure 4–1. Conflict resolution with a Central Coordinating Committee

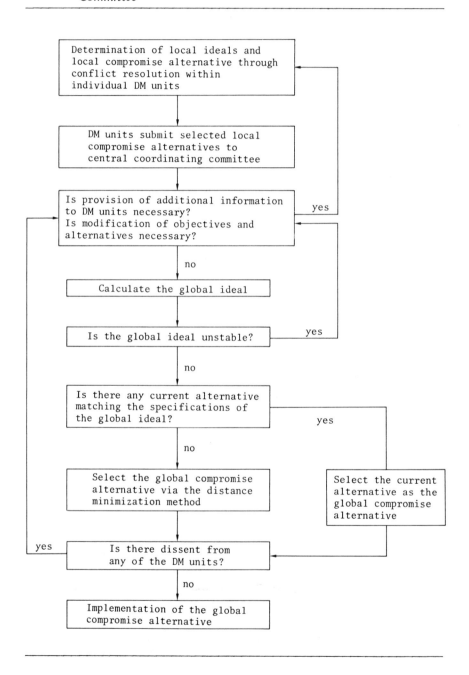

units. This type of iterative, interactive process may continue until no further adjustments are necessary. The coordinating committee then proposes the "global ideal" (to be discussed later) based on all the DM units' local compromise solutions. Stability of the global ideal is then evaluated. Should the global ideal be unstable, modification of DM units' standards, objectives, or alternatives may be necessary. A new iterative process of internal and external conflict resolution is then triggered again.

After the global ideal has been determined, the "global compromise solution" (to be discussed later) may be obtained by selecting the alternative closest to the global ideal. The result is then submitted to individual DM units for approval. Should there be any dissent, minor modifications may be necessary or the whole conflict-resolution process may have to repeat again. Though the whole conflict-resolution process is divided into two stages, they are actually highly interdependent and recursive.

Figure 4–1 summarizes the major steps of the process. Its formalization is detailed in the remaining part of this section.

Let $Z = \{z_1, \ldots, z_k, \ldots, z_l\}$ be the group of DM units. In the first stage, for DM unit z_k, let

$$X = \{x_1, \ldots, x_i, \ldots, x_n\}$$

be the set of initial feasible alternatives, and

$$Y = \{y_1, \ldots, y_j, \ldots, y_m\}$$

be the set of initial objectives by which the merit of an alternative is evaluated. Let

$$
\begin{bmatrix}
S(x_1, y_1) & \ldots & S(x_1, y_j) & \ldots & S(x_1, y_m) \\
 & & & & \\
 & & & & \\
S(x_i, y_1) & \ldots & S(x_i, y_j) & \ldots & S(x_i, y_m) \\
 & & & & \\
 & & & & \\
S(x_n, y_1) & \ldots & S(x_n, y_j) & \ldots & S(x_n, y_m)
\end{bmatrix}
\qquad (4-1)
$$

be the achievement matrix whose element $S(x_i, y_j)$ represents the achievement level, a numerical score, of alternative x_i with respect to objective y_j. Based on a concept of compromise solution (Zeleny 1974), the *local ideal* for DM unit z_k may be defined as

$$x_k^* = (S^*(y_1), \ldots, S^*(y_j), \ldots, S^*(y_m)), \tag{4-2}$$

whose element

$$S^*(y_j) = \max_{x_i \in X} S(x_i, y_j) \tag{4-3}$$

indicates the maximum level, ideal value, of achievement of objective y_j by current feasible alternatives. Thus, the local ideal designates the consummate alternative with respect to all objectives for DM unit z_k. It is an ideal alternative because it possesses the highest achievement levels with respect to all individual objectives. It is local because it may be inferior to other DM units' local ideals. In general, such an alternative is infeasible, especially in the presence of conflicting objectives or conflicting interest groups. Consequently, an alternative which has the smallest deviation from the local ideal is a natural compromise alternative for DM unit z_k.

To make the ideal operational, a proximity measure indicating the closeness of an alternative's achievement level to the ideal value of an objective needs to be sepcified first. A distance function between an alternative and the ideal alternative is then defined and minimized accordingly.

A common measure of proximity (Zeleny 1976) is

$$d(x_i, y_j) = \frac{S(x_i, y_j) - S_*(y_j)}{S^*(y_j) - S_*(y_j)}, \quad \forall\ x_i \in X,\ \forall\ y_j \in Y, \tag{4-4}$$

where

$$S_*(y_j) = \min_{x_i \in X} S(x_i, y_j), \tag{4-5}$$

and

$$d(x_i, y_j) = 1 \quad \text{if} \quad S^*(y_j) = S_*(y_j). \tag{4-6}$$

The problem of this measurement is twofold. First, it only serves as a normalization and proportionality assignment which fails to measure proximity in a manner varying according to the nature—for instance, the importance—of the objectives. For example, for identical $S_*(y_i)$ and $S^*(y_j)$, the same level of achievement, $S(x_i, y_j)$, an alternative has should probably be perceived to be closer to the ideal value with respect to a less important objective than to that of a more important objective, since the magnitude of deviation from the former objective may not matter too much. However, equations (4–4), (4–5) and (4–6) do not possess such a differentiating mechanism. To account for varying degrees of importance, a weighting scheme is ordinarily required in conventional analysis (Zeleny 1974). Second, it fails to account for the value-based decisionmaking processes in which vague concepts, such as axiological objectives, and qualitative criteria prevail and natural language plays an important role in decisionmaking. In this situation, proximity is often characterized by linguistic terms, such as "close to," "very close to," or "somewhat close to," which are words or sentences in our common language. To incorporate these two features in a single measure, a concept of a linguistic variable (Zadeh 1975a, 1975b, and 1975c) can be employed to characterize proximity.

Treating proximity as a linguistic variable, its value, a linguistic term, can be characterized by varying mathematical functions in accordance with objectives having varying degrees of importance. Taking the linguistic term "close to" as an example, here "close to" means close to being considered as an ideal value, the defining membership function

$$\mu_{close\ to}\ (S(x_i, y_j)) = \exp - k\left(\frac{S(x_i, y_j) - S^*(y_j)}{S^*(y_j)}\right)^4,$$

$$k > 0, \quad x_i \in X, \quad y_j \in Y. \tag{4–7}$$

induces a higher degree of differentiation of the relative merits of an alternative's achievement level of an objective than the following function:

$$\mu_{close\ to}\ (S(x_i, y_j)) = \left[1 + k\left(\frac{S(x_i, y_j) - S^*(y_j)}{S^*(y_j)}\right)^2\right]^{-1},$$

$$k > 1, \quad x_i \in X, \quad y_j \in Y. \tag{4–8}$$

See Figure 4–2 for the membership functions of "close to."

Equation (4–7) may serve as a proximity measure of an important objective, while equation (4–8) is probably more appropriate for

Figure 4—2.   Membership Functions of "Close to"

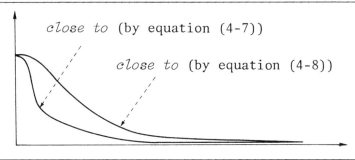

that of a less important objective. Thus, the weighting scheme is implicitly embedded in the value-based rule.

Once the linguistic term "close to" is defined, other terms such as "very close to," "extremely clost to," and "somewhat close to" can be derived by applying operations such as concentration, dilation, or contrast intensification to modify the meaning of "close to" (Leung 1982). Such a procedure allows decisionmakers to evaluate and select alternatives in accordance with the relative importance of objectives by varying the value-based rule. This is especially important when a central coordinating committee does not exist and conflict resolution depends on negotiation. (This point is detailed in the next section.) Thus, the value-based measure of proximity, such as the functions in equations (4—7) or (4—8), is in fact more flexible than the conventional formulations such as those in equations (4—4), (4—5), and (4—6).

Once the approximation of proximity, such as "close to," is determined, a family of distance functions for any alternative x_i with respect to the local ideal may be defined as

$$\left[\sum_j (1 - \mu_{close\ to} (S(x_i, y_j)))^p\right]^{1/p}, \qquad 1 \leqslant p \leqslant \infty. \qquad (4-9)$$

With respect to the parameter p, the function in equation (4—9) is in fact a distance between two fuzzy subsets, with the fuzzy subset $(1, \ldots, 1, \ldots, 1)$ representing the ideal alternative x_k^*.

Taking all alternatives into consideration, for a specific value of the parameter p, the local compromise solution for DM unit z_k is x_k^c which minimizes the distance function in equation (4—9). For

$$x_k^c = (S(x_k^c, y_1), \ldots, S(x_k^c, y_j)), \ldots, s(x_k^c, y_m)) \qquad (4-10)$$

where $S(x_k^c, y_j)$ is the achievement level of x_k^c with respect to objective y_j, the following condition

$$\left[\sum_{j=1}^{n} (1 - \mu_{close\ to}\ (S(x_k^c, y_j)))^p\right]^{1/p}$$

$$= \min_{x_i \in X} \left[\sum_{j=1}^{n} (1 - \mu_{close\ to}\ (s(x_i, y_j)))^p\right]^{1/p}, \qquad 1 \leqslant p \leqslant \infty.$$

$$(4-11)$$

is satisfied.

Nevertheless, the alternative x_k^c, as previously discussed, may possibly be selected only after several displacements of the initial local ideal have taken place.

In the second stage, the local compromise solutions of all the DM units are submitted to the central coordinating committee. An achievement matrix

$$\begin{bmatrix} S(x_1^{c'}, y_1) & \cdots & S(x_1^c, y_j) & \cdots & S(x_1^c, y_m) \\ \cdot & & \cdot & & \cdot \\ \cdot & & \cdot & & \cdot \\ \cdot & & \cdot & & \cdot \\ S(x_k^c, y_1) & \cdots & S(x_k^c, y_j) & \cdots & S(x_k^c, y_m) \\ \cdot & & \cdot & & \cdot \\ \cdot & & \cdot & & \cdot \\ \cdot & & \cdot & & \cdot \\ S(x_l^c, y_1) & \cdots & S(x_l^c, y_j) & \cdots & S(x_l^c, y_m) \end{bmatrix} \qquad (4-12)$$

containing all DM units' local compromise alternatives is constructed. The major objective of this stage is to find a global compromise solution for all DM units based on their local compromise solutions. The procedure of conflict resolution is similar to that of the individual DM units.

The central coordinating committee will first derive the global ideal

$$x^* = (S^*(y_1), \ldots, S^*(y_j), \ldots, S^*(y_m)), \qquad (4-13)$$

where

$$S^*(y_j) = \max_{x_k^c \in X} S(x_k^c, y_j) \qquad (4-14)$$

denotes the maximum level of achievement of objective y_j by the current local compromise alternatives.

Again, value-based proximity measures along the line of reasoning of equations (4–7) and (4–8) may be employed. The corresponding distance function similar to equation (4–9) may be constructed. For a specific value of the parameter p, the global compromise solution for all the DM units is

$$x^c = (S(x^c, y_1), \ldots, S(x^c, y_j), \ldots, S(x^c, y_m)) \qquad (4\text{–}15)$$

which minimizes the distance function

$$\left[\sum_{j=1}^{m} (1 - \mu_{close\ to}\ (S(x_k^c, y_j)))^p\right]^{1/p}, \qquad 1 \leqslant p \leqslant \infty. \qquad (4\text{–}16)$$

The alternative x^c will then be submitted to the DM units for approval. DM unit z_k may request partial modifications of the alternative, depending on which objective is not satisfactorily achieved. Alternatively, a generalized decision rule may be specified as follows:

Accept x^c as the compromise alternative if

for each $S(x_k^c, y_j)$ in x_k^c, and each

$S(x^c, y_j)$ in x^c,

$$|S(x_k^c, y_j) - S(x^c, y_j)| \leqslant \alpha_j, \qquad (4\text{–}17)$$

for $j = 1, \ldots, m$;

reject, otherwise.

The value, α_j, is the maximum permissible level for the global compromise solution x^c to deviate from the local compromise solution x_k^c in achieving objective y_j.

As previously discussed, it may not be possible to ascertain x^c until a certain number of displacements of the initial global ideal and local ideals are made.

CONFLICT RESOLUTION WITHOUT COMMITTEE

Conflicts among DM units are often resolved without any master control such as a central coordinating committee discussed in the previous section. Negotiation and bargaining seem to be peaceful approaches for conflict resolution in this situation. Over the years,

Figure 4–3.   A DM Unit's Conflict-Resolution Procedure without the Coordination of a Central Committee

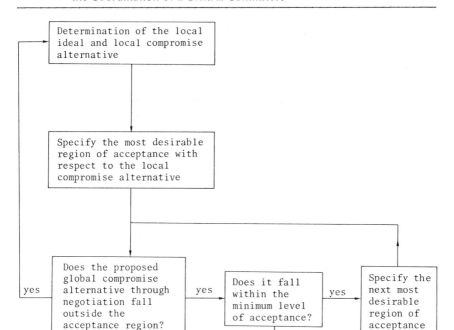

the problem has mostly been analyzed in the framework of n-person games (Rapoport 1974). Though the theory is basically appealing, its complicated concepts such as core, kernel, and bargaining set are pragmatically difficult, if not impossible, to obtain.

In this section, a simpler approach based on the concept of local ideals and value-based satisfying principles is proposed to analyze the problem. The process, comprising the major steps depicted in Figure 4–3, consists of two stages.

The first stage is conflict resolution within individual DM units, and is similar to the first stage of the process discussed in the previous section. DM units $z_1, \ldots, z_k, \ldots, z_l$ formulate their own local ideals and derive the local compromise solutions $x_1^c, \ldots,$ $x_k^c, \ldots, x_l^c$ through an iterative process of ideal displacement. The local compromise solutions will then be employed by the DM units as a basis of negotiation in the second stage.

The second stage is a negotiation phase through which the global compromise solution is selected in relation to all DM units' local compromise solutions. Due to time and budget constraints, a resolution process which requires an infinite number of rounds of negotiation is impossible. Instead, negotiation with a finite number of rounds, usually a few, guided by some satisfying principles is a common practice.

Since the negotiation process is not administered by a central coordinating committee, and a DM unit's alternative preferences may not be completely revealed, then the global ideal for all DM units cannot be derived. Without referring to a global ideal as a basis, compromise solutions have to be proposed among the DM units. To ensure that the proposed global compromise solution will not deviate too much from its local compromise solution, acceptance regions reflecting different levels of satisfaction that a DM unit may have with respect to the proposed global compromise solution may be employed as criteria for decisionmaking.

Based on the rationale that each DM unit would like to select the global compromise solution as close as possible to its local compromise solution, the acceptance region which allows the smallest deviation from the local compromise solution is employed first. Should the employment of an acceptance region with a higher level of satisfaction fail to reach a consensus, an acceptance region of a lower level of satisfaction becomes effective in the next step of the negotiation process.

For DM unit z_k, acceptance regions with varying value-based levels of satisfaction may be specified by the following sequence of membership functions: let

$$w = \sum_{j=1}^{m} (S(x^c, y_j) - S(x_k^c, y_j)), \qquad (4-18)$$

where x^c and x_k^c are the proposed compromise alternative for all DM units and the local compromise solution for DM unit z_k, respectively. Then, for DM unit z_k, the following set of value-based rules:

$$\mu_{extremely\ satisfied}\ (w) = 1, \qquad \text{for} \quad -\alpha_1 \leqslant w \leqslant \alpha_1,$$

$$= \left(\frac{\alpha_2 + w}{\alpha_2 - \alpha_1}\right)^4, \qquad \text{for} \quad -\alpha_2 \leqslant w \leqslant -\alpha_1,$$

$$= \left(\frac{\alpha_2 - w}{\alpha_2 - \alpha_1}\right)^4, \qquad \text{for} \quad \alpha_1 \leqslant w \leqslant \alpha_2,$$

$$= 0, \qquad \text{otherwise}; \qquad\qquad (4\text{--}19)$$

$$\mu_{very\ satisfied}\ (w) = 1, \qquad \text{for} \quad -\beta_1 \leqslant w \leqslant \beta_1,$$

$$= \left(\frac{\beta_2 + w}{\beta_2 - \beta_1}\right)^2, \qquad \text{for} \quad -\beta_2 \leqslant w \leqslant \beta_1,$$

$$= \left(\frac{\beta_2 - w}{\beta_2 - \beta_1}\right)^2, \qquad \text{for} \quad \beta_1 \leqslant w \leqslant \beta_2,$$

$$= 0, \qquad \text{otherwise}; \qquad\qquad (4\text{--}20)$$

$$\mu_{somewhat\ satisfied}\ (w) = 1, \qquad \text{for} \quad -\gamma_1 \leqslant w \leqslant \gamma_1,$$

$$= \left(\frac{\gamma_2 + w}{\gamma_2 - \gamma_1}\right)^{0.5}, \qquad \text{for} \quad -\gamma_2 \leqslant w \leqslant -\gamma_1,$$

$$= \left(\frac{\gamma_2 - w}{\gamma_2 - \gamma_1}\right)^{0.5}, \qquad \text{for} \quad \gamma_1 \leqslant w \leqslant \gamma_2,$$

$$= 0, \qquad \text{otherwise}; \qquad\qquad (4\text{--}21)$$

may be constructed as a basis for negotiation (see Figure 4–4).

In the initial round of negotiation, DM unit z_k will employ equation (4–19) as the decisionmaking criterion. Should w be within the interval $[-\alpha_1, +\alpha_1]$, for example, $w = w_o$ in Figure 4–4, the proposed global compromise alternative x^c will be accepted

Figure 4–4. Membership Functions of the Acceptance Regions

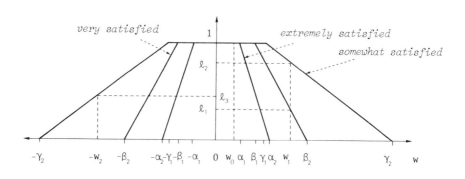

with the highest level of satisfaction, for instance, $\mu_{extremely\ satisfied}$ $(w) = 1$). The degree of satisfaction monotonically decreases to zero within the intervals $[-\alpha_2, -\alpha_1]$ and $[\alpha_1, \alpha_2]$. Should w be outside $[-\alpha_2, \alpha_2]$, for instance, $w = w_1$ in Figure 4–4, the global compromise alternative will not be accepted under the rule *extremely satisfied*. Either a new global compromise solution has to be proposed or acceptance with lower level of satisfaction has to be activated. For instance, at $w = w_1$, a global compromise alternative can be accepted at l_1 degree of satisfaction under the level *very satisfied*, and at l_2, with $l_2 > l_1$, degree of satisfaction under *somewhat satisfied*. By the same token, for $w = -w_2$ in Figure 4–4, a compromise alternative can only be accepted with l_3, degree of satisfaction under the level *somewhat satisfied*. From equations (4–19) to (4–21), when the level of satisfaction changes from *extremely satisfied* to *somewhat satisfied*, the acceptance regions extend from α_2 to γ_2 and from $-\alpha_2$ to $-\gamma_2$. That is, the regions of acceptance expand with the relaxation of satisfaction requirements. Throughout the entire negotiation process, DM unit z_k may specify a minimum acceptance level α, $\alpha \in [0, 1]$. Should $\mu_A(w) < \alpha$, where A is a label of satisfaction level, the proposed global compromise solution is rejected. If the compromise solution falls below at least one DM unit's minimum level of acceptance, a consensus is not reached. The negotiation process may have to start again by reformulating DM units' local ideals and the local compromise solutions, and the associated acceptance regions.

Remark

During each round of negotiation, there are no guarantees that each DM unit will employ the acceptance region with the same level of satisfaction. That is, some DM units may employ acceptance regions with higher levels of satisfaction while others may use regions with lower levels of satisfaction. Since a few rounds of negotiation is assumed, and value-based satisfying principles are employed, the global compromise alternative x^c is very likely not a Pareto-optimal solution. This conflict resolution result may not be theoretically desirable but probably occurs frequently in real-life conflict resolution, involving multiple objectives and multiple DM units, without a central coordinating committee. Thus, from the conflict management point of view, some channels of communication which encourage better information exchange among the DM units should probably be established.

CONCLUSION

The chapter combines a concept of a displaced ideal and linguistic variables in the study of conflict resolution involving multiple conflicting objectives and multiple decisionmaking units with conflicting interests. Linguistic variables are embedded in the extended model of displaced ideal to resolve group conflicts with and without a central coordinating committee. In the presence of a central coordinating committee, the notions of local ideal and local compromise solution are formulated as a basis for conflict resolution within a DM unit. The global ideal, derived from a set of local compromise solutions, and the global compromise solution are constructed to resolve conflicts among DM units. The whole conflict-resolution process is iterative and interactive. Value-based decisionmaking criteria are employed as rules rather than exceptions in such an environment.

When a central coordinating committee does not exist, conflicts are resolved through simple value-based satisfying principles. Since DM units' alternative preferences are not fully disclosed, the formation of coalition throughout the negotiation process is not analyzed here. If DM units had complete knowledge of each other's alternative preferences, coalition would be likely to occur. The value-based approach may possibly be extended to analyze such situations.

Though the possibility of incorporating linguistic variables in conflict analysis has been suggested by a number of researchers (Gale 1975; Leung 1980; Nijkamp 1979; and Zeleny 1976), and its versatility is demonstrated in the present analysis, some basic problem of the linguistic variable approach such as the inexactness of the membership function defining a linguistic term (Leung 1981a, 1981b, 1981c), especially when applied to conflict resolution, require further research. As a whole, fuzzy sets theory appears to be a viable framework for decision analysis in general and conflict analysis in particular.

REFERENCES

Gale, S. 1975. "Boundaries, Tolerance Spaces, and Criteria for Conflict Resolution." *Journal of Peace Science* 1:95–115.

Isard, W., and T.E. Smith. 1966. "On the Resolution of Conflicts Among Regions of a System." *Papers of the Regional Science Association* 17:19–46.

Leung, Y. 1980. "A Fuzzy Set Procedure for Project Selection with Hierarchical Objectives." In *Fuzzy Sets—Theory and Applications to Policy Analysis and Information Systems*, edited by P.P. Wang and S.K. Chang. New York: Plenum.

———. 1981a. "An Empirical Analysis of Linguistic Hedges—I." *Proceedings, International Conference on Policy Analysis and Information Systems*: Taiwan: Tamkang University, 237–249.

———. 1981b. "An Empirical Analysis of Linguistic Hedges—II." *Proceedings, International Conference on Policy Analysis and Information Systems*: Taiwan: Tamkang University, 251–262.

———. 1981c. "On the Exactness of Membership Functions in Fuzzy Sets Theory." *Proceedings, International Conference on Policy Analysis and Information Systems*: Taiwan: Tankang University, 765–775.

———. 1982. "Approximate Characterization of Some Fundamental Concepts of Spatial Analysis." *Geographical Analysis* 14:29–40.

Nijkamp, P. 1978. "Compromise Choices in Spatial Interaction and Regional Planning Models." In *Spatial Interaction Theory and Planning Models*, edited by A. Karlqvist, L. Lundqvist, F. Snickars, and J.W. Weibull. Amsterdam: North Holland.

———. 1979. "A Multidimensional Approach to Environmental Analysis: A Non-technical Survey." *Man, Environment, Space and Time* 1:64–95.

Rapoport, A. (ed.) 1974. *Game Theory as a Theory of Conflict Resolution*. Dordrecht: D. Reidel.

Yu, P.L. 1973. "A Class of Solutions for Group Decisions Problems." *Management Science* 19:936—946.

——. 1974. "Cone Convexity, Cone Extreme Points, and Nondominated Solutions in Decision Problems with Multiobjectives." *Journal of Optimization Theory and Applications* 14:573—584.

Zadeh, L.A. 1965. "Fuzzy Sets." *Information and Control* 8:338—353.

——. 1975a. "The Concept of a Linguistic Variable and Its Application to Approximate Reasoning—I." *Information Science* 8:199—249.

——. 1975b. "The Concept of a Linguistic Variable and Its Application to Approximate Reasoning—II." *Information Science* 8:301—357.

——. 1975c. "The Concept of a Linguistic Variable and Its Application to Approximate Reasoning—III." *Information Science* 9:43—80.

Zeleny, M. 1974. "A Concept of Compromise Solutions and the Method of the Displaced Ideal." *Computers and Operations Research* 1:479—496.

——. 1976. "The Theory of the Displaced Ideal." In *Multiple Criteria Decision Making, Kyoto 1975*, edited by M. Zeleny. Berlin: Springer-Verlag.

5 Decisionmaking Under Conflict in Project Evaluation

Yoshimi Nagao, Katsuhiko Kuroda, and Ikujiro Wakai

It is often the case that the decisionmaker has to choose the "best" from a number of alternatives regarding location, scale, and structural type of such public facilities as roads, ports and harbors, airports, and so on. However, conflicts usually occur among interest groups in choosing the "best alternative" because each of the interest groups evaluates from different points of view. Under such situations there can be two cases from which the decisionmaker chooses the best alternative. One is the case where all the feasible alternatives, including the alternative to abandon the project itself, are presented to the interest groups and all the interest groups play the game of choosing the best one. In practice the interest groups will send their representatives to play the game. In this chapter this is referred to as the "opened case." The other case is when all of the alternatives are not opened to the public in order to avoid confusing political and economical options. In this case the executing organization, such as the agency of public works (that is, decisionmaker), can open only one alternative after the final decision. Of course, the decisionmaker must use logic to make all interest groups consent to accept the proposed alternative. The decisionmaker assumes that conflicts among the interest groups result from different weights on the attributes in evaluating alternatives based on different viewpoints of different groups, and thus there are certain groups who reject whichever alternative is proposed. For such situations, the decisionmaker should choose the alternative corresponding to Least Favorable Weights based on the Maxmin Principle. Here this case is called the "non-opened case."

This chapter formulates these two kinds of situations by the theory of games. Some numerical examples and discussions are presented for two cases.

CURRENT STATE OF STUDIES

Cost-benefit analysis or cost-effectiveness analysis has often been used for evaluating projects. In cost-benefit analysis it is difficult to evaluate many cost- and -benefit measures and condense them into a single composite measure, since various benefits are incommensurable units and not much can be done with coalescing these separate entities. In cost-effectiveness analysis no attempt is necessary to combine the various benefit measures into a single, composite benefit measure. However, difficulties will still remain in analyzing the trade-offs among them.

The advanced case is the situation where multi-objective decisions occur. In this study, multi-objectives of a unitary decisionmaker or many interest groups can be described in terms of their attributes and evaluated through preference (or value or utility) analysis. This method has, however, the crucial problem of reconciling different assesments of preference (or value of utility) for these attributes by different individuals or groups.

Neither cost-benefit, cost-effectiveness, or multi-objective decision analysis has presented the methodology for managing the conflict among the interest groups. The reasons why the current methods cannot reconcile this conflict are, first, that there is an incomplete choice of attributes for evaluating alternatives and a lack of consideration to the fact that different preference (or value or utility) for the alternatives will be assessed by different individuals or groups; and, second, that current methods fail to present the way to reconcile conflict among the interest groups. Taking into account these problems, this study intends to develop two kinds of methodology for managing conflict. One is for the case when all the planned alternatives are opened to the public prior to the final decision. The other is the case when all the planned alternatives cannot be opened to the public in advance.

OPENED CASE

Alternatives and Utilities

There are a number of alternatives that need to be considered for a public project such as the construction of various transportation facilities and the objectives of various interest groups. For example, suppose there are the alternatives $\{a_j, \ j = 1, \ 2, \ldots, m\}$ such as various types of design of roads, and the interest groups

$$N = \{1, 2, \ldots, k, \ldots, n\} \tag{5-1}$$

such as government, users, operators, residentials, and environmentalists. When the alternatives $\{a_j, \ j = 1, \ 2, \ldots, m\}$ are opened to the public, all the interest groups, say k, evaluate them from their own viewpoint. In some cases, the most preferred alternative may be the case to abandon the project itself. Thus, the set A of all the feasible alternatives must contain this case as one of the alternatives. Let this case be the alternative a_0. Therefore, the set of all the alternatives is given by

$$A = \{a_0, a_1, \ldots, a_m\}. \tag{5-2}$$

As just mentioned, each of the interest groups evaluates the alternatives from a particular viewpoint. In other words, a group has its own set of attributes for evaluating the alternatives. Let θ^k be the set of attributes of group k, where,

$$\theta^k = \{\theta_1^k, \theta_2^k, \ldots, \theta_{L_k}^k\} \tag{5-3}$$

According to Keeney and Raiffa (1976), the group k's utility resulting from a choice of an alternative a_j can be defined as

$$U^k(a_j) = \sum_{i=1}^{L_k} \lambda_i^k u_{ij}^k(\theta_i^k, a_j), \tag{5-4}$$

where $u_{ij}^k(\theta_i^k, a_j)$ is k's utility function associated with the attribute θ_i^k and the alternative a_j and is given by a real number; λ_i^k is the weight on the attribute θ_i^k, and satisfies

$$0 \leqslant \lambda_i^k \leqslant 1, \quad \sum_{i=1}^{L_k} \lambda_i^k = 1. \tag{5-5}$$

Pay-offs of a Coalition and Majority Power Rule

It can often be seen that some of the interest groups form a coalition in order to get greater power for presenting their points of view. When no restriction for making coalitions is assumed, $(2^n - 1)$ coalitions are possible. Let the set of possible coalitions be $\mathscr{S}$, any two elementary coalitions be S and T, and the number of members of the coalitions S and T be $[S]$ and $[T]$. The Majority Power Rule can then be defined as:

S has greater power than T if and only if

$$[S] > [T] \tag{5-6a}$$

S and T have equal power if and only if

$$[S] = [T] \tag{5-6b}$$

S has less power than T if and only if

$$[S] < [T]. \tag{5-6c}$$

In the decisionmaking process, the Majority Power Rule should be reflected in the characteristic function which defines the pay-offs of the game for choosing an alternative. Assuming that the group utility is given by the summation of individual utilities, then the characteristic function $v(S)$ of a coalition S is defined as

$$v(S) = \max_{a_j \in A} \sum_{k \subset S} U^k(a_j) \qquad \text{for} \quad [S] > [\bar{S}] \tag{5-7a}$$

where $\bar{S}$ is the complement of the coalition set S, and

$$v(S) = \sum_{k \subset S} U^k(a_0) + \max_p \min_q$$

$$\left[\sum_{j=0}^{m} \sum_{k \subset S} \{U^k(a_i) - U^k(a_0)\} p_j q_j \right]$$

$$\text{for} \quad [S] = [\bar{S}]$$

where

$$p = (p_0, P_1, \ldots, p_m)$$

$$q = (q_0, q_1, \ldots, q_m)$$

and

$$0 \leqslant p_j \leqslant 1 \quad (j = 1, 2, \ldots, m)$$

$$\sum_{j=0}^{m} p_j = 1$$

$$0 \leqslant q_j \leqslant 1 \qquad (j = 1, 2, \ldots, m)$$

$$\sum_{j=0}^{m} q_j = 1$$

and

$$v(S) = \sum_{k \subset S} U^k(a_*^{\bar{S}}) \qquad \text{for} \quad [S] < [\bar{S}] \qquad (5-7c)$$

where $a_*^{\bar{S}}$ is the alternative that gives the maximum resultant utility to the coalition $\bar{S}$, that is,

$$U(a_*^{\bar{S}}) = \max_{a_j \in A} \sum_{k' \subset S} U^{k'}(a_j) \qquad (5-8)$$

Equation (5–7) means that the coalition S considers the $v(S)$ as their minimum security level.

Choice of Alternative Based on Nucleolus

Schmeidler (1969) presents a concept of nucleolus associated with the imputation of an n-person game as the extension of the concept of "Core" or "Kernel." This concept can be applied to the problem of selecting the best alternative, that is, to choose the alternative which satisfies

$$\min_{a_j \in A} \max_{S \in \mathscr{S}} \left\{ v(S) - \sum_{k \subset S} U^k(a_j) \right\}. \qquad (5-9)$$

In the above equation, $v(S) - \sum_{k \subset S} U^k(a_j)$ means the dissatisfaction of a coalition S with an alternative a_j. Therefore the principle of selecting the best alternative is to minimize the maximum dissatisfaction that a coalition S has.

Allotment and Compensation

When the alternative a^* that satisfies equation (5–9) is chosen, each interest group k will get the utility $U^k(a^*)$, and the total utility that society gets is given by $U^N = \sum_{k \subset N} U^k(a^*)$. Obviously, there are still some groups who are dissatisfied with the alternative a^* because not all of the interest groups will have initially supported that alternative. Therefore, some compensation is required so that the alternative a^* will be supported by all of the interest groups. For this reason, Kuroda et al. (1981) formulate the compensation as the ideal allotment of the total utility U^N to each interest group. Denoting the ideal allotment to a group k by $x(k)$, $(k = 1, 2, \ldots, n)$, then $x(k)$ must satisfy the conditions

$$x(k) \geqslant v(k) \qquad (k = 1, 2, \ldots, n) \quad \text{and}$$

$$\sum_{k \subset N} x(k) = \sum_{k \subset N} U^k(a^*) = U^N. \tag{5-10}$$

In the foregoing equations, the first means the individual rationality, and the second means the Pareto optimality.

Again the concept of nucleolus is introduced to determine the ideal allotment $x(k)$, that is,

$$\min_{x} \max_{k \in N} [v(k) - x(k)] \tag{5-11}$$

subject to the constraints given in equation (5–10).

Let the solution of equation (5–11) be $x^*(k)$, $(k = 1, 2, \ldots, n)$. The difference amount

$$c(k) = x^*(k) - U^k(a^*), \qquad (k = 1, 2, \ldots, n) \tag{5-12}$$

must be reallocated as compensation, either as money or some other new alternatives.

It should be noted in equation (5–10), that in an n-person cooperative game, Pareto optimality is given by

$$\sum_{k \subset N} x(k) = \max_{a_j \in A} \sum_{k \subset N} U^k(a_j) = v(N) \tag{5-13}$$

and that the value of $x(k)$ is called "imputation." However, in the present theory, it is not always assured to satisfy

$$v(N) = U^N(a^*). \tag{5-14}$$

Of course, it goes without saying that the alternative which will give $v(N)$ should be chosen from the viewpoint of social optimality, if all the interest groups could cooperate.

Illustrative Example (1)

Suppose there is a government project to improve existing urban transportation conditions. The government has a plan to construct a new highway through a residential district. Initially one alternative (say, a_1) is presented (see Figure 5–1). However, the government is afraid that this new project may be rejected by the residents because of its anticipated bad environmental impacts. Therefore, alternatives (say, a_2, a_3, a_4, a_5) are proposed (see Figure 5–1). If the case of abandoning this project is included as one of the alternatives (say, a_0), then the set A of all the alternatives is given by

$$A = \{a_0, a_1, a_2, a_3, a_4, a_5\}.$$

Further, let's suppose the interest groups are government (G), users (U), and residents (R), that is,

$$N = \{G, U, R\}.$$

Each alternative is evaluated by the representatives of all the interest groups. The results of the evaluation are given in Table 5–1, which shows the corresponding utility to the attributes θ_i^k and the alternatives a_j. The resultant utility of each interest group is then computed as shown in Table 5–2.

The set of available coalitions is given by

$$\mathscr{S} = \{G, U, R, GU, GR, UR, GUR\}$$

and the corresponding characteristic function $v(S)$ is computed from equation (5–7a) and Table 5–2, with the results in Table 5–3.

The amounts of dissatisfaction each coalition has with each alternative are also presented in Table 5–3.

Applying the results of Table 5–3 to equation (5–9), the alternative a_2 should be selected. This gives a total utility of 900, that is,

$$U^N = \sum_{k \subset N} U^k(a_2) = 900.$$

By substituting this result into equation (5–11), the ideal allotment is computed as shown in Figure 5–2. Using Table 5–2 and Figure 5–2, the amounts of compensation of each interest group are computed as shown in Table 5–4.

Figure 5–1.   Alternatives

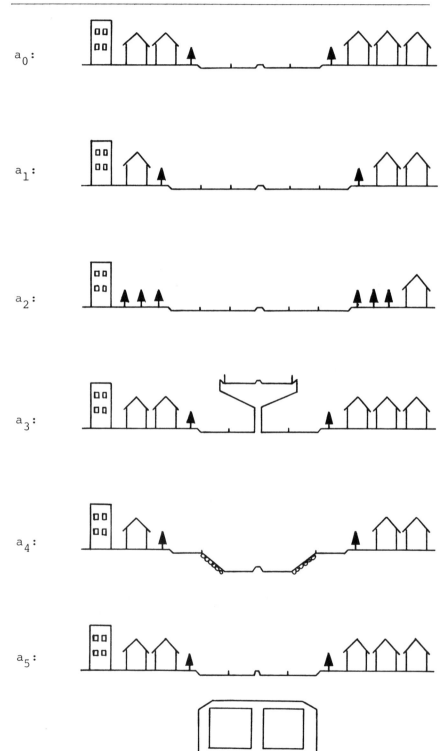

Table 5–1.   Utility Functions

Government	θ^G	λ^G	a_0	a_1	a_2	a_3	a_4	a_5
Regional development (long-range effects)	θ_1^G	20	−10	8	10	8	8	8
Stimulation of economy (short-range effects)	θ_2^G	20	−10	5	7	9	8	10
Reduction of regional traffic jam	θ_3^G	10	−10	9	10	6	7	5
Noise	θ_4^G	10	0	−5	−1	−3	−1	−2
Vibration	θ_5^G	10	0	−7	−1	0	0	0
Air pollution	θ_6^G	5	0	−4	−1	−2	−1	−1
Construction cost	θ_7^G	15	0	−1	−8	−8	−7	−10
Construction period	θ_8^G	10	0	0	−1	−4	−2	−8
Total $U^G(a_j)$			−500	195	285	200	250	155

Users	θ^U	λ^U	a_0	a_1	a_2	a_3	a_4	a_5
Reduction of travel time	θ_1^U	60	−8	10	10	8	10	8
Safety in driving	θ_2^U	40	−5	8	10	−3	7	−7
Total $U^U(a_j)$			−680	920	1000	360	880	200

Residents	θ^R	λ^R	a_0	a_1	a_2	a_3	a_4	a_5
Failure of community	θ_1^R	30	10	−10	−10	−8	−10	10
Noise	θ_2^R	15	−1	−10	−5	−10	−8	−7
Vibration	θ_3^R	15	−1	−10	−5	−5	−4	−1
Air pollution	θ_4^R	15	−2	−10	−2	−10	−8	−5
Traffic accidents	θ_5^R	10	−1	0	0	0	0	0
Traffic jam reduction of local road	θ_6^R	10	−1	1	1	−1	−1	−1
Regional development	θ_7^R	5	0	2	2	2	2	1
Total $U^R(a_j)$			220	−730	−385	−615	−600	100

Table 5–2.   Resultant Total Utility

	a_0	a_1	a_2	a_3	a_4	a_5
(G) Government	-500	195	285	200	250	155
(U) Users	-680	920	1000	360	880	200
(R) Residents	220	-730	-385	-615	-600	100
Social utility	-960	385	900	-55	530	455

Table 5–3.   Characteristic Function and Dissatisfaction

S	$v(S)$	a_0	a_1	a_2	a_3	a_4	a_5
G	285	785	90	0	85	35	130
U	200	880	-720	-800	-160	-680	0
R	-385	85	345	0	230	215	-485
G + U	1285	2465*	170	0	725	155	930*
G + R	255	535	790*	355*	670	605*	0
U + R	615	1075	425	0	870	335	315
G + U + R	900	1860	515	0	955*	370	445
Maximum dissatisfaction		2465	760	355** (minmax)	955	605	930

Table 5–4.   Ideal Allotment and Adjustment

k	$x(k)$	$U^k(a_2)$	$c(k)$
G	$\dfrac{1655}{3}$	285	$+\dfrac{800}{3}$
U	$\dfrac{1400}{3}$	1000	$-\dfrac{1600}{3}$
R	$-\dfrac{355}{3}$	-385	$+\dfrac{800}{3}$
		900	0.0

Figure 5–2.   Graphical Solution of Ideal Allotment

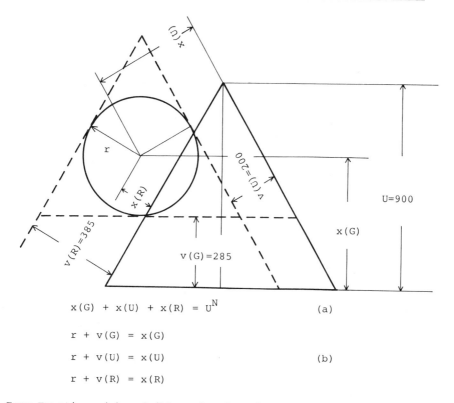

$$x(G) + x(U) + x(R) = U^N \tag{a}$$

$$r + v(G) = x(G)$$
$$r + v(U) = x(U) \tag{b}$$
$$r + v(R) = x(R)$$

From Equations (a) and (b), r is given by

$$r = \frac{1}{3}[\ U^N - v(G) - v(U) - v(R)\ ] \tag{c}$$

From Table 2 and 3,

$$U^N = U(a_2^*) = 900$$
$$v(G) = 285$$
$$v(U) = 200 \tag{d}$$
$$v(R) = -385$$

Substituting (d) into (c), we obtain $r = \dfrac{800}{3}$.

Therefore, the ideal allotments are

$$x(G) = \frac{1655}{3}, \quad x(U) = \frac{1400}{3}, \quad x(R) = -\frac{355}{3}$$

NON-OPENED CASE

Alternatives and Utilities

In the previous case, the theory is formulated on the assumption that all of the considered alternatives can be opened to the public before the final decision and that each of the interest groups will behave so as to maximize its utility by making coalitions. However, it is often the case in practical problems that not all alternatives can be opened to the public before getting the final decisions. If all alternatives are opened, then: (1) people feel uneasy designing their socioeconomic activities and their life styles due to areas of uncertainty; (2) land prices will rise due to speculation; (3) political friction will occur among regions nominated and their local governments; and so forth. With such situations being anticipated, the decisionmaker must present only that alternative which is expected to be accepted by the interest groups. In this case the agency of public works asks professionals or specialists to make utility functions from the anticipated viewpoints of the interest groups. The resultant total utility of an interest group from an alternative is assumed to be given by the weighted summation of single attribute utility. Consequently, each of the interest groups will want to weight their own attributes so that their most preferred alternative is selected. Nagao et al. (1981) identified this as a gaming situation between the decisionmaker and the interest groups.

The Idea of Decisionmaker

In order to select the one alternative to be opened, the decisionmaker (agency of public works) should evaluate all of the considered alternatives from a broader standpoint, taking into account conflicts that exist among the interest groups. The decisionmaker knows that there are many interest groups who have placed different weightings on the attributes. As discussed in the previous section, the utility $u_{ij}(\theta_i, a_j)$ $(i = 1, 2, \ldots, L, j = 1, 2, \ldots, m)$ is given by the professionals or specialists. Therefore, the total utility of a group (say, k) resultant from an alternative a_j is given by

$$U^k(a_j) = \sum_{i=1}^{L} \lambda_i^k u_{ij}(\theta_i, a_j) \qquad (5-15)$$

where $\lambda_i^k (i = 1, 2, \ldots, L)$ is the weight constants of group k. In the expression of equation $(5-15)$ different groups (say, k and k') can be symbolized by the different weight vectors $\overline{\lambda}^k$ and $\overline{\lambda}^{k'}$. The decisionmaker faces the problem of deciding what weight vector to use in choosing the best alternative. If an appropriate weight vector (say, $\overline{\lambda}^*$) is given a priori, then the decisionmaker can choose the alternative which maximizes the total utility, that is,

$$U(a^*) = \max_{a_j \in A} \sum_{i=1}^{L} \lambda_i^* u_{ij}(\theta_i, a_j) \tag{5-16}$$

Under this situation, the decisionmaker may be thinking: "If I use a weight vector $\overline{\lambda}^k$ and choose the alternative a_*^k which gives maximum total utility under that weight vector $\overline{\lambda}^k$, some groups may claim to use it, but instead use another weight vector $\overline{\lambda}^{k'}$ in order to reject to proposed alternative a_*^k. If $\overline{\lambda}^{k'}$ is used, the alternative a_*^k does not become optimal and another alternative might be chosen. However, if I use the weight vector $\overline{\lambda}^{k'}$ instead of $\overline{\lambda}^k$ and propose another alternative $a_*^{k'}$ as the optimal, then some other groups may bluff again. Consequently, the strategy for the groups who reject any proposed alternative must be to insist the use of the weight vector which minimizes the resultant total utility." After these considerations the decisionmaker might decide to use the weight vector $\overline{\lambda}$ which satisfies

$$\max_{a_j \in A} \min_{\overline{\lambda} \in \Lambda} \sum_{i=1}^{L} \lambda_i u_{ij}(\theta_i, a_j) \tag{5-17}$$

in which Λ is the set of $\overline{\lambda}$.

The idea of this decisionmaking process is the same as that in Statistical Decision Theory where the decisionmaker uses the least favorable subjective probability under an uncertain state of nature. Thus in this chapter, that vector which satisfies equation $(5-17)$ is called the "Least Favorable Weights (L.F.W.)."

Choice of Alternative based on L.F.W.

Suppose the utility function $u_{ij}(\theta_i, a_j)$ is given by some professionals and specialists. Let the set of attributes be $\Theta = \{\theta_1, \theta_2, \ldots, \theta_L\}$ and the set of the considered alternatives be $A = \{a_0, a_1, \ldots, a_m\}$ where a_0 is the alternative defined in the previous case. Let the probability distribution function defined on A be δ, that is,

$$\delta = \{\delta_1, \delta_2, \ldots, \delta_m\}$$

$$0 \leqslant \delta_j \leqslant 1 \qquad (j = 1, 2, \ldots, m) \tag{5-18}$$

$$\sum_{j=1}^{m} \delta_j = 1$$

and let the set of δ be Δ.

Denoting $\bar{\lambda} = \{\lambda_1, \lambda_2, \ldots, \lambda_L\}$ as the weight vector used by any interest group and Λ as the set of $\bar{\lambda}$, the number of the elements of the set Λ is the number of interest groups. Using these notations, the solution equivalent to equation (5–17) is given by

$$U(a^*) = \max_{\bar{\lambda} \in \Lambda} \; \min_{\delta \in \Delta} EU(\delta, \bar{\lambda})$$

$$= \min_{\delta \in \Delta} \; \max_{\bar{\lambda} \in \Lambda} \; EU(\delta, \bar{\lambda}) \tag{5-19}$$

where $EU(\delta, \bar{\lambda})$ is the expected utility given by

$$EU(\delta, \bar{\lambda}) = \sum_{j=1}^{m} \sum_{i=1}^{L} \lambda_i u_{ij}(\theta_i, a_j) \delta_j \tag{5-20}$$

in which

$$0 \leqslant \lambda_i \leqslant 1 \qquad (i = 1, 2, \ldots, L)$$

$$\sum_{i=1}^{L} \lambda_i = 1. \tag{5-21}$$

It is not to say that there is an equilibrium solution $(\delta^*, \bar{\lambda}^*)$ which satisfies the equation (5–19).

It is sometimes recognized that there exists some order of importance of the attributes. For such cases, the following constraints should be added to equation (5–21).

$$\lambda_i - \lambda_{i+1} \geqslant 0 \qquad (i = 1, 2, \ldots, L-1) \tag{5-22}$$

which means the attribute λ_i is understood to be more important than the attribute λ_{i+1} by all the interest groups.

As is well known, the solution of equation (5–19) is subject to the constraints expressed within equations (5–21) and (5–22), which can be obtained by using linear programming. However, it should be noted that the solution is not necessarily given by a nonrandomized (pure) alternative but a randomized (mixed) alternative. Therefore, the decisionmaker must choose an alternative through a random mechanism which satisfies the solution. If he does not wish to use the random mechanism, he must solve the following equations:

for the case without the constraint of equation (5–22)

$$U(a^*) = \max_{a_j \in A} \min_{\theta_i \in \Theta} u_{ij}(\theta_i, a_j), \text{ and} \qquad (5\text{–}23)$$

for the case with the constraint of equation (5–22)

$$U(a^*) = \max_{a_j \in A} \min_{\overline{\lambda} \in \Lambda} \sum_{i=1}^{L} \lambda_{ij}^* u_{ij}(\theta_i, a_j) \qquad (5\text{–}24)$$

where λ_{ij}^* are the solutions of the linear programming:

$$\min_{\overline{\lambda} \in \Lambda} \sum_{i=1}^{L} \lambda_{ij} u_{ij}(\theta_i, a_j) \qquad (5\text{–}25)$$

subject to equation (5–22).

From these, the decisionmaker will get the solution of the non-ramdomized alternative.

It should be noted that even if the decisionmaker were to propose the alternative obtained from the solution of equations (5–19) and (5–23) or (5–24), there will still be some groups who reject it. Therefore, some form of compensation must be considered, as discussed in the previous case.

Illustrative Example (2)

Suppose the national government makes a plan of a new offshore airport. Three locational alternatives, including the existing off-shore airport, are considered, taking into account each locations accessibility, geotechnical issues, environmental impacts, constructional costs, and so forth. Let these three alternatives be (a_0, a_1, a_2).

In evaluating these alternatives, the government asks specialists and professionals to make lists of attributes and to prepare utility functions from the viewpoints of concerned interest groups. In Table 5–5 is the pay-off matrix as presented to these groups. Given this pay-off matrix, the government then uses the maxmin principle and selects the best alternative by using equation (5–19), without the constraint of equation (5–22). The computed solution is given in Table 5–6. As can be understood from this table, the best

Table 5–5.   Pay-off Matrix (Normalized Utility Value)

Interest Groups	Attributes			Alternatives		
				a_0 δ_0	a_1 δ_1	a_2 δ_2
Users	Accessibility	θ_1	λ_1	0.894	0.821	0.562
Construction agency	Air control & navigation	θ_2	λ_2	0.729	0.801	0.912
	Construction cost	θ_3	λ_3	0.700	0.782	0.853
Inhabitants	Environmental impacts	θ_4	λ_4	0.700	0.841	0.829
Navigators & fishermen	Adjustment of present benefit	θ_5	λ_5	0.668	0.852	0.618
Regional people	Comprehensive regional plan	θ_6	λ_6	0.653	0.865	0.779
	Regional development	θ_7	λ_7	0.664	0.851	0.750

Table 5–6.   Case without Constraint on Importance of Attributes (U = 0.790)

Alternatives	a_0			a_1			a_2
δ	0			0.882			0.118

Attributes	θ_1	θ_2	θ_3	θ_4	θ_5	θ_6	θ_7
λ	0.215	0	0.785	0	0	0	0

Note. The second best solution: $U^* = 0.782$, Alternative a_1).

Table 5–7.   Case with Constraint on Importance of Attributes (U = 0.801)

Alternatives	a_0	a_1	a_2
δ	0	1.00	0

Attributes	$\theta_1 \geqslant \theta_2 \geqslant \theta_3 \geqslant \theta_4 \geqslant \theta_5 \geqslant \theta_6 \geqslant \theta_7$						
$\bar{\lambda}$	$\frac{1}{3}$	$\frac{1}{3}$	$\frac{1}{3}$	0	0	0	0

alternative is given by the randomized one: alternative a_1 with a probability of 0.882 and alternative a_2 with a probability of 0.118. This solution suggests that the government has to choose a_1 or a_2 by using some random mechanism.

If this random choice is not preferred, then the second best solution should be obtained by equation (5—23), which in this case is the alternative a_1 with the weight vector:

$$\bar{\lambda} = \{\lambda_1 = 0.215, \lambda_2 = 0.0, \lambda_3 = 0.785, \lambda_4 = \lambda_5 = \lambda_6 = \lambda_7 = 0.0\}.$$

Table 5—7 shows the given order of importance of attributes for the situation when the constraint is applied. In this case, the constraint of λ_i corresponding to equation (5—22) is given by

$$\lambda_1 \geqslant \lambda_2 \geqslant \lambda_3 \geqslant \lambda_4 \geqslant \lambda_5 \geqslant \lambda_6 \geqslant \lambda_7.$$

The best alternative is also given by a_1 with the probability 1.0, while the corresponding weight vector $\bar{\lambda}$ is given by

$$\bar{\lambda} = \{\lambda_1 = \lambda_2 = \lambda_3 = \tfrac{1}{3}, \lambda_4 = \lambda_5 = \lambda_6 = \lambda_7 = 0.0\}.$$

DISCUSSION AND CONCLUDING REMARKS

This chapter presents ideas to resolve conflicts among interest groups in choosing an alternative. One idea is formulated by an n-person non-zero sum game and the other by statistical decision theory. Both of the ideas intend to make clear the conflicts present among the interest groups and to give a method of resolving the conflicts aimed at public welfare while societal efficiency is pursued. It is well recognized that whatever alternative is proposed, there still exist some groups or individuals who will not agree. Therefore, in executing any public project, some compensation or other adjustments of interest between the groups will become necessary. While this chapter presents the procedure for such compensation or adjustments, there remain some problems for practical uses such as how to adjust the utility difference by a monetary amount or some other alternative. Notwithstanding, it is still useful for the decisionmaker to be able to obtain information about what the conflicts among interest groups are, what the level of dissatisfactions in the groups are, and what additional alternatives to consider in order to get consensus from all the groups.

Finally, with an expression of gratitude to Professor D.E. Boyce of the University of Illinois for his discussions on this chapter, the authors offer this thought: in light of the practical conditions, the government may want the non-opened case, but the people themselves may prefer the opened case. While further discussion on this point is beyond our scope here, it might be suggested that the government make efforts to use the opened case except where problems of important national security arise. These points and their applicability to practical problems should be discussed and examined further.

REFERENCES

Keeney, R.L., and H. Raiffa. 1976. *Decisions with Multiple Objectives— Preferences and Value Tradeoffs.* New York: Wiley.

Kuroda, K.; Y. Nagao; and I. Wakai. 1981. "A Game Theoretic Interpretation of an Incidental Policy of Public Transportation Projects." *Proceedings of the 3rd Annual Meeting on Civil Engineering Systems & Planning* (in Japanese), JSCE, pp 78–85.

Nagao, Y.; A. Asaoka; and I. Wakai. 1981. "A Method of Synthetic Evaluation for Alternatives with Unknown Weight in Evaluation Items." *Proceedings of JSCE.* No. 313 (in Japanese), JSCE, pp 89–100.

Schmeidler, D. 1969. "The Nucleolus of a Characteristic Function Game." *SIAM, Journal of Applied Mathematics* 17, no. 6:1163–1170.

6 Regional Development and Investments in Infrastructure—The Evaluation of Conflicting Impacts

Rolf H. Funck and Ulrich Blum

In this chapter a concept is developed in order to relate regional production to regional infrastructure equipment and evaluate the conflicting impacts induced. It can be shown that the level of production of a region strongly depends on its infrastructure facilities and the degree of utilization of the infrastructure capacities. Thus it seems justified to define a regional production function which describes the importance of the various infrastructural categories for the regional income potential. The knowledge of these relationships can be used to define regional growth strategies and balance them against other interests—especially in the environmental field—if transformation functions for these other impacts can be found in order to include them in a decision model.

The first part of this chapter focuses on an adequate definition of infrastructure and gives a brief description of the level of infrastructure investments based on the West German experience. The second part briefly describes productive and environmental regional impacts of infrastructure investments. The third part is dedicated to the providing of a decision model which can be used to balance productive and environmental interests against each other in the planning and implementing of infrastructure investments. The fourth part of the chapter concentrates on the designing of a model which can be used to measure the regional effects of infrastructure investments with respect to production and land use; these serve as two examples for conflicting impacts. The fifth part is dedicated to providing empirical evidence for this concept using selected data for West Germany for the year 1976.

IMPORTANCE OF INFRASTRUCTURE

Definition

An infrastructure system can be defined as a set of specific categories of assets and abilities, the availability of which are necessary preconditions for making productive or consumptive use of all other existing assets. In West Germany infrastructure assets are mainly provided by the public sector. Depending on the quantity and the quality of infrastructure facilities available, a suprastructure may evolve.[1]

Infrastructure systems can be classified into two groups:

1. Immaterial infrastructure includes human capital and the system of social organization as well as the institutional structures of the public sector, and the set of rules which constitutes the framework of economic and social activities: human or personal, institutional, and social infrastructure.

2. Material or physical infrastructure includes all fixed assets, the services of which can be regarded as public goods for private production and consumption: infrastructure capital.

In the following, we will concentrate on the regional importance of material infrastructure, which can be characterized by three concepts (Funck 1978: 290–294):

1. Agglomerative or locational infrastructure comprises facilities which supply public goods from fixed locations. Individuals or groups residing or working in the supply area of the facilities are required to commute to the respective location in order to make use of the public goods offered. Typical examples of this first type of infrastructure are schools, theaters, recreational facilities, hospitals, and so on. This type of infrastructure is called agglomerative or locational since a strong relationship between its capacity

---

1. This dependency of the suprastructure on the infrastructure will be one of the starting points for the modeling of regional production systems in part four of this chapter.

and the degree of agglomeration of residential and productive activities can be assumed.

2. Network infrastructure comprises all facilities designed to link together different locations, thus forming a network structure. Typical examples of this second type of infrastructure are transportation and communication systems.

3. Nodal infrastructure comprises all nodes in network systems which transform flows within the network. Typical examples are ports, airports, railroad stations, and so forth.

Financial Volume of Investments in the Infrastructure in the Federal Republic of Germany

Table 6–1 gives an impression of the financial volume of investments in the infrastructure in the Federal Republic.

Figure 6–1 displays the development of transport investments in West Germany over time.

Table 6–1.   Investments in the Infrastructure in the Federal Republic of Germany (Billion DM)

Investment	1978
Schools	6.3
Universities (Hochschulen)	2.3
Hospitals	3.4
Waste water and waste disposal	6.0
Federal interstate highways	3.3
Federal, state, county, or community roads	12.1
Waterways and port facilities	1.9

Source: Statistisches Bundesamt (1982: 422–423).

Effects of Investments in the Infrastructure

The equipment of a region with infrastructure is, as mentioned before, strongly related to its suprastructure, especially to the latter's productive part. Even with a steady-state infrastructure, this suprastructure will change; however, investments in the infrastructure can be seen as a dynamic stimulus for influencing regional development. The following effects are worth mentioning:

Figure 6—1.   Gross Investments in transportation in the Federal Republic of Germany

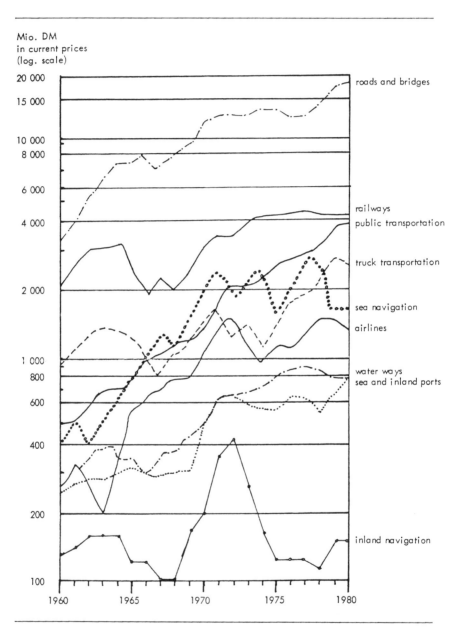

Source: Bundesminister für Verkehr (1981).

1. Income effects: a primary income effect of an investment in the infrastructure stems from the spending of financial means; a secondary income effect may occur through changes in attractivity leading to additional consumptive activities.

2. Capacity effects: an investment in the infrastructure increases the production capacity and thus gives a chance for additional income, if this potential is used through additional productive activities.

IMPACTS OF INVESTMENTS IN THE INFRASTRUCTURE

The Impact on Production

As already mentioned, an adequate equipment with infrastructure facilities is a necessary condition for the enhancement of regional production.

From a regional point of view, the regional equipment with infrastructure—as well as with certain other locational factors and parts of the labor force—belongs to a class of spatially immobile production factors called "input potentials." This designation has been chosen since there is evidence of a strong relationship between a region's equipment with input potentials and its economic development potential due to a high degree of limitationality between input potentials and all other (attractable) production factors (Blum 1982; Funck and Blum 1980). Thus an improvement of a region's infrastructure base will increase the economic development potential. Actual growth can only occur, however, if the new infrastructure capacities are adequately utilized—for instance, through additional traffic flows issuing from dissolved bottlenecks or newly induced transportation demands. This leads to the concept of regional growth stated in Figure 6–2 (Blum 1982:96–101; Funck and Blum 1980: 216–222).

The actual level of production activities in region i and period t is given by x_{it} (for example, by the regional gross value added). This level of activity will increase to the value of x_{it}, if an infrastructure investment is implemented, as savings in outlays induced by the investments (for example, transport cost reduction) allow for new investments, and the compensation of those disadvantaged

Figure 6–2.   Regional Growth Process Induced by an Investment
in the Infrastructure

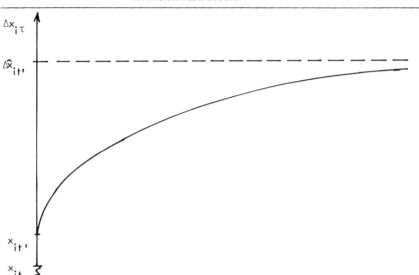

Note: Abbreviations and subscripts are explained in the text.

by the investment. Additional growth $\Delta x_{i\tau} \, \epsilon \, [x_{it'}, \Delta \hat{x}_{it'}]$, $\tau = t' + 1$, $t' + 2, \ldots$ will only occur if the production factors, especially the new infrastructure capacities, are adequately used. Infrastructure investments therefore have two effects: (1) they enlarge regional production capacities and thus create growth potentials; and (2) if adequately used, they induce regional growth. These two effects must be distinguished if they are to be related to an environmental impact analysis: land use for infrastructure investments is related to the capacities; harrassments such as noise or pollution depend on the degree of capacity utilization.

Impact on the Regional Environment

The most immediate impact of infrastructure investments is on the use of land. Generally speaking, the impacts on the regional environment very highly depend on the category of infrastructure investment, the degree of utilization of the new capacities, and the layout

Figure 6–3.   Impact Matrix for Transportation Investments

impacts strategies	economic growth	air quality	water quality	noise level	scenery	recreation	land use
road investments							
rail investments							
investment in inland waterways							
new siting							
.							
.							
.							
.							

planned by architects and civil engineers. In the case of an investment in the transport infrastructure, the following (incomplete) list of impacts other than on economic growth may be relevant:

Positive	Negative
decrease of noise	increase of noise
decrease of air pollution	increase of air pollution
energy savings	land use
savings in travelling time	severance effects
modal split changes	modal split changes
decrease of traffic accidents	

GROWTH-ORIENTED REGIONAL STRATEGIES

The Problem

A stimulation of regional economic growth can be achieved by investment strategies changing the regional factor equipment. Earlier these strategies were related to their impacts on production and the environment. In what way can these effects be analyzed?

One way of describing the influences of infrastructure investments is the establishing of an impact matrix (see Nijkamp 1976: 2) for every relevant project. In this context, the matrix could have the form shown in Figure 6–3.

The economic evaluation of the costs and benefits of economic growth induced by infrastructure investments might be fairly convincing if all impact data were given in monetary terms. This, however, is not the case. Market prices often do not exist for input potentials. Solow (1971: 498) has argued that with respect to natural and environmental resources a pricing mechanism will work only if ecological damage has already occurred; otherwise these resources will be treated as free goods.

One possible response to this situation might be in the introduction of social-environmental standards, and taxes reflecting the external, social, and ecological costs. Such a procedure would, however, imply a serious loss of flexibility in public decisionmaking.

In cases where two—or more—conflicting goals have to be evaluated, an aggregate, scalar-valued goal function can be introduced by monetary or nonmonetary weighting of all components. The weights can be fixed by expert judgments, through a technique of interviewing the concerned citizens or by any other sensible method (see, for example, Funck and others 1975). This means that out of any two projects, either of the two may become the more advantageous one, depending on the weighting system applied, as long as one of the projects does not dominate the other one.

The Model

A model which can be used to define an optimum regional investment strategy can be developed in the following way. Based on the concept of vector maximization, infrastructure investment strategies (investments into input potentials) are linked to production levels and environmental impacts, that is, all effects of an investment into input potentials are included in a vector-valued goal function under a technical restriction system. Then, all functionally efficient strategies—that is, those strategies, the impacts of which cannot be ordered with respect to the relation "$\geqslant$"[2] –are possible solutions to the investment project in question.

It can be shown (see Blum 1982: 115 ff.) that all functionally efficient strategies can be found by varying the weighting vector of certain classes of substitute functions which aggregate the weighted impacts. The following assumptions are needed to describe the problem (Blum 1982: 115–116):

Assumption 1.   There exist at least two social or political groups with conflicting goals regarding an investment into regional input potentials.

Assumption 2.   For every group a transformation function exists which relates the investment into input potentials to the goals. The input potentials of region i in period t are given by a vector $\hat{v}_{it} = (\hat{v}_{1it}, \hat{v}_{2it}, \ldots, \hat{v}_{mit}) \in \mathbb{R}_+^m$.

Assumption 3.   The degree of goal achievement can, for group k, be described by the expression

$$\lambda_{kit} = h_{kit}(\hat{v}_{it}) \in [0, 1], \qquad (6\text{–}1)$$

$$h_{kit} \text{ strictly monotonic, and}$$

$$\sum_{k=1}^{K} \lambda_{kit} = 1.$$

Assumption 4.   Every group has a utility (urgency) function

$$u_k: \mathbb{R} \times [0, 1] \rightarrow \mathbb{R}_+, \qquad (6\text{–}2)$$

$$\lambda_{kit} \rightarrow u_k(\lambda_{kit})$$

with the following properties: u_k is strictly monotonic with respect to λ_{kit}; and $U = \Psi(u_1, u_2, \ldots, u_k)$ is bounded and convex, and Ψ is an aggregation function increasing with respect to each u_k, $k = 1, 2, \ldots, K$.

2. For example, $\begin{pmatrix} 2 \\ 2 \end{pmatrix} > \begin{pmatrix} 1 \\ 1 \end{pmatrix}; \begin{pmatrix} 2 \\ 2 \end{pmatrix} \geqslant \begin{pmatrix} 2 \\ 1 \end{pmatrix}; \begin{pmatrix} 2 \\ 1 \end{pmatrix} \not\geqslant \begin{pmatrix} 1 \\ 2 \end{pmatrix}.$

Assumption 5.   The regional investment strategies are

$$
\begin{cases}
\hat{v}_{it'} \in \hat{V}_{it} \subseteq \mathbb{R}_+^m, \quad \text{and} \\
(\hat{v}_{it'} - \hat{v}_{it}) > 0, \quad t' = t + \tau, \quad \tau = 1, 2, \ldots \\
\qquad\qquad\qquad t' > t.
\end{cases}
\tag{6-3}
$$

The subset $\hat{V}_{it}$ comprises all possible and feasible combinations of investment strategies as well as the actual equipment with input potentials in region i.

Assumption 6.   The transformation functions of all groups are included in the vector-valued master function which is to be maximized:

$$
F : \hat{v}_{it} \rightarrow W_{it} \in \mathbb{R}_+^K.
\tag{6-4}
$$

Under a technical restriction system, maximization of the master function will supply the set of all functionally efficient strategies:

Definition 1.   For a vector maximum problem,

$$
E = \{\hat{v}_{it}^* \in \hat{V}_{it} \subseteq \mathbb{R}_+^m \mid \nexists\ \hat{v}_{it} \in \hat{V}_{it} \subseteq \mathbb{R}_+^m \mid F(\hat{v}_{it}^*) \leqslant F(\hat{v}_{it})\}
\tag{6-5}
$$

is called the *set of functionally efficient strategies.*

The problem, then, is to choose one "optimal" solution from the set of functionally efficient strategies. This task can be solved by defining a substitute problem for region i in period t which is to be maximized:

This substitute problem values the results of all functional efficient strategies:

$$
\Phi : F(\hat{v}_{it}) \in \mathbb{R}_+^K \rightarrow \Phi(F(\hat{v}_{it})) \in \mathbb{R}_+,
\tag{6-6}
$$

and Φ strictly increasing.

It can be shown that using an additive function for Φ will give all functional efficient $\hat{v}_{it}$, by varying the weighting vector $a_{it} \in \mathbb{R}_+^K$:

$$
\Phi(F(\hat{v}_{it})) = \sum_{k=1}^{K} F_k(\hat{v}_{it}) \cdot a_{kit}
\tag{6-7}
$$

A direct computation of weights $a_{it} \in \mathbb{R}_+^K$ faces several problems. First, problems of dimensionality arise, as the terms $F_k(\hat{v}_{it})$, $k = 1, 2, \ldots, K$ are not normalized. Second, expressions (6–3), (6–6), and (6–7) do not consider the starting position of each group nor the desired size of changes in the equipment with input potentials. This is why we prefer to achieve maximization by using the utility functions (6–2) and assumption (7).

Assumption 7.   For all $k = 1, 2, \ldots, K$, the master function is related to the utility function as follows:

$$\frac{\partial \Psi(u_1, u_2, \ldots, u_K)}{\partial u_k} > 0 < = > \frac{\partial \Phi(F(\hat{v}_{it}))}{\partial F_k(\hat{v}_{it})} > 0, \qquad (6\text{–}8)$$

and

$$\frac{\partial \Psi(u_1, u_2, \ldots, u_K)}{\partial u_k} \not> 0 = > \quad \begin{array}{l} \text{Group } k \text{ is irrelevant} \\ \text{for the decision model} \end{array} \qquad (6\text{–}9)$$

The problem thus becomes:

$$\text{max:}\ \Psi(u_1(\lambda_{1it}), u_2(\lambda_{2it}), \ldots, u_K(\lambda_{Kit}))$$

$$\text{sub:}\ \sum_{k=1}^{K} \lambda_{kit} = 1 \qquad (6\text{–}10)$$

$$\lambda_{kit} \in [0, 1].$$

A function for Ψ can be given by

$$\Psi(u_1(\lambda_{1it}), \ldots, u_K(\lambda_{Kit})) \qquad (6\text{–}11)$$

$$= \prod_{k=1}^{K} \lambda_{kit}^{d_{kit}},$$

with $d_{kit} \in \mathbb{R}$, $k = 1, 2, \ldots, K$ as weights chosen according to a method discussed later.

The result is given by expression

$$\lambda_{kit}^* / \lambda_{k'it}^* = r_{kit}^*, \qquad k = 1, 2, \ldots, K,$$

$$k' = 1, 2, \ldots, K, \qquad (6\text{–}12)$$

$$k \neq k'.$$

According to these ratios r_{kit}^* an "optimal" investment strategy $\hat{v}_{it'}$ can be computed for region i in period t, according to the following instruction:

$$\left\{\begin{array}{l} \text{Find (optimal) solution } \hat{v}_{it}, \\[6pt] \text{for } \lambda^*_{kit} = b_{kit}(\hat{v}_{it}), \qquad k = 1, 2, \ldots, K, \\[6pt] \hat{v}_{it} \in \hat{V}_{it}, \\[6pt] \lambda^*_{kit}/\lambda^*_{k'it} = r^*_{kit}, \qquad k = 1, 2, \ldots, K, \\[6pt] \qquad\qquad\qquad\qquad k' = 1, 2, \ldots, K, \\[6pt] \qquad\qquad\qquad\qquad k' \neq k. \end{array}\right. \qquad (6\text{--}13)$$

As mentioned, the substitute function (6—6) aggregates the weighted impacts of a given strategy $\hat{v}_{it}$ in such a way that a scalar evaluation of strategies becomes possible. As utility weights we propose the marginal rates of substitution which are a measure of scarcity for all factors included in a production analysis and average rates of substitution for all other factors relevant to the social and ecological environment when the marginal rates of substitution are not available.

INVESTMENTS IN THE REGIONAL INFRASTRUCTURE

Analysis of Production

The following assumptions are needed to interpret the mechanisms of regional production[3] :

Assumption A.   All regions belong to a market economy.

Assumption B.   All attractable factors are priced at marginal costs.

Assumption C.   Input potentials are priced according to costs and political influences.

Assumption D.   Input potentials are limiting with respect to the input of attractable factors.

---

3. Assumptions (A) to (G) and their deductions were proposed and discussed at length by Blum (1982: 24 ff).

Assumption E.   In every region maximization of output is an objective for achievement. In the environment of full employment, cost functions have a convex slope.

Assumption F.   Total output corresponds to total potential output of all regions, that is, only the distribution of potential and actual output varies interrregionally.

Assumption G.   Subsidies are financed by taxes.

Under assumptions (A) to (G) an interpretation is developed with the following deductions:

The regional equipment with input potentials determines (and limits) regional economic development. Attractable factors are combined with input potentials in fixed proportions according to the underlying technology, and are always fully employed.

A regional production function thus only needs to contain input potentials as exogenous variables. The parameters of the chosen production function can be estimated by a cross-section analysis of all regions. Once all input potentials have been valued by their maximum capacity, the parameters of the production function may be estimated. As no data on potential regional products are available, it is assumed that the sum of potential outputs, $\sum_i \hat{x}_{it}$, will be equal to the sum of actual outputs, $\sum_i x_{it}$, thus the latter can be used in a regression as an endogenous variable. In doing so, efficiency in production is not necessarily given; this leads to differences between actual and potential regional products caused by bottlenecks in the regional factor equipment or to interregional price discrimination with respect to the utilization of input potentials.

The following production function was computed for the cross-section of all of the 325 German counties in 1976:

$$P(\hat{v}_{it}) = \hat{x}_{it} = 3.58 \cdot \hat{v}_{1it}^{0.5007} \cdot \hat{v}_{2it}^{0.1100} \cdot \hat{v}_{3it}^{0.3241} \cdot$$

$$\cdot \hat{v}_{4it}^{-0.0737} \cdot \hat{v}_{5it}^{0.0065} \cdot \hat{v}_{6it}^{0.0363} \cdot \hat{v}_{7it}^{0.0718} \cdot$$

$$\cdot \hat{v}_{8it}^{-0.0765} \cdot \hat{z}_{it}, \qquad i = 1, 2, \ldots, 325,$$

$$t = 1976,$$

$$(6-14)$$

with $\hat{z}_{it} = \hat{z}_{1it} \cdot \hat{z}_{2it} \cdot \hat{z}_{3it}$,   (6—14a)

and $\hat{z}_{1it} = 1.20$ for "Oberzentrum" (high ranked central place),

   $\hat{z}_{2it} = 1.13$ for "Sitz der Bezirksregierung" (site of the district government),

   $\hat{z}_{3it} = 1.43$ for "Sitz der Bundes oder der Landesregierung" (site of the federal or a state government),

   and $\hat{z}_{jit} = 1, j = 1, 2, 3$ if the county's city has neither of these ranks.

Table 6—2 explains the variables used in the production function.

Table 6—2.   Variables Used in the Production Analysis

Abbreviation	Name	Measurement
$\hat{x}_{it}, x_{it}$	Potential regional product, actual regional product	Potential gross value added, actual gross value added (million DM)
$\hat{v}_{1it}$	Agglomeration	Inhabitants per Area (Pers./km^2)
$\hat{v}_{2it}$	Long-distance roads	See formula 6—15
$\hat{v}_{3it}$	Other roads	See formula 6—16
$\hat{v}_{4it}$	Railroad	Number of freight stations
$\hat{v}_{5it}$	Navigation	Potential turnover (Million metric tons)
$\hat{v}_{6it}$	New sites	New industrial and commercial sites for short and medium term use (square km)
$\hat{v}_{7it}$	Information and Recreation	Hotel bed capacity
$\hat{v}_{8it}$	Natural environment	Rural area of total area (%)
$\hat{z}_{it}$	Central place	See formula 6—14a

Note. For further details on the methods by which the data were gained and a description of the indicators see Funck and Blum (1980: 99—106, 135—167) and Blum (1982: 42—65).

The formulae for computing the values of the two input potentials measuring road infrastructure are given as

$$\hat{v}_{2it} = \left(\sum_{h=1}^{H1} 1_{hit}^{BAB} \cdot Q_{hit}^{BAB} + \sum_{h=1}^{H2} 1_{hit}^{BS} \cdot Q_{hit}^{BS} \right) \cdot q_{it}, \qquad (6-15)$$

and

$$\hat{v}_{3it} = \sum_{h=1}^{H3} 1_{hit}^{SS} \cdot Q_{hit}^{SS}, \qquad (6-16)$$

with: $1_{hit}^{BAB}, 1_{hit}^{BS}, 1_{hit}^{SS}$: Length of section h of the regional system of federal highways; interstate: $h = 1, 2, \ldots, H1$; intrastate: $h = 1, 2, \ldots, H2$; other roads: $h = 1, 2, \ldots, H3$;

$Q_{hit}^{BAB}, Q_{hit}^{BS}, Q_{hit}^{SS}$: Respective capacity weights;

q_{it} : Nodal weight: total regional number of network links at highway intersections.

Bottlenecks in the regional factor equipment were identified by computing the regional marginal rate of substitution between all $j = 2, 3, \ldots, 8$ input potentials, and agglomeration if the respective input potential proved to be substitutional with respect to agglomeration:

$$MRS_{1jit} = -\frac{\partial \hat{v}_{1it}}{\partial \hat{v}_{jit}} = \frac{a_{jt} \cdot \hat{v}_{1it}}{a_{1t} \cdot \hat{v}_{jit}} > 0, \qquad j = 2, 3, \ldots, 8,$$

$$i = 1, 2, \ldots, 325,$$

$$t = 1976. \qquad (6-17)$$

As the marginal rate of substitution shows the approximate increase of input potential $\hat{v}_{jit}$ necessary to compensate for a unit decrease of input potential $\hat{v}_{1it}$, this formula is suitable to describe and identify bottlenecks of input potentials on a regional level. As a criterion, the following definition is proposed (Funck and Blum 1980: 131):

Definition 2. A bottleneck of input potential $\hat{v}_{jit}$ may be identified by

$$MRS_{1jit} > c \cdot \overline{MRS}_{1jt}, \qquad c \geq 1, \qquad (6-18)$$

with:

$$\overline{MRS}_{1jt} = \frac{a_{jt} \cdot \frac{1}{325} \cdot \sum\limits_{i=1}^{325} \hat{v}_{1it}}{a_{1t} \cdot \frac{1}{325} \cdot \sum\limits_{i=1}^{325} \hat{v}_{jit}} \qquad (6\text{--}19)$$

as average marginal rate of substitition for the cross-section (West Germany) and $c \geqslant 1$ as a factor arbitrarily chosen according to statistical or political considerations.

The Analysis of the Regional Environment

As already mentioned, an investment in the regional infrastructure influences regional natural and environmental qualities. Attempts to quantify some of these impacts have been made by Funck and others (1975), Nijkamp and others (1976), Forschungsgesellschaft für das Straßenwesen (1980), and others. Since a quantification of all impacts would go beyond the scope of this chapter, we shall concentrate on the problem of land use for transport infrastructure and new production locations.

Every implementation of a new transportation or siting project for industrial or commercial development of a region uses up land, up to then mostly used for agricultural, forestry, recreational, residential, industrial, or commercial purposes. As a possible measure of land scarcity, the value of discounted earnings can describe the material value only; this market price is, however, the result of an incomplete market. It has been argued (Solow 1971) that for most natural resources, "true" prices exist only if these resources approach depletion.

As a social indicator of land scarcity, we propose to use the average rate of substitution of regional rural land against regional agglomeration; this indicator is independent from changes in taste and from utility-dependent functions such as climate, water, or oxygen reservoirs or preferences for recreation.

The average rate of substitution does not refer to a constant production level. It is given by

$$ARS_{1jit} = \frac{\hat{v}_{1it}}{\hat{v}_{j*it}} > 0, \qquad j^* = 9, 10, \ldots$$

$$i = 1, 2, \ldots, 325,$$

$$t = 1976, \qquad (6\text{--}20)$$

Figure 6–4.   Relation between Road Capacity and Land Use

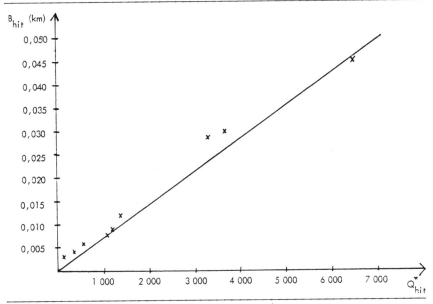

Note: All crosses refer to selected road types; Q^*_{hit} gives the capacity of road section h in region i in period t in number of cars per hour and direction.

and $\hat{v}_{j*it}$ is an input potential not related to production, but to environmental potentials.

While a bottleneck situation regarding a particular input potential has been defined earlier, a bottleneck with respect to a natural resource (excluding its production impact) can be defined as follows:

Definition 3.   A bottleneck in natural resource $\hat{v}_{j*it}$ exists if

$$ARS_{1j*it} > c \cdot \overline{ARS}_{1j*t}, \qquad c \geqslant 1, \qquad (6-21)$$

with:

$$\overline{ARS}_{1j*t} = \frac{\frac{1}{325} \cdot \sum_{i=1}^{325} \hat{v}_{1it}}{\frac{1}{325} \cdot \sum_{i=1}^{325} \hat{v}_{j*it}} \qquad (6-22)$$

as the average rate of substitution of the cross-section, and c as a parameter chosen according to statistical, technological or regional political considerations.

Figure 6–4 relates road capacity (Q^*_{hit}) to the width of a road

(B_{hit}) (computed from data by Forschungsgesellschaft für das Straßenwesen 1980).

An ordinary least-squares regression produces the following estimate of the relationship:

$$B_{hit} = 7.02 \cdot 10^{-6} \cdot Q^*_{hit}, \qquad b = 1, 2, \ldots$$

$$i = 1, 2, \ldots, 325,$$

$$t = 1976. \qquad (6\text{--}23)$$

Considering the relationship between capacity weights and capacity per hour (Blum 1982: 120), the land-use formulae for the two road categories become:

$$LU_1(\hat{v}_{it}) = \frac{\hat{v}_{2it}}{q_{it}} \cdot 0.00702, \qquad (6\text{--}24)$$

$$LU_2(\hat{v}_{it}) = \hat{v}_{3it} \cdot 0.00702. \qquad (6\text{--}25)$$

The area for new sites is given in square kilometers, so that

$$LU_3(\hat{v}_{it}) = \hat{v}_{6it} \qquad (6\text{--}26)$$

can be stated.

Measures of Urgency for the Weighting in a Utility Function

Under the assumption of flexible prices, the price ratio between two input potentials equals the ratio of their marginal rates of substitution in the production point. The difference between the marginal rate of substitution and the average rate of substitution lies in the inverse ratio of the respective production elasticities, which means that the average rate of substitution can be attributed to the same measuring concept.

In order to exclude influences of dimensionality, all measures of urgency have to be normalized by subtracting the interregional mean and dividing this difference by the interregional standard deviation (σ). As the starting position of every group and the desired size of the investment (or disinvestment) should be included in the measure of urgency, the latter is dependent on the marginal (average) rates of substitution at the starting position and the final position. If all these prerequisites are to be fulfilled, the formula for measures of urgency becomes (for example: highway infrastructure, $j = 2$; land use, $j = 9$; t: base period; $t' > t$: period, in which all investments are concluded):

$$d_{1it} = \frac{\frac{1}{2} \cdot (MRS_{1,2,it} + MRS_{1,2,it'}) - \overline{MRS}_{1,2,t}}{\sigma(MRS_{1,2,it})} , \qquad (6{-}27)$$

and $\qquad MRS_{1,2,t} = (MRS_{1,2,1,t}, MRS_{1,2,2,t}, \ldots, MRS_{1,2,325,t}),$

$$d_{2it} = \frac{\frac{1}{2} \cdot (ARS_{1,9,it} + ARS_{1,9,it'}) - \overline{ARS}_{1,9,t}}{\sigma(ARS_{1,9,it})} , \qquad (6{-}28)$$

and $\qquad ARS_{1,9,t} = (ARS_{1,9,1,t}, ARS_{1,9,2,t}, \ldots, ARS_{1,9,325,t}).$

AN APPLICATION OF THE MODEL

Description of the Region Investigated

The region of Pirmasens in the Southwest of the Rhineland-Palatinate suffers from an underutilization of productive capacities and an insufficient equipment with transportation infrastructure. It has, therefore, been proposed to link the two counties to the West German interstate highway system. Figure 6–5 gives an impression of the investments proposed.

Table 6–3 lists the data necessary for an evaluation of the two highway projects $A8$ and $A62$ with respect to production and land use.

The secondary data computed using the methods described in the previous section are listed in Table 6–4.

The set of normalized measures of urgency thus becomes:

$$d_{1,166,t} = \frac{\frac{1}{2} \cdot (5.5 + 1.04) - 0.022}{2.5} = 1.2200, \qquad (6{-}29)$$

$$d_{1,179,t} = \frac{\frac{1}{2} \cdot (0.08 + 0.005) - 0.022}{2.5} = 0.0082, \qquad (6{-}30)$$

$$d_{2,166,t} = \frac{\frac{1}{2} \cdot (13.0 + 13.0) - 0.74}{16.0} = 0.7663, \qquad (6{-}31)$$

$$d_{2,179,t} = \frac{\frac{1}{2} \cdot (0.13 + 0.13) - 0.74}{16.0} = -0.0381. \qquad (6{-}32)$$

Figure 6—5.   The Region of Pirmasens in the Southwest of the Rhineland-Palatinate and the Interstate Highway Projects A8 and A62

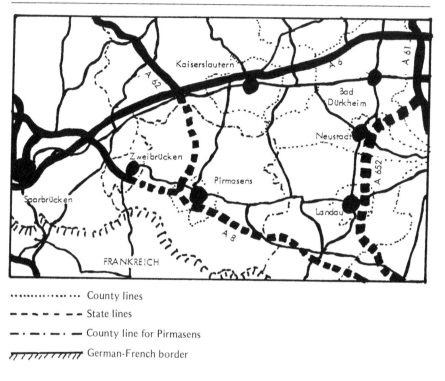

··············· ··· County lines

— — — — — — — State lines

— · — · — · — County line for Pirmasens

⫻⫻⫻⫻⫻⫻⫻ German-French border

Solution of the Problem

The solution of the optimization problem gives the following results: for the city of Pirmasens, the degree of achievement in production is:

$$\lambda_{1,\,166,\,t} = 0.61. \tag{6—33}$$

the degree of achievement regarding the environment is:

$$\lambda_{2,\,166,\,t} = 0.39. \tag{6—34}$$

For the county of Pirmasens, since land—even with an interstate highway built—remains abundant (the respective weight is negative), the degree of achievement in production is here.

$$\lambda_{1,\,179,\,t} = 1.00. \tag{6—35}$$

Table 6–3. Data for the Evaluation of Two Highway Projects in the Region of Pirmasens (Primary Data)

Variable	City of Pirmasens		County of Pirmasens	
	$t = 1976$	$t' = ?$	$t = 1976$	$t' = ?$
Agglomeration	864.2 (Pers/km^2)	864.2 (Pers/km^2)	104.1 (Pers/km^2)	104.1 (Pers/km^2)
Interstate highw.	—	12 km	—	38 km
Capacity weight	4.1	4.1	4.1	4.1
Other highways	10.4 km	10.4 km	86.9 km	86.9 km
Capacity weight	1.1	1.1	1.1	1.1
Nodal weight	3	3	3	19
Long distance roads ($\hat{v}_{2it}$)	34.32	181.92	286.77	4776.41
Other roads	190.8 km	190.8 km	975.8 km	975.8 km
Capacity weight	0.5	0.5	0.5	0.5
Other roads ($\hat{v}_{3it}$)	95.4	95.4	487.9	487.9
Natural environment ($\hat{v}_{8it}$)	0.724	0.720	0.847	0.846
Gross value added (x_{it})	984 (mill. DM)		969 (mill. DM)	

Table 6–4. Secondary Data for the Region of Pirmasens

	City of Pirmasens ($i = 166$)		County of Pirmasens ($i = 179$)		Mean	Standard Deviation of all regions
	$t = 1976$	$t' = ?$	$t = 1976$	$t' = ?$		
Potential regional product (mill. DM)	1201	1443	1150	1576		
Long-distance highways	(+) 5.50	(+) 1.04	(+) 0.08	0.005	0.022	2.5
Rural land	(+) 13.0	(+) 13.0	0.13	0.13	0.740	16.0

Note. +: bottleneck; see formulae (6–18) and (6–21).

Figure 6–6.   The Impact of Highway Infrastructure on Production

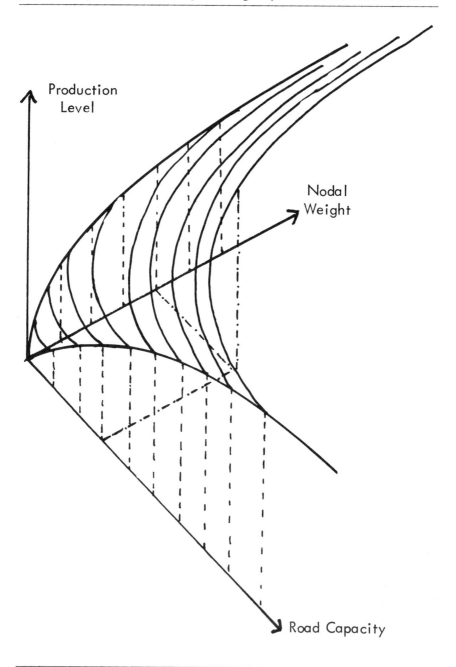

Figure 6–7. The Impact of Highway Infrastructure on Land Use

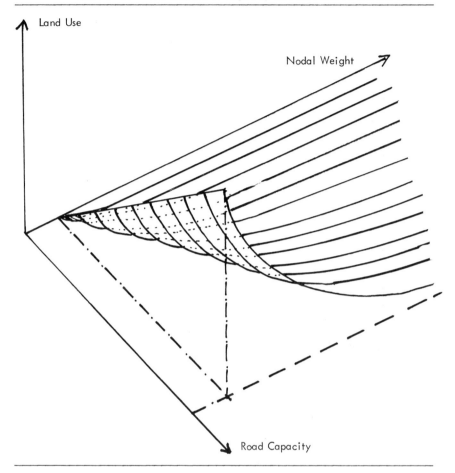

With the vector maximum problem given by

$$\text{``max''} \begin{bmatrix} P(\hat{v}_{it}) \\ \dfrac{1}{LU_1(\hat{v}_{it})} \end{bmatrix} = F(\hat{v}_{it}) \qquad (6\text{–}36)$$

$$\text{sub:} \ \hat{v}_{it} \in \hat{V}_{it} \subseteq \mathbb{R}^m_+, \qquad i = 166, 179,$$

$$t = 1976,$$

where the inverse of land-use function (land-savings function) was taken in order to comply with formula (6–8) in assumption 7, a

Figure 6–8.   Display of $F(\hat{v}_{it}) \in \mathbb{R}_+^2$

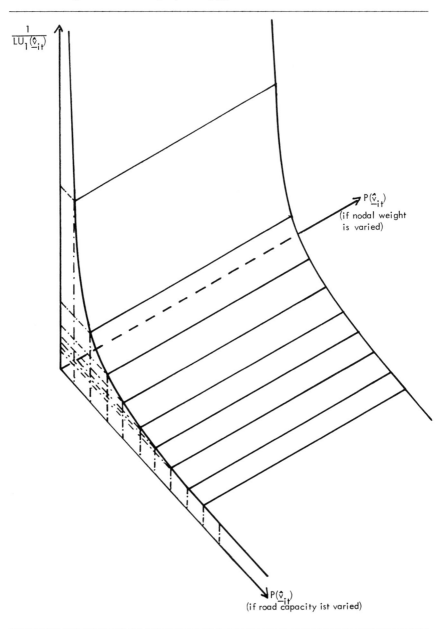

Note. The hyperbolic limitation of $F(\hat{v}_{it})$ on the right is shown only in order to improve the three-dimensional impression of the figure.

solution to the problem using the weighting system computed has to be found by following the instructions given in formula (6–13). Since only interstate highways, which are incorporated in the indicator $\hat{v}_{2it}$, are varied in this example, it is worth noting that the value of this indicator is a multiplicative function of the road capacity and a nodal weight (see formula 6–15). Both elements have a positive impact on production, but only the first one uses up land.

These asymmetric effects—as displayed in Figures 6–6 and 6–7— become understandable when one realizes that only road capacity, through the necessary width of the road, is land-consuming.

This consideration leads to an approach toward solving the vector maximum problem: "best" strategies are those strategies, which, if rural land is scarce, combine the highest degree of improvement in the regional highway network system with the lowest degree of additional road lengths. This can easily be seen from a display of $F(\hat{v}_{it})$ given in Figure 6–8. High production levels can be achieved at no loss of land if the regional network linkage is improved.

This leads to the "best" strategy (see Table 6–5):

1. Reduce long-distance highway investments within the city of Pirmasens to 61 percent of the level planned.

2. Leave the intersection of the interstate highways $A62$ and $A8$ within the city limits to provide for an optimal linkage to the city center.

Table 6–5. "Best" Strategy for Investment in the Interstate Highway Infrastructure in Pirmasens

Variable	City of Pirmasens	County of Pirmasens
Interstate highways	6.2 km	43.8 km
Capacity weights	4.1	4.1
Other highways	10.4 km	86.9 km
Capacity weights	1.1	1.1
Nodal weight	3.0	19.0
Long distance highway infrastructure $(\hat{v}_{2it'})$	110.6	5228.2

REFERENCES

Blum, U. 1982. *Regionale Wirkungen von Infrastrukturinvestitionen.* Karlsruhe Institut für Wirtschaftspolitik und Wirtschaftsforschung der Universität Karlsruhe (TH).

Bundesminister für Verkehr. 1981. *Verkehr in Zahlen 1981.* Bonn: Bundesminister für Verkehr.

Forschungsgesellschaft für das Strassenwesen. 1980. *Richtlinien für die Anlage von Straßen*, RAL 1974, RAS-W. (draft), Köln.

Funck, R. 1978. "Multidimensional Entscheidungsfunktionen in der Planung der regionalen Infrastrukturausstattung." In *Konkurrenz zwischen kleinen Regionen*, edited by W. Buhr and P. Friedrich. Baden-Baden: Nomos verlagsgesellschaft.

Funck, R., and U. Blum. 1980. *Die Berücksichtigung von Wachstums- und Struktureffekten in den Richtlinien für wirtschaftliche Vergleichsrechnungen im Straßenwesen* (RAS-W). Karlsruhe: Institut für Wirtschaftspolitik und Wirtschaftsforschung der Universität Karlsruhe (TH).

Funck, R., H.G. Retzko, K. Schaechterle, et al. 1975. *Prioritäten für den Ausbau des Hamberger Schnellbahnnetzes,* Karlsruhe, Darmstadt, München: Institut für Wirtschaftspolitik und Wirtschaftsforschung der Universität Karlsruhe (TH).

Nijkamp, P. (ed.) 1976. *Environmental Economics*, 2 vols., Leiden: Martinus Nijhoff.

Solow, R.M. 1971. "The Economist's Approach to Pollution and its Control." *Science* 173.

Statistisches Bundesamt. 1982. *Statistisches Jahrbuch 1981 für die Bundesrepublik Deutschland*, Stuttgart und Mainz: Verlag W. Kohlhammer.

7 International Conflict Analysis*

Peter Nijkamp

International conflict analysis aims at identifying the discrepancies among nations (or groups of nations) which might potentially explain the economic or political conflicts among these nations. Changes in (dis)similarities among nations may be a result of either internal forces or external interdependencies. Even if it were possible consistently to aggregate national interests to a master control of a global welfare function (which is contradicted by Arrow's theorem), a meaningful reconciliation of national interests is often an illusion due to the interwoven structure of international systems. Consequently, any change in one component of the global system will (directly or indirectly) affect the states of the other components (see, for instance, Herman and Montroll 1972).

Theoretically speaking, one might argue that the neoclassical Pareto principle extended with the compensation principle might lead to a balanced international system characterized by a Pareto equilibrium among the actors. In reality, however, this situation does not occur because (1) there is no system (neither a market system nor an institutionalized system) that shapes the conditions

*The author is indebted to Marcel van Handenhoven and Willem Zoetmulder for their stimulating comments on an earlier draft of this chapter and to Wouter van Veenendaal for his computational assistance.

for the fulfillment of such an equilibrium situation; and (2) the actors in the international system do have such strongly conflicting interests that harmony or cooperation strategies are less likely than international competition and power conflicts.

Because international consensus lies beyond the possibilities of our present international system, it is extremely important to determine the extent to which nations or groups of nations differ mutually. Even if different nations would have entirely diverging interests, it may be in their self-interest to seek for compromise strategies with other nations. This is essentially a problem of multiperson game theory (or, in a dynamic setting, differential gaming). A necessary input, however, for any international conflict analysis will be the indentification of the major discrepancies among the entities of the international system. In respect to this, the calculation of discrepancy measures among these entities is an extremely important step toward gaining more insight into the components, backgrounds, and strategies of international conflicts.

INTERNATIONAL COMPLEXITIES

The international pattern of relationships between countries offers a diffuse picture of a complex network. This complexity is *inter alia* due to:

- the interwovenness of economic competition (among others, supply–demand conditions) and political conflicts (for instance, East–West relationships).
- the dominance of economic factors, so that the international economic structure (for instance, the skew distribution of welfare) determines to a major extent the development perspectives of countries (as a case in point, North–South relationships).
- the multiplicity of national and international political issues and objectives, so that goal conflicts are mostly likely to arise (for instance, between economic growth and environmental quality).
- the skew distribution of raw materials and energy, so that only a few countries control the supply of necessary inputs for production systems everywhere in the world (for instance, the dependence of countries in the Organization for Economic Cooperation and Development (OECD) on OPEC countries).

- the fact that many countries may play different roles in different international institutions (for example, the European Economic Community (EEC), OECD and United Nations) at the same time.
- the unsystematic way in which international conferences are being held, so that there is hardly any coordination in terms of issues to be discussed at successive international meetings in different forums (for instance, the United Nations Committee on Trade and Development (UNCTAD) and the General Agreement on Trade and Tariffs (GATT)).
- the diffuse role of many international institutions and agencies in international development strategies (for instance, the International Monetary Fund (IMF), World Bank, and the International Energy Association (IEA) and the dominance of some countries in these institutions (for instance, the dominating role of OECD countries in the IMF, and the minor role of less developed countries in the IMF).

The foregoing remarks indicate that a more thorough analysis or the positions of the successive countries (for instance, a strength-weakness analysis), the dominating issues in international policies, the interrelationships between countries and issues, and the identification of clusters of parallel interests and of groups of countries is a prerequisite for getting more insight into the long-run international decisions, activities, conflicts, and strategies (either in an institutionalized way or not). This is illustrated in a simple way in Figure 7—1.

Figure 7—1 indicates that a wide variety of international policy

Figure 7—1.   A Pattern of Relationships Between Countries

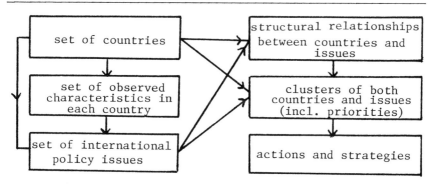

issues associated with a set of countries can be related to a series of national (mainly economic) features of each country. The position of each country and their mutual relationships determine the emergence of clusters of countries or of related international policy issues, which determine in turn the actions and strategies of countries (or blocks of countries).

Figure 7–1 presents a static network which might be adjusted *inter alia* for international dynamics, the simultaneous operation in different institutions by several countries and international institutionalized decision structures. In the next sections, a more extended exposition of the contents and the structure of an international discrepancy analysis among countries (and groups of countries) will be given, which may be used as one of the building stones of Figure 7–1.

INTERNATIONAL MULTICRITERIA PROFILES

The international political situation is strongly dominated by economic factors associated with the scarcity of money, commodities, energy, food, or raw materials. The topics discussed at most international conferences indicate that many political conflicts at a global scale are to a large extent a consequence of discrepancies among countries with regard to finances and money, food, raw materials, energy, and commodities. All these issues have played an important role in discussions at past meetings of many institutions such as IMF, UN, OECD, OPEC, EEC, and IEA.

It has to be added, however, that all these issues are multidimensional in nature; they are the result of targets set by the various nations and of the economic situation of these countries. Therefore, it is necessary to relate each of these issues to a large set of national characteristics which determine implicitly or explicitly the successive issues discussed at international conferences. This is also a prerequisite to identify the discrepancies between countries. For instance, the energy issue has to be related to the supply of oil, the oil price, the demand for energy, the use of the financial surplus by OPEC countries, and so on; international trade has to be related to the international tariff system, trade policies, comparative advantages and so on; raw materials have to be related to price stabilization, food supply, and so on; money and finance have to be related to international loans, IMF conditions, aid in case of deficits on the balance of payment, and so on; development aid has to be related to program lending, financing of international funds, and the realization of the 0.7 percent target for development aid from the rich countries (see also Van Handenhoven and Zoetmulder 1980).

Consequently, all these issues require a painstaking and accurate data collection on all their relevant attributes at a national scale. The attitude of a certain country with regard to a given international issue is then the result of a set of forces exerted by the set of national attributes. The values of these attributes also determine the degree at which a certain country is prepared to cooperate with other countries in regard to a certain joint relevant alternative. This is also a useful way to analyze international interaction patterns between OPEC countries, developing countries, and the Western countries.

Formally speaking, one may define an *issue profile* (a set of topics regularly being discussed at international conferences) and an *attribute* profile (a set of national characteristics which determine the attitude of countries regarding the issues). This is illustrated in Figure 7–2.

A closer examination of Figure 7–2 requires three steps: (1) the assessment of the values of all national attribute profiles; this means the estimation of all elements a_{ni}^j, where a_{ni}^j represents the level of the ith attribute (related to the issue j) for country n; (2) the assessment of the functional linkages between all attributes of each individual country (an intranational model); (3) the assessment

Figure 7–2. A Profile Representation of Attributes and Issues

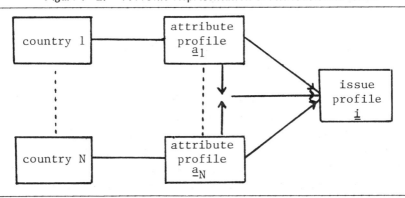

of the functional linkages between the attribute profiles of successive countries (an international model).

The lack of a reliable set of international (time-series and cross-section) data hampers the application of steps (2) and (3), so that only step (1) can be realized. But it has to be added that the information contained in step (1) can be used to identify correspondence and discrepancy patterns between countries or main issues. Consequently, the analysis of interdependencies among and within nations has to be made by means of an analysis of the positions of all nations regarding all attributes related to each international issue. In this respect multivariate cluster techniques may be extremely useful methods of gaining more insight into complex international policy structures (see Wang and Lake 1978).

There is, however, an additional problem. Due to a lack of reliable statistics, much information contained in the national attribute profiles is rather "soft" and inaccurate in nature. Very often one has to deal with ordinal scores only. Consequently, many traditional multivariate techniques such as principal component analysis and interdependence analysis cannot be applied. Fortunately, however, a whole series of soft data techniques has recently been developed which allows the application of normal numerical and mathematical operations on (transformed) ordinal data. Especially, the class of *multidimensional scaling methods* is extremely important (see, among others Nijkamp 1979, and Nijkamp and Voogd 1979), although alternative methods such as *logit analysis* might be used as well (see Nijkamp and Rietveld 1981). Later an introduction into multidimensional scaling analysis will be given. First, however, more detailed attention will be paid to the components of the issue profile and the attribute profiles in each country.

INTERNATIONAL POLICY ISSUES AND NATIONAL ATTRIBUTES

As mentioned before, the issue profile is composed of the following elements: (1) international trade; (2) raw materials and food; (3) energy; (4) money and finance; and (5) development aid.

Each issue can be associated with an *attribute* profile which determines the national interest attached to a certain international issue. The choice of the specific attributes related to each issue is mainly made on economic grounds. These attributes characterize the position of the country at hand with regard to the item concerned from the economic viewpoint of the country itself. For the richer countries the scores on these attributes reflect also their economic power position; for the less developed countries these scores can also be seen as a proxy for their needs. The information on these items is mainly based on several international statistical yearbooks published *inter alia* by IMF, UN, OECD, OPEC, IEA, and so forth (see also Van Handenhoven and Zoetmulder 1980). The following attribute profiles can be distinguished:

International trade profile

1. a preferential tariff system for all developing countries;
2. differentiation according to degree of development of countries;
3. further elaboration of results of multilateral trade negotiations (MTN);
4. treatment of own raw materials by developing countries themselves;
5. financing of commodity trade and of domestic treatment of raw materials;
6. access for developing countries to world markets;
7. adjustment of international trade system in favor of developing countries;
8. choice of UNCTAD as the main forum for international negotiations.

Raw materials and food profile

1. market stabilization via an integrated raw materials program;
2. revenue stabilization;
3. financing of an international raw materials fund;
4. linkage of product prices to Western inflation;
5. financing of domestic treatment of raw materials;
6. new exploration and exploitation of raw materials;
7. a system of own raw materials for multinationals;
8. aid for purchasing food;
9. commercial treatment of food.

Energy profile

1. linkage of oil prices to Western inflation;
2. preferential oil prices for developing countries;
3. predictable and gradual evolution of oil prices;
4. agreements on supply and demand of energy;
5. institutionalization of supply and demand of energy;
6. cooperation on alternative energy research;
7. creation of an energy authority in the UN framework;
8. protection of assets in Western countries.

Money and finance profile

1. increase of SDR assignments (special drawing rights);
2. regular and sufficient SDR assignments for reserve needs;
3. alternative distribution of SDR assignments;
4. new medium-term balance-of-payment facilities;
5. revision of criteria for determining financial quota (including more control over IFM and World Bank);
6. extension of refunding period;
7. improvement of quantitative restrictions on obtaining funds;
8. relating conditional capital loans to causes of deficit on balance of payment;
9. a new system of conditions for financial support;
10. improvement of IMF compensatory facility;
11. creation of a substitution account;
12. long-term facilities for purchasing capital goods;
13. better access to commercial credit provisions;
14. financing of trade;
15. better guarantees in case of nationalization.

Development aid profile

1. 0.7 percent of Gross National Product (GNP) for development aid from Western countries;
2. improvement of financial aid conditions for developing countries;
3. binding commitments for a longer period;

4.   more program lending instead of financing of projects;
5.   reduction of financial burden for developing countries;
6.   creation of supplementary international funds.

The scores on these attribute profiles for a whole set of countries are contained in a tentative form in the Annex (see also Van Handenhoven and Zoetmulder 1980). These scores are ordinal in nature, but have been assessed after a careful analysis of many international documents, especially as far as their impacts on the balance-of-payment or growth perspectives of the successive countries are concerned. These scores are running from 1 to 7, where a value of 4 reflects an average (intermediate) position.

Now the essential problem of this study is to identify discrepancies among countries, issues, and attributes in order to assess the possibilities for compromise (cluster) strategies among countries. This requires an ordinal discrepancy analysis by using, for instance, a multidimensional scaling analysis (see also Adelman and Morris 1974). The latter technique will be exposed in greater detail in the next section.

INTRODUCTION TO MULTIDIMENSIONAL SCALING METHODS

Multidimensional scaling (MDS) methods have originally been developed in psychometrics. The rationale behind the use of MDS methods was to *transform ordinal data*, that describe in a $N \times N$ paired comparison table the (dis)similarity between N objects, into *cardinal units*. Assuming, for instance, a symmetric paired comparison table and omitting the self-dissimilarities on the main diagonal, one has in fact $\frac{1}{2}N(N-1)$ ordinal dissimilarity relationships. The only way to represent these N objects as (cardinal) coordinates in a Euclidean space is to reduce the number of dimensions. Suppose that the Euclidean space is K-dimensional with $K < \frac{1}{2}N(N-1)/N = \frac{1}{2}(N-1)$. Then the coordinates of the N objects in a K-dimensional space can be estimated due to the fact that the transition from higher to lower dimensions implies in general the emergence of degrees of freedom which can be used to extract cardinal information from the underlying ordinal data structure. The main criterion for assessing the coordinates of the N objects in the new K-dimensional space is that these N points must have a configuration so that the interpoint distances bear a maximum correspondence to the rankings in the initial dissimilarity data.

If the ordinal dissimilarities are denoted by $\delta_{nn'} (n > n')$, the paired comparison table Δ for dissimilarities between items is:

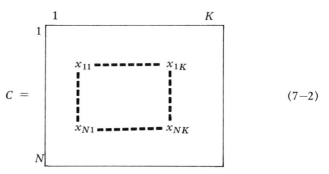

$$\Delta = \qquad (7-1)$$

If this symmetric matrix is supposed to have a *complete* ordinal ranking without ties, the highest rank number is $\frac{1}{2}N(N--1)$ and the lowest 1. It should be noted that the assumption of the absence of ties is by no means necessary and that it can easily be relaxed. In such a table of ordinal dissimilarities the transitivity conditions are not necessarily satisfied. Suppose now that the N objects are to be represented in a K-dimensional Euclidean space. Then one has to construct the following $N \times K$ configuration table which represents the coordinates of the N points in this space:

$$C = \qquad (7-2)$$

Next one may define a distance measure (for example, a Euclidean distance metric) between all N points of the righthand side of $(7-2)$:

$$d_{nn'} = \left\{ \sum_{k=1}^{K} (x_{nk} - x_{n'k})^2 \right\}^{1/2} \qquad (7-3)$$

The best way to achieve an optimal fit between the ordinal data from $(7-1)$ and the cardinal data from $(7-2)$ is to impose the condition that the geometric configuration of $(7-2)$ should be such that the distances represented in $(7-3)$ do not violate the dissimilarity conditions from (7–1). This best fit can be achieved by means of some sort of least-squares procedure, by minimizing the (normalized) residual variance ("stress"). This stress function (or loss function) may have the following shape (although a more general Minkowski metric is also allowed):

$$s = \left\{ \frac{\sum\limits_{n,n'} (d_{nn'} - \hat{d}_{nn'})^2}{\sum\limits_{n,n'} d_{nn'}^2} \right\}^{1/2}, \qquad n \neq n' \qquad (7\text{–}4)$$

where $d_{nn'}$ is already defined in (7–3) and where $\hat{d}_{nn'}$ are order-isomorph values (so-called disparities) which should be determined subject to the condition that $\hat{d}_{nn'}$ is in agreement with $\delta_{nn'}$; in other words, $\hat{d}_{nn'} \leqslant \hat{d}_{nn''}$, whenever $\delta_{nn'} < \delta_{nn''}$. Such a stress function may be regarded as a measure for the degree at which the information from C contradicts that from Δ. One possible way to determine $\hat{d}_{nn'}$ may be a monotone regression which can be formalized as:

$$\min_{\hat{d}_{nn'}} = \sum_{n,n'} |d_{nn'} - \hat{d}_{nn'}|$$

$$\text{s.t.} \qquad\qquad\qquad (7\text{–}5)$$

$$\delta_{nn'} > \delta_{nn''} \rightarrow \hat{d}_{nn'} > \hat{d}_{nn''}.$$

An alternative procedure is *inter alia* a rank-image method. Instead of linear distance functions, any other nonlinear distance metric may be used as well. Before (7–5) can be applied, a first "guess" of $d_{nn'}$ has to be made. This guess can be made after the determination of an initial configuration of (7–2); this configuration is often the result of a principal component analysis with K components applied to (7–1). Given the initial configuration, the initial distances between the points of a configuration can be calculated and substituted into (7–5); these distances are normally measured with respect to an ideal point which is specific for each individual. Next, the monotone regression may be carried out in order to assess an initial value for $\hat{d}_{nn'}$, so that the disparities are in accordance with the (dis)similarities. Thus, $\hat{d}_{nn'}$ is not a specific distance but a number that is as close as possible to the original distance $d_{nn'}$ while being in accordance with the (dis)similarities.

When the initial values of $\hat{d}_{nn}$ are substituted into (7–4), a minimum stress can be calculated (in terms of x_{nk}) by means of a

Figure 7–3.   Simplified Representation of an MDS Procedure

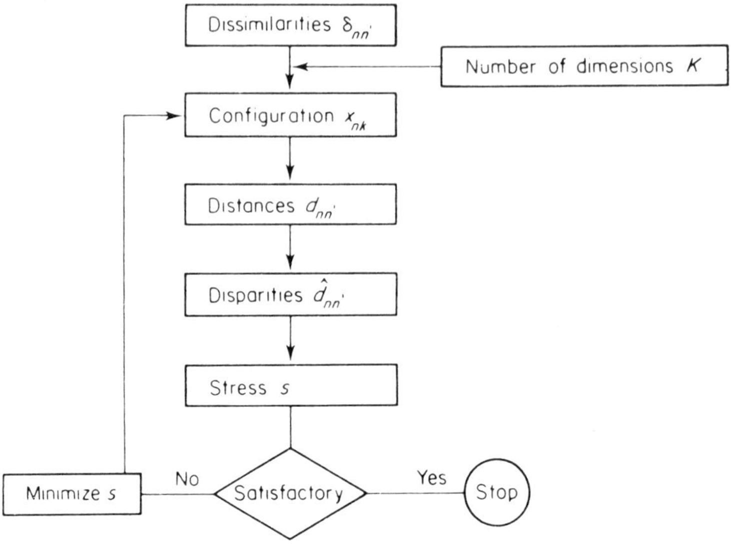

Source: Nijkamp (1979: 104)

numerical solution procedure for minimizing (7–4) (for example, by means of a gradient method). The resulting values of the configuration can again be used to assess a new value of $\hat{d}_{nn'}$ and so on, until after a number of runs the whole procedure converges.

So the MDS procedures are based on a whole series of successive steps: (1) the construction of a paired comparison table of dissimilarities $\delta_{nn'}$; (2) the calculation of an initial configuration which is successively manipulated in order to obtain a monotone relationship between the original dissimilarities and the ultimate distances $d_{nn'}$; (3) the use of a set of intermediate variables $\hat{d}_{nn'}$ (so-called disparities) which are determined in accordance with the (dis)similarities and which are used in a stress function (a loss function) so as to minimize the discrepancies between the unknown distances and the disparities; (4) the use of an iterative algorithm which guarantees ultimately a convergence. The whole procedure is represented in a simplified manner in Figure 7–3.

The conclusions that can be drawn from the ultimate value of the stress function are slightly subjective, so certain rules of thumb may be helpful:

s percent	Goodness of Fit
20	poor
10	fair
5	good
$2\frac{1}{2}$	excellent
0	perfect

Another subjective element concerns the choice of the dimension K. Clearly one should strive at a minimum stress with a minimum number of dimensions involved. It is clear that the ultimate interpretation of the configuration is also a matter of personal inventiveness of the researcher, so that here again subjective elements may enter. Like in factor analysis, some of the results are invariant against a translation and rotation of the axes (provided that a Euclidean distance metric is used). A more extensive discussion of MDS can be found in Nijkamp (1979).

RESULTS

The data for the international conflict analysis and the results of a two-dimensional MDS procedure for the ordinal rankings of the issues for a (condensed) series of countries are contained in the Appendix.

These results give rise to the following brief conclusions.

International trade

1. The EEC countries appear to form a cluster of joint interests, while the United States, Canada, and Japan have also positions closely related to the EEC countries.

2. Cuba, China, Egypt, Brazil, and Mexico appear to have almost similar positions as the EEC while Yugoslavia, Korea, India, and Pakistan also form a cluster of joint interests.

3. The attributes of international trade give rise to the following three clusters: (1) preferential tariffs for developing countries + better access to international markets, (2) elaboration of results of MTN + treatment of raw materials by developing countries + financing of domestic production and raw materials treatment,

and (3) improvement of international trade system + transformation of UNCTAD into a new forum.

Raw materials and food

1. The EEC countries reflect again a cluster of joint interests shared with Japan, Egypt, Mexico, and Brazil, among others.
2. The United States and Canada have a slightly eccentric position.
3. India and Pakistan form a close cluster.
4. The following clusters of attributes appear to exist: (1) market stabilization + revenue stabilization + new raw materials system for multinationals, and (2) financing of domestic raw materials treatment + aid for purchasing food.

Energy

1. The pattern of the energy item is as such less clear, especially because the energy interests are related as necessary conditions for all other items.
2. The OPEC countries have apparently a joint interest (on the supply side), but this interest is shared by other countries as the demand side (*inter alia* by several EEC countries). This indicates that energy plays a crucial role in international conflict management for both the demand side and the supply side.
3. The attributes of the energy issue do not demonstrate here a clear cluster, so that a uniform picture of solutions for the energy question is less likely to obtain.

Money and finance

1. The developing countries (LDC's and NIC's) show a clear joint configuration of similar interests.
2. Rich countries have a more eccentric position, while the OPEC countries have an intermediate position.
3. The attributes of this issue have a diffuse pattern, particularly because many of them are related as prerequisites for other items of the international issue profile.

Development aid

1. The majority of EEC countries appear to have a relatively eccentric position compared to the LDC's and NIC's, while the OPEC countries again have an intermediate position.

2. There is a clear cluster of four attributes jointly characterizing this issue: fixed share of development aid + improvement of financial conditions + more program lending + reduction of financial burden.

It should be noted that in addition to a separate analysis of the five successive issues also various combinations of these issues can be examined. This is extremely important for identifying joint strategies for international conferences dealing with different items. The results of these experiments, however, will not be described here in this brief framework, but they can be found elsewhere (see Van Handenhoven and Zoetmulder 1980).

CONCLUSION

The conflict analysis described in this chapter appears to be a helpful way of identifying discrepancies and similarities among countries and among important international issues as well. In addition, the attributes of the successive items can also be studied in greater detail by making use of MDS techniques. In this way, international strategies can be provided with a more rational basis, though it has to be added that such a rationalization is a necessary but by no means sufficient condition for solving global conflicts. The previous analysis has also indicated that seemingly intangible and qualitative policy considerations might be studied in a more appropriate way by identifying the underlying economic interests and positions reflected by the profiles of issues and attributes. In this way, the potential conflict and compromise strategies may become more transparent, particularly when the above-mentioned analysis would be extended with complementary soft statistical methods and soft econometric techniques (see Nijkamp and Rietveld 1981) in order to assess also the structural functional relationships between countries with common interests or common economic positions.

REFERENCES

Adelman, I., and C.T. Morris. 1974. "The Derivation of Cardinal Scales from Ordinal Data." In *Economic Development and Planning* edited by W. Sellekaarts, pp. 1–39. London: MacMillan.

Handenhoven, M. van, and W.A. Zoetmulder. 1980. *Standpuntenbepaling door Landen en Blokken van Landen in het Internationale Overleg en de Gevolgen voor de Structuur van Internationale Conferenties.* Research Report, Bureau Berenschot, Utrecht.

Herman, R., and E.W. Montroll. 1972. "A Manner of Characterizing the Development of Countries." *Proceedings, National Academy of Science, U.S.A.*, vol. 69, pp. 3019–3023.

Nijkamp, P. 1979. *Multidimensional Spatial Data and Decision Analysis.* London/New York: Wiley.

Nijkamp, P., and P. Rietveld. 1981. *Ordinal Data Analysis*, Professional Paper 81–2, IIASA, Laxenburg.

Nijkamp, P., and J.H. Voogd. 1979. "The Use of Psychometric Techniques in Evaluation Procedures." *Papers of the Regional Science Association*, vol. 42, pp. 119–138.

Wang, P.C.C., and G.E. Lake. 1978. "Application of Graphical Multivariate Techniques in Policy Sciences." *Graphical Representation of Multivariate Data*, edited by P.C.C. Wang, pp. 13–58. New York: Academic Press.

APPENDIX A: DATA AND RESULTS OF A TWO-DIMENSIONAL MDS PROCEDURE FOR COUNTRIES AND ISSUES

Table 7–A1. Data and Results of Two-Dimensional MDS Procedure for Countries and Trade Attributes

Countries	Ordinal Rankings of International Trade Data								Results of Two-Dimensional MDS Procedure for Countries	
	A1	A2	A3	A4	A5	A6	A7	A8		
USA	7.0	7.0	2.0	4.5	3.0	7.0	4.5	1.0	0.4306	0.5407
Canada	5.5	3.0	5.5	8.0	5.5	5.5	1.5	1.5	0.8510	0.4174
Japan	6.0	8.0	2.5	2.5	2.5	6.0	6.0	2.5	0.1029	−0.5164
France	7.5	5.0	5.0	5.0	2.5	7.5	2.5	1.0	0.4111	−0.2494
England	6.5	6.5	6.5	3.5	3.5	6.5	1.5	1.5	0.3677	−0.1147
FRG	7.0	7.0	4.0	4.0	4.0	7.0	2.0	1.0	0.3282	−0.3052
Italy	7.5	4.5	4.5	1.5	1.5	7.5	4.5	4.5	0.2445	−0.1538
Netherlands	5.5	7.5	7.5	3.0	3.0	5.5	1.0	3.0	0.6707	0.0078
Algeria	1.0	3.0	7.0	7.0	5.0	3.0	7.0	3.0	−0.4720	1.0000
Yugoslavia	6.5	1.5	6.5	1.5	6.5	3.5	3.5	6.5	0.1113	0.1620
Cuba	1.0	6.0	6.0	4.0	2.5	2.5	–	6.0	−0.5652	−0.0980
China	1.0	6.0	6.0	4.0	2.5	2.5	–	6.0	−0.5652	−0.0980
Korea	6.0	1.5	6.0	1.5	6.0	6.0	6.0	3.0	0.1113	0.1621
India	5.5	2.0	5.5	2.0	5.5	2.0	5.5	8.0	0.0159	0.1419
Pakistan	5.5	2.5	5.5	1.0	5.5	2.5	5.5	8.0	0.0291	0.1216
Egypt	1.0	7.0	5.5	3.0	3.0	3.0	5.5	6.0	−0.6617	−0.2627
Brazil	1.0	2.5	5.5	5.5	5.5	2.5	5.5	8.0	−0.4653	0.2895
Mexico	1.5	6.5	4.0	4.0	4.0	1.5	6.5	8.0	−0.4706	−0.0464

Results of Two-Dimensional MDS Procedure for Trade Attributes

A1	−0.4855	0.2822
A2	0.0714	0.6621
A3	−0.1717	−0.4971
A4	−0.1446	−0.3554
A5	−0.1504	−0.3877
A6	−0.4551	0.2698
A7	0.6665	0.0086
A8	0.6694	0.0176

Table 7A—2. Data and Results of Two-Dimensional MDS Procedure for Countries and Raw Materials and Food Attributes

Countries	Ordinal Ranking of International Raw Materials and Food Data									Results of Two-Dimensional MDS Procedure for Countries	
	B1	B2	B3	B4	B5	B6	B7	B8	B9		
1. USA	3.0	3.0	5.5	3.0	5.5	7.0	1.0	8.5	8.5	−0.3685	−0.3052
2. Canada	1.5	1.5	3.0	4.0	7.5	5.5	5.5	7.5	9.0	−0.7403	−0.5573
3. Japan	6.0	6.0	6.0	2.5	2.5	8.5	8.5	2.5	2.5	0.0200	0.7521
4. France	5.5	5.5	5.5	2.0	2.0	8.5	2.0	5.5	8.5	−0.2122	0.2262
5. England	6.5	6.5	8.5	3.0	3.0	8.5	3.0	3.0	3.0	0.2131	0.3274
6. FRG	5.5	5.5	5.5	1.0	5.5	9.0	2.0	5.5	5.5	−0.2963	0.1414
7. Italy	7.0	7.0	7.0	4.0	1.5	9.0	4.0	1.5	4.0	0.1264	0.5822
8. Netherlands	6.5	6.5	6.5	1.0	3.0	9.0	3.0	3.0	6.5	−0.1166	0.3381
9. Saudi-Arabia	—	—	—	—	—	—	—	1.0	2.0	−0.0336	0.1266
10. Iran	—	—	—	—	—	—	—	1.5	1.5	0.1649	0.0327
11. Venezuela	—	—	—	—	—	—	—	2.0	1.0	0.3638	−0.0606
12. Nigeria	—	—	—	—	—	—	—	1.5	1.5	0.1669	0.0327
13. Algeria	7.5	7.5	7.5	7.5	3.5	3.5	3.5	1.0	3.5	0.4612	0.4202
14. Yugoslavia	3.0	3.0	7.0	3.0	9.0	2.0	3.0	7.0	7.0	−0.1009	−0.6650
15. Cuba	7.0	7.0	9.0	4.5	2.5	7.0	4.5	2.5	1.0	0.4644	0.4275
16. China	5.5	5.5	7.0	—	1.0	3.0	—	3.0	3.0	0.8910	0.8091
17. Korea	3.5	3.5	6.5	3.5	9.0	3.5	1.0	8.0	6.5	−0.0278	−0.6559
18. India	3.5	3.5	7.5	3.5	7.5	3.5	3.5	9.0	3.5	0.4345	−0.6498
19. Pakistan	3.5	3.5	7.0	3.5	8.5	3.5	3.5	8.5	3.5	0.4158	−0.6542
20. Egypt	7.5	7.5	7.5	7.5	3.0	3.0	3.0	3.0	3.0	0.4241	0.1938
21. Brazil	5.5	5.5	5.5	5.5	5.5	5.5	5.5	1.0	5.5	−0.1272	0.3602
22. Mexico	3.5	3.5	8.0	3.5	3.5	3.5	3.5	8.0	8.0	0.0921	−0.1450

Results of Two-Dimensional MDS Procedure for Raw Materials and Food Attributes

B1	−0.1956	−0.4313
B2	−0.1864	−0.4432
B3	−0.8561	0.0340
B4	−0.4663	−0.0217
B5	0.0289	0.8180
B6	0.8806	−0.5472
B7	−0.1516	−0.4102
B8	0.0265	0.8192
B9	1.0000	0.1825

Table 7A–3. Data and Results of Two-Dimensional MDS Procedure fro Countries and Energy Attributes

Countries	Ordinal Rankings of International Energy Data								Results of Two-Dimensional MDS Procedure for Countries	
	C1	C2	C3	C4	C5	C6	C7	C8		
1	4.0	3.0	6.0	6.0	1.5	5.0	1.5	6.0	−0.1062	0.1905
2	2.0	8.0	7.0	5.0	3.0	5.0	1.0	5.0	−0.6453	−0.0489
3	5.0	1.0	6.0	6.0	2.5	6.0	6.0	2.5	−0.0221	0.2137
4	3.5	1.0	3.5	7.0	3.5	3.5	7.0	7.0	0.2984	1.0000
5	2.0	7.0	5.0	5.0	2.0	5.0	2.0	8.0	−0.7532	0.5274
6	2.5	4.0	6.5	6.5	1.0	6.5	2.5	6.5	−0.3426	0.3549
7	6.5	1.0	6.5	6.5	3.0	3.0	6.5	3.0	−0.0129	0.2236
8	6.5	3.5	6.5	6.5	3.0	3.0	1.0	6.5	−0.0681	0.2339
9	6.5	1.5	6.5	6.5	3.0	1.5	4.0	6.5	−0.0029	0.3545
10	6.0	3.0	3.0	6.0	8.0	1.0	3.0	6.0	0.5763	0.5124
11	6.0	3.5	3.5	3.5	7.5	7.5	1.0	3.5	−0.0520	0.1271
12	3.5	5.5	3.5	1.5	7.5	7.5	1.5	3.5	−0.0618	0.0721
13	2.5	2.5	2.5	2.5	6.0	6.0	6.0	—	0.0309	−0.1717
14	2.5	2.5	5.5	1.0	5.5	5.5	5.5	—	−0.0126	−0.0615
15	2.0	3.5	3.5	1.0	6.0	6.0	6.0	—	0.0400	−0.3969
16	—	3.0	—	1.0	4.5	4.5	2.0	—	−0.0741	0.0600
17	3.5	3.5	6.5	1.0	6.5	3.5	3.5	—	−0.0492	0.1272
18	2.0	5.5	3.5	1.0	5.5	7.0	3.5	—	−0.1709	−0.2025
19	2.5	4.5	2.5	1.0	6.0	7.0	4.5	—	−0.0697	−0.4171
20	1.0	6.5	3.5	3.5	3.5	6.5	3.5	—	−0.3649	−0.2071
21	6.0	6.0	3.5	1.0	6.0	2.0	3.5	—	0.2081	−0.7094
22	2.5	2.5	2.5	2.5	6.5	5.0	6.5	—	0.0309	−0.1716

Results of Two-Dimensional MDS Procedure for Energy Attributes

C1	−0.6035	−0.1311
C2	0.4805	0.2774
C3	0.5449	0.0081
C4	−0.0135	−0.4012
C5	−0.5846	0.4184
C6	0.5636	0.1650
C7	−0.5717	0.0113
C8	0.1843	−0.3480

Table 7A—4.   Data and Results of Two-Dimensional MDS Procedure for Countries and Mone—Finance Attributes

Countries	D1	D2	D3	D4	D5	D6	D7	D8	D9	D10	D11	D12	D13	D14	D15	Results of Two-Dimensional MDS Procedure for Countries	
						Ordinal Rankings of International Money and Finance Data											
1	4.5	12.5	11.0	6.0	2.0	2.0	8.0	8.0	2.0	8.0	4.5	12.5	15.0	8.0	14.0	0.4703	0.6019
2	6.0	1.5	6.0	11.5	11.5	11.5	11.5	6.0	14.5	1.5	6.0	6.0	6.0	14.5	6.0	−0.5293	−0.6394
3	11.0	4.5	11.0	4.5	11.0	4.5	15.0	11.0	11.0	4.5	4.5	11.0	11.0	1.0	4.5	0.0437	−0.0173
4	5.0	5.0	14.5	1.0	5.0	11.0	11.0	11.0	14.5	5.0	5.0	11.0	5.0	5.0	11.0	−0.0517	−0.0423
5	4.5	8.5	2.0	14.0	5.5	8.5	8.5	8.5	4.5	2.0	2.0	12.0	14.0	8.5	14.0	1.0000	0.0934
6	5.5	11.5	1.0	14.5	5.5	5.5	5.5	5.5	5.5	5.5	5.5	11.5	14.5	11.5	11.5	0.8229	0.6096
7	8.5	2.5	2.5	13.5	13.5	8.5	15.0	8.5	8.5	8.5	2.5	8.5	8.5	2.5	8.5	−0.1020	−0.5617
8	4.5	4.5	13.5	13.5	13.5	9.5	4.5	4.5	13.5	1.0	4.5	13.5	9.5	4.5	9.5	−0.0587	−0.4391
9	2.5	2.5	2.5	2.5	6.5	9.5	—	—	—	—	8.0	—	5.0	—	6.5	0.2105	−0.7412
10	2.0	2.0	5.0	5.0	7.0	—	—	—	—	—	8.0	—	5.0	—	2.0	−0.0395	−0.4489
11	2.5	2.5	5.0	5.0	7.0	—	—	—	—	—	8.0	—	5.0	—	1.0	−0.0462	−0.4835
12	2.5	2.5	4.5	4.5	6.5	—	—	—	—	—	8.0	—	6.5	—	1.0	−0.0220	−0.4169
13	14.5	6.5	11.5	6.5	11.5	14.5	6.5	2.0	11.5	11.5	1.0	6.5	3.0	6.5	6.5	−0.2966	0.1352
14	15.0	3.5	8.5	8.5	8.5	2.0	8.5	8.5	8.5	13.5	1.0	3.5	13.5	8.5	8.5	−0.0540	0.2466
15	13.5	5.0	10.0	10.0	10.0	3.0	13.5	7.5	13.5	13.5	1.5	7.5	1.5	5.0	5.0	−0.0580	0.2245
16	14.5	5.0	11.5	11.5	11.5	2.5	2.5	8.0	8.0	14.5	1.0	8.0	11.5	5.0	5.0	−0.0518	0.2845
17	14.5	7.5	3.5	7.5	11.5	3.5	3.5	11.5	7.5	7.5	1.0	3.5	11.5	11.5	11.5	−0.0689	0.2845
18	14.0	10.5	6.5	3.5	3.5	1.5	6.5	6.5	10.5	14.0	1.5	6.5	10.5	10.5	14.0	−0.0341	0.2626
19	13.5	8.5	4.0	8.5	4.0	2.0	13.5	8.5	8.5	13.5	1.0	4.0	13.5	8.5	8.5	−0.0264	0.2494
20	10.5	10.5	10.5	6.0	6.0	14.5	14.5	3.0	10.5	10.5	1.0	6.0	10.5	3.0	3.0	−0.0623	0.1925
21	13.5	9.0	4.5	4.5	2.0	2.0	9.0	15.0	9.0	9.0	2.0	9.0	9.0	9.0	13.5	0.0697	0.2786
22	14.5	9.0	9.0	3.5	2.0	9.0	9.0	9.0	9.0	9.0	1.0	9.0	14.5	3.5	9.0	0.0055	0.1986

Results of Two-Dimensional MDS Procedure for Money—Finance Attributes

D1	0.3984	−0.3871
D2	−0.4395	−0.2854
D3	0.5599	−0.0858
D4	0.3670	−0.2396
D5	0.5555	0.0696
D6	0.5844	0.2609
D7	−0.4839	0.7190
D8	−0.3725	−0.3243
D9	0.4679	0.7016
D10	−0.184	−0.4336
D11	−0.0204	0.3302
D12	−0.6314	0.5154
D13	−0.5817	−0.1801
D14	0.0846	−0.3952
D15	−0.4069	−0.2651

Table 7–A5. Data and Results of Two-Dimensional MDS Procedure for Countries and Development Air Attributes

Countries	Ordinal Rankings of Development Aid Data						Results of Two-Dimensional MDS Procedure for Countries	
	E1	E2	E3	E4	E5	E6		
1	3.5	3.5	5.0	2.0	1.0	6.0	−0.7447	0.1590
2	2.5	2.5	6.0	2.5	2.5	5.0	−0.5961	−0.3755
3	3.0	3.0	5.0	3.0	1.0	6.0	−0.9907	0.0735
4	3.0	3.0	3.0	3.0	3.0	6.0	−0.2152	1.0000
5	3.5	3.5	3.5	3.5	3.5	3.5	0.3000	0.3201
6	3.5	3.5	6.0	3.5	1.0	3.5	−0.2436	−0.6940
7	4.0	4.0	4.0	4.0	1.0	4.0	−0.1642	−0.3103
8	1.5	4.5	4.5	4.5	4.5	1.5	0.6810	−0.6501
9	2.0	−	−	−	−	1.0	0.2992	−0.4313
10	5.0	2.0	2.0	2.0	−	4.0	0.9869	0.7832
11	1.0	−	−	−	−	2.0	−0.2738	−0.0138
12	1.0	−	−	−	−	2.0	−0.2738	−0.0138
13	4.0	4.0	4.0	1.0	4.0	4.0	0.2444	0.4337
14	4.5	2.5	6.0	2.5	1.0	4.5	−0.7121	−0.0984
15	3.0	1.5	6.0	4.5	1.5	4.5	−0.7756	−0.4482
16	−	4.5	4.5	2.5	1.0	2.5	0.1982	−0.5516
17	4.5	3.0	6.0	1.5	1.5	4.5	−0.2413	−0.2415
18	4.0	1.5	6.0	4.0	1.5	4.0	−0.5255	−0.5184
19	4.0	1.5	6.0	3.0	1.5	5.0	−0.7916	−0.1066
20	4.0	4.0	4.0	1.0	4.0	4.0	0.2444	0.4337
21	4.5	2.0	6.0	2.0	2.0	4.5	−0.6080	−0.0876
22	4.5	4.5	4.5	1.5	4.5	1.5	0.9525	−0.4563

Results for Two-Dimensional MDS
Procedures for Development and Attributes

E1	−0.4155	−0.0057
E2	−0.4346	−0.0168
E3	0.7899	0.9694
E4	−0.4014	0.0220
E5	−0.5097	−0.1178
E6	0.9712	−0.8511

8 Resolution of Mutual Loss Conflict Induced by the Embargo Threat

Noboru Sakashita

The response by resource-importing countries to the embargo threat of resource-exporting countries, which takes the form of a precautionary cutback of the quantity imported or of additional storage of imported resources, was, for example, analyzed by Nordhaus (1974), and Tolley and Wilman (1977). But neither article considered the impact of reduced imports on the world market, which might suppress the international equilibrium price of the resource in question. This impact will hurt the trading position of exporting countries, who as a group are forced to adopt monopolistic behavior in order to maintain the level of international price. This behavior will induce further contraction of that resource on the world trade market.

This chapter attempts to analyze these secondary and tertiary effects of an embargo threat and also to search for some instruments to solve this mutual loss conflict in the world (north-south) trade market. The first section analyzes the behavior of a resource-importing country under the embargo threat. The change of international trade equilibrium when exporting countries show passive response is discussed in the second section. Further shrinkage of the world trade market when exporting countries assume a monopolistic behavior is examined in the third section. Finally, in the fourth section, possible resolution of resultant mutual loss conflict is discussed, which then leads to the chapter's conclusion.

ANALYSIS OF AN IMPORTING COUNTRY

Imagine a resource-importing country which has a long-run demand function of the following linear form:

$$q_0 = a - bp_0, \qquad p_0 = \bar{p} + t, \qquad (8-1)$$

where

q_0: quantity imported during non-embargo period,
p_0: domestic price of the resource during non-embargo period,
$\bar{p}$: international price of the resource,
t: rate of import tariff.

The short-run demand function starting from an initial combination of (p_0, q_0) can be expressed as:

$$q_1 - q_0 = -b\lambda(p_1 - p_0), \qquad (8-2)$$

where

q_1: quantity imported during embargo period,
p_2: domestic price during embargo period,
λ: ratio of the short-run price coefficient to the long-run price coefficient, $0 < \lambda < 1$.[1]

Apparently, the loss in the economy as a whole induced by an import tariff, L_T, is expressed as:

$$L_T = \tfrac{1}{2} t\, [(a - b\bar{p}) + \{a - b(\bar{p} + t)\}] - t\{a - b(\bar{p} + t)\}$$
$$= \tfrac{1}{2} bt^2 \qquad (8-3)$$

The first term in the middle line of equation (8–3) shows the decrease in demander's surplus, and the second term expresses the revenue from the import tariff which offsets the surplus loss. On the other hand, the loss evoked by the realization of the embargo, L_E, is given by the following formula:

$$L_E = \tfrac{1}{2}(p_1 - p_0)(q_1 + q_0)$$
$$= \frac{1}{2} \frac{(1-\mu)}{b\lambda} q_0(\mu + 1) q_0 = \frac{(1-\mu^2)}{2b\lambda} \{a - b(\bar{p} + t)\}^2,$$

$$(8-4)$$

---

1. The difference between long-run and short-run demand functions is, of course, the fixedness of certain factors of production in the latter case which are employed by the resource demander as a producer of some final commodity. Even if the demander is supposed to be a consumer, we can assume the presence of similar "factors" in the consumption activities.

where

μ: given contraction rate of import during embargo period,

$$q_1 = \mu q_0, \qquad 0 < \mu < 1.$$

The content of L_E is, needless to say, the decrease in demander's surplus when the quantity of the resource supplied is suddenly cut to q_1 from q_0. Here we are assuming that the gain from the short-run increase of resource price is entirely taken by foreign traders and not by domestic traders.

The total loss evoked by the possibility (not by the realization) of an embargo and corresponding import-cutback policy of the importing country, is the sum of (8—3) and (8—4), that is,

$$L(t) = L_T + \pi L_E = \tfrac{1}{2} b t^2 + \theta \{a - b(\bar{p} + t)\}^2, \qquad (8-5)$$

where

π: given realization probability of embargo

$$\theta = \frac{\pi(1 - \mu^2)}{2 b \lambda}$$

The optimal rate of import tariff which minimizes $L(t)$ is given by:

$$t^* = \frac{2\theta(a - b\bar{p})}{1 + 2\theta b}$$

after letting

$$\frac{dL(t)}{dt} = 0.$$

Now we assume the following values for the parameters:

$$\pi = 0.2, \quad \lambda = 0.2, \quad a = 10, \quad b = 0.8, \quad \mu = 0.75 \quad (\theta \cong 0.27).$$

$$(8-7)$$

Then the optimal rates of import tariff under the different values of international price of the resource are shown in Table (8—1).

Table 8—1. Optimal Rates of Import Tariff and Related Quantities

	$\bar{p}$	t^*	$\bar{p} + t^*$	q_0	$q(\bar{p})^{a)}$	$q(\bar{p}) - q_0^{b)}$
Case 1	$1.50	$3.32	$4.82	6.14	8.8	2.66
Case 2	$7.00	$1.66	$8.66	3.07	4.4	1.33

Table 8–2.   Calculation of Losses under Alternative Trade Policies for Case 1

	t	q_0	L_T	πL_E	L
1. Laissez-faire	0	8.80	0	20.91	20.91
2. Optimal tariff	3.32	6.14	4.41	10.19	14.60
3. Autarky (no import)	11	0	48.40	0	48.40

Table 8–1 implies that the sensitivity of import-cutback policy is a decreasing function of the initial international price of the resource, $\bar{p}$.

Calculation of the losses under alternative trade policies are shown in Table 8–2 for Case 1. Of course, the loss is minimized under the optimal rate of import tariff.

We should notice with Table 8–2 that the cost of an autarchy policy is much bigger than that of a laissez-faire policy in this case, which can be a warning to the extremist on the side of a "foreign independence" policy.

ANALYSIS OF EXPORTING COUNTRIES AND CONTRACTED EQUILIBRIUM

Here we introduce a long-run supply function LRS:

$$q^S = -0.2 + 6p \qquad (8-8)$$

which produces the long-run international equilibrium price $\bar{p} = 1.5$ assumed earlier combined with the long-run demand function LRD given in the previous section:

$$q^D = 10 - 0.8p. \qquad (8-9)$$

Under the import-cutback policy employed by the importing country, however, the assumed equilibrium price, $\bar{p} = 1.5$, never realizes. Therefore, in the presence of an embargo threat, actual equilibrium of the world resource market is given as a solution of the following three equations:

$$\tilde{q} = 10 - 0.8(\tilde{\tilde{p}} + t^*) \qquad \text{LDR} \qquad (8-10)$$

$$\tilde{q} = -0.2 + 6\tilde{\tilde{p}} \qquad \text{LSR} \qquad (8-11)$$

$$t^* = 3.804 - 0.304\tilde{\tilde{p}} \qquad \text{optimal tariff policy.} \qquad (8-12)$$

We can contrast the international equilibrium with an embargo threat—(8–10), (8–11), (8–12)—with the same without that threat— (8–8) and (8–9)—as follows:

$$\tilde{\tilde{p}} = 1.09, \quad t^* = 3.47, \quad \tilde{q} = 6.35 \qquad \text{with embargo threat}$$

$$(8\text{–}13)$$

$$\bar{p} = 1.5, \quad t = 0, \quad \bar{q} = 8.8 \qquad \text{without embargo threat} \quad (8\text{–}14)$$

The losses borne by both parties caused by the transition from a state without an embargo threat to one with an embargo threat *which is not realized* will be calculated as follows:

$$L_D = \tfrac{1}{2}\{(\tilde{\tilde{p}} + t^*) - \bar{p}\}\{q^D(\bar{p} + t^*) + q^D(\bar{p})\}$$
$$-t^* \cdot q^D(\tilde{\tilde{p}} + t^*) = 1.1632 \qquad (8\text{–}15)$$

The loss for the exporting countries are:

$$L_S = \tfrac{1}{2}(\bar{p} - \tilde{\tilde{p}})\{q^s(\bar{p}) + q^s(\tilde{\tilde{p}})\} \qquad (8\text{–}16)$$
$$= 3.0942$$

Obviously the cost of an embargo threat hurts exporting countries themselves more severely if they do not take further retaliatory action after the threat in this case.

MONOPOLISTIC BEHAVIOR BY EXPORTING COUNTRIES

Under the circumstance just described, the exporting countries will realize that the *effective* demand function which they face is the following one deduced by the substitution of (8–12) into (8–10):

$$q = 6.957 - 0.557p \qquad (8\text{–}17)$$

The marginal revenue associated with this effective demand function is:

$$MR = p + \frac{dp}{dq}q = 12.500 - 3.594q \qquad (8\text{–}18)$$

and the corresponding marginal cost as derived from equation (8–11) is:

$$MC = 0.033 + 0.167q \qquad (8\text{–}19)$$

The exporting countries will adopt monopolistic behavior in which they equate MR and MC given in equations (8–18) and (8–19), with the resultant equilibrium quantity and price:

$$\hat{p} = 6.543, \quad \hat{t}^* = 1.813, \quad \hat{q} = 3.315 \qquad (8–20)$$

The *absolute* gain for the exporting countries in this situation is calculated as follows:

$$\hat{G}_S = \hat{p}\hat{q} - \int_0^{\hat{q}} (MC)\,dq = 20.665 \qquad (8–21)$$

The *absolute* gain for the importing country is also calculated as follows:

$$\hat{G}_D = \int_0^{\hat{q}} (12.5 - 1.25q)\,dq - (\hat{p} + \hat{t}^*)\hat{q} + \hat{t}^*\hat{q} = 12.880 \qquad (8–22)$$

Corresponding absolute gains for both parties in the case of no-threat and no-tariff are given as follows:

$$\bar{G}_S = \bar{p}\bar{q} - \int_0^{\bar{q}} (MC)\,dq = 6.453 \qquad (8–23)$$

$$\bar{G}_D = \int_0^{\bar{q}} (12.5 - 1.25)q\,dq - \bar{p}\bar{q} = 48.4. \qquad (8–24)$$

The world gain, which is the sum of G_S and G_D, naturally decreases from 54.853 to 33.545 when both parties move from the laissez-faire situation to the tariff and monopoly situation. We should notice, however, that the distribution of the world gain is more drastically changed from one situation to the other.

COMPARISON OF POLICIES AND RESOLUTION OF THE CONFLICT

Comparison of equations (8–14), (8–13), and (8–20) shows us the course of retaliatory actions initiated by the embargo threat of exporting countries, which reduces sequentially the quantity imported. We can construct the pay-off matrix shown in Table 8–3 associated with alternative policies adopted by the importing country and the exporting countries.

The pay-off matrix as shown in Table 8–3 is clearly that of a non-zero-sum game, and from this matrix a possible resolution of the mutual loss conflict can be derived. An incentive for exporting

Table 8–3. Pay-off Matrix

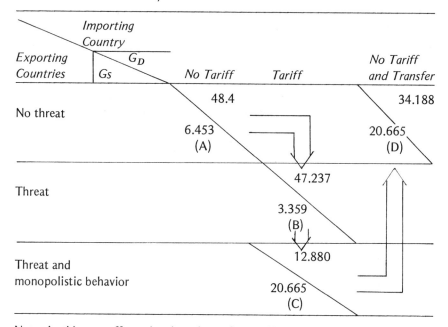

Note. In this pay-off matrix, the values of pay-off for unrealistic or unimportant combinations of policies are not calculated.

countries to make an embargo threat is the unequal distribution of gain from the international trade, as indicated by the pay-off in Case (A). Sequential retaliatory actions lead to the worst situation for the importing country, as shown by the pay-off in Case (C). In order to avoid this worst situation, the importing country should take an initial move to transfer approximately 30 percent of its gain in Case (A) to the exporting countries. This action will prevent the latter countries' embargo threat by inducing them and the importing country itself to the situation in Case (D). Of course, Case (D) is much better for the importing country compared to Case (C), and at the same time, maximum world gain from the international trade is preserved.

CONCLUSION

In the preceding sections, a heuristic discussion which leads to a possible way of resolving the mutual loss conflict initiated with an embargo threat, has been developed. The final calculation of the amount of initial transfer necessary to prevent the worst situation, of course, depends upon the specific values of the parameters given in the text, but the general principle of logic remains the same with different cases.

The most important point in this analysis is that both parties should analyze the outcome of alternative combinations of different policies adopted by themselves *beforehand*, and should start the process of negotiation before the adoption of any retaliative action and not after it. The hypothetical pay-off matrix approach described earlier would be, I think, very indicative as a datum for such a negotiation.

REFERENCES

Nordhaus, W.D. 1974. "The 1974 Report of the President's Council of Economic Advisors; Energy in the Economic Report." *American Economic Review* 64: 558–565.

Tolley, G.S., and J.D. Wilman. 1977. "The Foreign Dependence Question." *Journal of Political Economy* 85: 323–346.

III Contributions to Conflict Analysis and Welfare

9 Theoretical and Empirical Analysis of the Differentiation Process in the Technology Gap Between Developed and Developing Nations

Hajime Eto and Kyoko Makino

SIGNIFICANCE OF TECHNOLOGY-GAP ANALYSIS IN PEACE SCIENCE

The economic gap between the developed and developing nations may threaten world peace. Unfortunately this gap has attracted only the attention of "humanitarian" idealists while realists tend to believe that the existence of poverty in the developing countries causes only local war with little effect on the developed countries. Although the prevailing belief is that the "vacuum" of military power causes war, the historical fact seems to have been ignored that the "vacuum" of wealth in a particular area has very often called for the intervention of opposing powerful nations, which tends to result in global war.

In both humanitarian and peace-seeking contexts, the international economic gap must seriously be analyzed. Through the various attempts to fill this gap (for instance, economic aid activity), it is now recognized that the most scarce resource in developing countries is technology (or skill) rather than capital. This recognition leads to considering international technology-gap analysis as a fundamental element of peace science.

METHOD

In general, the availability of technological data is quite low; therefore, methods which require highly organized data (for instance, time series data) are often useless. Since there has been no widely accepted definition of how to measure technology, its definition varies through time. This makes time series analysis quite unreliable. The method proposed in this chapter avoids this difficulty by inferring dynamics from static (that is, nontime series) data. Firstly, a conceptual framework of the structure of technology development is formulated as a hypothesis or an assumption to which a stochastic process is applied to yield a statistical distribution. If this theoretical distribution is found to have a good fit to the real static distribution, then the dynamics underlying this stochastic process can be considered to have the explanatory power of the real distribution.

STRUCTURE OF TECHNOLOGY DEVELOPMENT

Technology is subject to the rule of self-multiplication. Once high technology resources exist in a country, it attracts excellent students, as well as scientists from abroad, and gives managers confidence to invest in technology development. Hence, technology in that country earns favorable conditions. Meanwhile, technology in another country faces unfavorable conditions because its excellent students tend to look for opportunities in other areas, and its managers lack confidence to invest in the field of technology. This situation in the latter country may give rise to brain drain. In this way, the country which has higher technology resources develops more favorable conditions at the sacrifice of the country possessing less technology resources. This differentiates the technology level between countries. This self-multiplication process may be expressed as in (9–1) under the condition that the technology resource at level x exists.

$$P(x \rightarrow x + 1, \ \Delta t) \sim \lambda x \Delta t \tag{9–1}$$

where the left side denotes the probability that the technology resource grows from x by a unit for the infinitesimal time interval, and λ on the right side denotes the positive parameter. The technology resource variable x is discrete here, not only for mathematical simplicity but also for the reality of our model. In technology, the most important and scarce resource is scientists and engineers; the second may be research institutes and sophisticated plants; while the most important performance indicator is patents and professional publications. These are all discrete. When our model is applied to small countries, institutes, and firms, the discrete model is desirable. On the other hand, the continuous model may be considered as an approximation for large countries, institutes, and firms, or as a model for technology resources normalized or divided by proper parameters (for example, population). The process described in (9—1) is called the Yule process.

This self-multiplication process typically works in the age of rapid innovation. In this age, the latest innovation gives direct and immediate rise to the next innovation, and therefore the country which experienced the latest innovation possesses the favorable conditions for the next. This differs from the situation in the age-of-technology stalemate, where the timelag between the preceding innovation and its further development is so long that the new innovation results mainly from an old one which has come to be widely adopted. In this sense, the Yule process works typically in the age of rapid innovation. The probability $q(t)$ that the duration time of the rapid innovation age is t in a country may be expressed as:

$$q(t) = \mu \exp(-\mu t) \quad \text{(exponential distribution)} \qquad (9-2)$$

where μ is positive. The structure underlying the exponential distribution (9—2) is that the duration of the rapid innovation age is only by accident brought to a halt. In fact, it is the solution to the following differential equation of the constant rate of accident:

$$dS(t)/dt = -\mu S(t),$$

where S denotes the length of the survival. This is known to be approximately valid for the duration time of telephone conversations and the lifetime of industrial products with no quality control, where the causes for death occur very rarely and at random (the Poisson process).

When the longer duration of the rapid innovation age tends to yield more favorable conditions for its further continuance (survival), the probability $q(t)$ is the density of the log-normal distribution to follow (Aitchison and Brown 1967: 23).

$$q(t) = \exp\left(-(\log t - m)^2 / 2\sigma^2\right)/(2\pi)^{1/2}\sigma t \qquad (9-3)$$

where m and σ^2 denote the mean and the variance, respectively.

When several factors support the duration of the rapid innovation age, where the duration time of each is subject to the exponential distribution (9–2), and when a certain (threshold) number of them cease to be in effect and thus lead to the end of the rapid innovation age (a kind of the majority circuit), the moment-generating function of the probability density in question $M_k(\theta)$ is expressed in terms of the exponential distribution $M_e(\theta)$ as follows (Yoda 1972: 20):

$$M_k(\theta) = (1 - \theta/v)^{-k} = (M_e(\theta))^k$$

where k denotes the threshold number. $M_k(\theta)$ yields the Gamma distribution whose density is the probability to be sought:

$$q(t) = v^k t^{k-1} \exp(-vt)/\Gamma(k) \qquad (9-4)$$

where Γ denotes the Gamma function.

THE YULE AND THE ULTRA-YULE DISTRIBUTIONS

The structural analysis of technology development in the foregoing section yields the realization of the technological resource distribution in the following way. Solving the equation (9–1) yields the probability $p(x|t)$ that the technological resource grows from x to $x + 1$ in time t with the initial condition of possessing the technological resource at level x (Yablonsky 1980):

$$p(x|t) = \exp(-\lambda t)(1 - \exp(-\lambda t))^{x-1} \qquad (9-5)$$

which may be called the pre-Yule quasi-probability. This has the following property:

Theorem 1

$$\int_0^\infty p(x|t)\, dt = 1/\lambda x. \qquad (9-6)$$

Proof.   Apply the integration by change of variable to the right side of (9–5).

Let $p^*(x|t)$ be defined as follows:

$$p^*(x|t) = \lambda x p(x|t). \qquad (9-7)$$

Corollary 1. $p^*(x|t)$ defined by (9–7) possesses the property of the probability.

By Corollary 1, $p^*(x|t)$ may be called the pre-Yule distribution. From the similarity between the Yule process and the deduction of the log-normal distribution as a proportional growth process, the asymptoticity of the pre-Yule distribution toward the log-normal distribution is anticipated. Indeed, it can be analytically and numerically verified.

Proposition 1. The pre-Yule distribution defined by (9–7) approaches asymptotically toward the log-normal distribution.

The probability $p(x)$ that a country acquires the technology resource at level x for a sufficient length of time (history) may be obtained by integrating the product of the associated probability in time t with the probability of the duration time of this process. The former probability is the pre-Yule quasi-probability, and the latter is one among (9–2), (9–3), and (9–4). The probability $p(x)$ is expressed as follows:

$$p(x) = \int_0^\infty p(x|t) q(t) \, dt. \qquad (9-8)$$

For theoretical simplicity, the exponential distribution (9–2) is now taken for $q(t)$ in (9–8). Hence

$$p(x) = \int_0^\infty \exp(-\lambda t)(1 - \exp(-\lambda t))^{x-1} \mu \exp(-\mu t) \, dt$$

$$= \mu B(x, 1 + \mu/\lambda)/\lambda = \alpha B(x, \alpha + 1) \qquad (9-9)$$

where

$$\alpha = \mu/\lambda \qquad (9-10)$$

$$B(x, \alpha + 1) = \int_0^1 y^{x-1}(1-y)^\alpha dy \quad \text{(Beta function)} \qquad (9-11)$$

The expression in (9–9) is called the density of the Yule distribution. As is well known, μ is the inverse of the mean of the duration time of the rapid innovation age. Recalling that λ denotes the productivity of innovation or the technology growth rate, the implication of α is as follows. In the case where α is large, the duration time of the rapid innovation age is relatively short and the productivity of innovation is relatively low. In the case where α is small, the duration time of the rapid innovation age is relatively long and the productivity of innovation is relatively high. That is the golden age of technology.

When α is large, the right tail of the Yule distribution is short. When α is small, it is longer than that of the other mathematically formulated distributions and it represents a very skewed distribution.

Proposition 2.   The Yule process with its exponential duration time yields the Yule distribution which is, for α small, more skewed than any well-known skewed distributions (exponential, log-normal, Gamma, Weibul, Beta, and so on).

As was discussed earlier, the Yule distribution is more skewed when μ is smaller, whereas the exponential distribution (9—2) is more skewed when μ is smaller. As the log-normal and the Gamma distributions for appropriate parameter values are skewed more than the exponential distribution, these facts together imply the following:

Theorem 2

Replacing (9—2) with (9—3) or (9—4) with appropriate parameter values in forming (9—8) yields distributions which are skewed more than the Yule distribution.

These distributions may be called the family of the ultra-Yule distributions.

CATCH-UP AND OVERTAKE

The integration is taken over the domain from zero to infinity in (9—8). Practically speaking, however, time prior to the latest decades is negligible in the integration under the condition of a monotonic increase of technology resource in time. Therefore the parameter value, say α, varies in historical time according to the degree of dominance of innovation age in the latest decades.

When α is small, that is, in the continued golden age in history of technology, the gap between nations is enlarging. It can be said that α was small in 1950s and 1960s.

When α is large, that is, in the continued stalemate of technology, the gap is diminishing. The technological catch-up can occur in such a situation. It can be said that α is large in the 1970s and around 1980. This may explain the catch-up and perhaps overtake of Japanese with Western technology, around 1980.

INTERNATIONAL GAP IN TECHNOLOGY RESOURCE

Technology resource can conceptually be classified into stock and flow. Different from the physical fields, however, stock in many cases cannot be measured in the social or human fields. Therefore, the triad of input, state, and output will be chosen hereafter. Input and output are mostly flows, while state is mostly stock which can only indirectly be measured by output. Measurable technology stocks are manpower, patent, and facilities like laboratories and plants, but the real technology stock is performance which is measured only through output or estimated by input. These are called the performance indices.

The international distributions of various technology resources and performance indices are analyzed, with empirical findings as follows (using data from World Bank 1980):

1. *Skewification.* For all the cases investigated, the distributions are more skewed than any mathematically well-known distributions (that is, the exponential, Gamma, log-normal, and so on). The Yule distribution gives a better fit than these distributions, and the family of the ultra-Yule distributions shows the best fit, as Figure 9—1 shows where the log-normal distribution (9—3) is taken for $q(t)$ in (9—8) as the ultra-Yule distribution.

2. *Polarization or Ramification.* In most cases the distributions are multimodal. More specifically there are separated clusters. In particular, the top cluster which denotes the richest group is often quite separate from the others. This is, of course, to be interpreted as the result of the self-multiplication or Yule process. The separation itself may not be important when it occurs at the right tail because it may be due to the fact that the sample size (about 120) is too small in comparison with the wide range of the distribution. In many cases the number of separated clusters exceeds two, that is, the second (or third) cluster which denotes the middle

Figure 9–1.   Fit to Distribution of Scientists and Engineers in 10^6 Persons

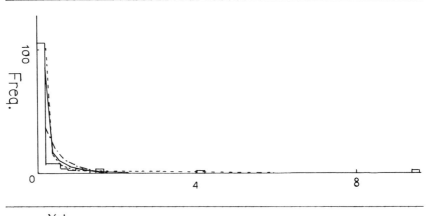

———; Yule
– – – –; Ultra-Yule
—·—·—; Exponential

Figure 9–2.   Percentage of Manufacturing Products in Exports

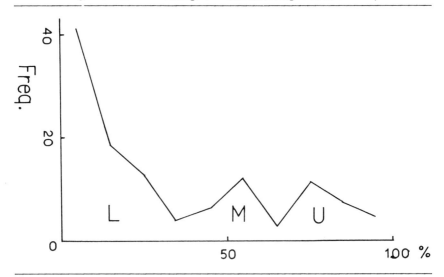

group, is separated or almost separated from the others on both sides. This fact can no longer be explained by the smallness of sample size because the density (the height of histogram) is not too low to have near-zero occurrence in the middle of the distribution. It may

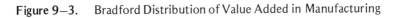

Figure 9–3.   Bradford Distribution of Value Added in Manufacturing

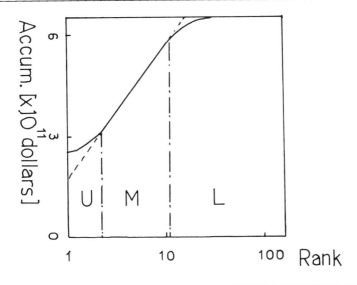

be explained by a decision-theoretic approach that the technology resource level is intentionally set in the light of the competitors' levels. In other words, the target of the technology resource level is set to rival the competitors but not to take too much risk by going significantly beyond competitors' level, which may be going beyond feasibility. This clusterization may be called the target-based technology development behavior (see Figure 9–2).

BRADFORD LAW IN TECHNOLOGY RESOURCES

The Bradford law, which is an empirical skew "distribution" in library science, gives a clear discrimination between the nucleus and the rest (Brookes 1969). In the case of incompleteness of bibliographic collection the rest is again divided into the middle and the peripheral parts. As technology development process is always incomplete, the incomplete case is applicable to our problem, yielding the three-clusterization pattern. In fact this fits the international technology distribution (Figure 9–3). The Bradford law is purely empirical while its theoretical explanation remains an open question.

PROSPECT OF GENERALIZED THEORY

The aforementioned polarization or ramification may be included in the branching process which is a special form of the Markov process especially developed for high-energy physics (Athreya and Ney 1972; Harris 1963; Sevastyanov 1971). The foregoing discussions can be restated in terms of the branching process as follows: an elementary particle with given initial energy experiences a series of fissions in a manner of cascades. Immigrating particles (new entries) also join the system. The transient rate may depend on age, and some particles are generated and extinguished at a certain rate. The resulting distribution is quite skewed and polarized or even ramified according to the parameter values. Here the structure of the process is

$$P(E, T, \epsilon, \iota, \rho)$$

where E and T denote the type of elementary particles and time, respectively, and ϵ, ι, and ρ denote the parameters of the initial energy, immigration rate, and transient rate, respectively.

In this way the special form of technology development process can be given a general expression common with the natural development process.

CONCLUSIONS

The technology development process is structured and formalized. This gives very skewed distributions which show the best fit to the real international gap of various technology resources than do any known distributions. The Bradford "distribution" is shown to fit the polarization and ramification which also characterize the international distributions of technology resources. The branching process frame is presented to connect with the natural development process.

REFERENCES

Aitchison, J., and J.A.C. Brown. 1957. *The Log-Normal Distribution*. Cambridge, England: Cambridge University Press.
Athreya, K.B., and P.E. Ney. 1972. *Branching Process*. Berlin: Springer.

Brookes, B.C. 1969. "Bradford's Law and the Bibliography of Science." *Nature* 244 (6): 953–956.

Harris, T.E. 1963. *The Theory of Branching Process*. Berlin: Springer.

Sevastyanov, B.A. 1971. *Branching Process* (in Russian). Moscow: Nauka.

Yablonsky, A.L. 1980. "On Fundamental Regularities of the Distribution of Scientific Productivity." *Scientometrics* 2 (1): 3–34.

Yoda, H. 1972. *Introduction to Reliability Theory* (in Japanese). Tokyo: Asakura Publishing Company.

World Bank. 1980. *World Development Report*. Washington, D.C.

10 Welfare Implications of Cost-Benefit Analysis*

Hisayoshi Morisugi

With few exceptions, the costs and benefits measured by monetary terms in standard cost-benefit analysis are simply added regardless of who receives them. As a result of this addition, a given project is always adopted if the benefits outweigh the costs.

One of the strongest justifications for this cost benefit criterion is based on a *compensation test*, in other words, *a potential Pareto improvement test*, which says that if the resulting algebraic sum is positive, gainers could more than compensate losers and still be better off after the project is undertaken. Thus it would be possible to redistribute the gainers' income to the losers so that no one is made worse off by the project (Mishan 1972).

This rather intuitive justification of the cost-benefit criterion was severely attacked by Boadway (1974). He showed that satisfying the cost-benefit criterion does not in general imply satisfaction of the compensation test. In his article Boadway defined "costs" and "benefits" in terms of the *compensating variation*, *CV*, which

*The author is much indebted to Professor Tony E. Smith, who has so kindly devoted his time to refine the structure of this chapter, including constructions of more elegant proofs and editing of the English text. Also the author is grateful for the helpful comments of Professors Masahisa Fujita, Thomas M. Fogarty, Roger E. Bolton, Yasoi Yasuda, and other members of Regional Theory Workshops held at the Department of Regional Science, University of Pennsylvania. Finally the auther expresses his gratitude for neat typing to Helen Neff, Kelly Herb, and Kathy Klingler.

corresponds to the amount of money which the gainer is willing to pay the loser in order to maintain the same welfare as before the change. As for the "compensating test," Boadway adopted the Kaldor version, in which the gainers are said to be able to compensate the losers whenever the final batch of goods can be redistributed in such a way as to make both persons better off than they were with the initial batch of goods. Hence, in more concrete terms, Boadway showed that the cost-benefit criterion based on the compensating variation (denoted by ΣCV) is *not* a sufficient condition for satisfaction of the compensation test of Kaldor (denoted by KT). At the same time, he showed that although it is not a sufficient condition, the positivity of net benefit as measured by the sum of consumers' compensating variation ΣCV, is indeed necessary for a proposed change to satisfy the Kaldor test.

In response to this negative conclusion for classical cost-benefit analysis, Mishan (1976) has attempted to argue that this technique can still be justified on other grounds. Although his argument is not very clear, it can be interpreted roughly in the following way.

If the total batches of goods for society both before and after the project are assumed to be given, then these quantity constraints must be taken into account when calculating compensating variation. Hence Mishan advocated the use of a *constrained* compensating variation rather than a pure compensating variation (which turns out to be equivalent to the national income evaluated by the prices resulting after the change). Moreover, as a compensation test, he advocated the use of the Hicksian version, HT, which says that a given change is socially preferred if those who would lose by this change cannot profitably bribe the gainers into rejecting it. He then shows that the cost-benefit criterion using the constrained compensating variation indeed provides a sufficient condition for satisfying the Hicksian test HT.

These findings by previous researchers leave open the question as to whether there exist cost-benefit criteria which are *sufficient* for the Kaldor test. Hence, our first result is to show that any cost benefit criterion which is sufficient for the Hicksian test is also sufficient for the Kaldor test—whenever these tests can meaningfully be defined. More concretely, it is shown in Proposition 1 that in all cases where the Hicksian and Kaldor test are *not* equivalent, it must be true that either the Hicksian and Kaldor test exhibits a "Scitovsky paradox," and hence cannot be meaningfully interpreted.

Thus, if attention is restricted to these cases in which both tests can be meaningfully defined (that is, are free of paradoxes), then satisfaction of the Hicksian test is *equivalent* to satisfaction of the Kaldor test. In particular, this result implies that Mishan's constrained compensating variation criterion is sufficient for the Kaldor test in such cases (as shown in Proposition 4).

More generally, this result shows that in all cases of interest, one may focus attention on those cost-benefit criteria satisfying the Hicksian test. With this in mind, our second result is to establish the sufficiency of an alternative cost-benefit criterion for the Kaldor test. This criterion designated as the *equivalent variation* (denoted by ΣEV) is defined to be the amount of money which the loser is willing to pay the gainer in order to prevent the proposed change from taking place. The proof of this sufficiency condition is developed in the fourth section.

Furthermore, it will be shown in the fifth section that a combined cost-benefit criterion using both compensating and equivalent variations yields a sufficient condition for the presence of a Scitovsky paradox in the Hicksian test. Hence, a necessary condition for the applicability of these results is that this condition fails to hold.

Finally, the chapter concludes with a comparative analysis of the equivalent variation and current national income indices. In particular, a "Pareto" axiom is proposed which reveals a clear superiority of the equivalent variation criterion in many cases.

FOUR COST-BENEFIT CRITERIA

If we assume that all goods are used for either private consumption or private factor supply, and that there exist no externalities, then the costs and benefits of any given social change can be defined in terms of individual consumer behavior as follows:

Let a given representative individual's ordinal utility function be denoted by

$$u = u(x_1, \text{-----}, x_n) = u(x) \qquad (10\text{--}1)$$

where x is a consumption and factor-supply vector of goods for the individual. We designate each component x_j of the vector x positive if x_j is a consumption good and negative if x_j is a factor supply. We can then derive both the individual's *demand and factor-supply functions* $x_j = x_j(p, y)$ for each good $j = 1, \ldots, n$, and his *indirect utility function* $u = v(p, y)$, given the price vector p and his lump sum income y.[1] Since $v(p, y)$ is a strictly increasing function of y, we can solve for y in terms of u and p to obtain the corresponding expenditure function $y = e(p, u)$, which may be interpreted as the minimal amount of income necessary to derive a specific utility level u at price p.

Now suppose that the consumer faces an initial price vector p^0 and a final price vector p^1, and money income y^0 and y^1, his consumption vectors x^0 and x^1 for respective situations. Then his compensating variation CV and equivalent variation EV can be defined as follows (Currie, Murphy, and Schmitz 1971):

CV: the amount of compensation, paid or received, which will leave the consumer in his *initial* welfare position *following the change in price and income*, if he is free to buy and supply any quantity of the commodity and the factor at the new price and income.

EV: the amount of compensation, paid or received, which will leave the consumer in his *subsequent* welfare position *in absence of the price and income change*, if he is free to buy and supply any quantity of the commodity and the factor at the old price and income.

These two measures can be expressed by both indirect utility and expenditure functions:

$$v(p^1, y^1 - CV) = v(p^0, y^0) \qquad (10\text{--}2)$$

or

$$CV = y^1 - e(p^1, v^0) \qquad (10\text{--}3)$$

where

$$v^0 = v(p^0, y^0), \qquad (10\text{--}4)$$

and

$$v(p^0, y^0 + EV) = v(p^1, y^1) \qquad (10\text{--}5)$$

1. Formally, the individual behavior can be represented by the following:

$$\max u(x) \quad \text{given} \quad px = y.$$

Substitute this solution $x_j = x_j(p, y)$ into the utility function $u(x)$. Then we obtain the indirect utility function $v(p, y) \equiv u(x(p, y))$.

or

$$EV = e(p^0, v^1) - y^0 \qquad (10-6)$$

where

$$v^1 = v(p^1, y^1) \qquad (10-7)$$

Notice that we define CV and EV in such a way that they are positive or negative depending on whether prices of consumption goods fall or rise, prices of supply factors rise or fall, and income rises or falls, respectively, so that we may designate these levels of CV and EV as *costs* when they are negative, and *benefits* when they are positive.[2] The corresponding social net benefits (denoted, respectively, by ΣCV and ΣEV) can then be obtained by summing up CV and EV algebraically over the affected individuals.

Although this discussion is sufficient to provide us with an exact definition of both costs and benefits, it is convenient to introduce two additional measures of welfare improvement. These measures are defined in terms of the initial and subsequent prices, respectively, as the *real income change* $RI = p^0 x^1 - p^0 x^0$ and the *current income change* $CI = p^1 x^1 - p^1 x^0$. The associated national incomes can then be obtained by summing up the associated individual income changes as denoted by RNI and CNI, respectively.

These four individual welfare indices can be illustrated by using a

---

2. Also notice that these definitions of costs and benefits can be interpreted in terms of the conventionally defined costs and benefits. As a simple illustration, consider a project which is socially financed by a lump sum tax Δy and which affects consumers only by decreasing the prices of certain consumption goods. Then the resulting compensating variation CV and equivalent variation EV for this case can be written simply as

$$CV = e(p^0, v^0) - e(p^1, v^0) - (y^0 - y^1)$$

$$= \oint_{p^1}^{p^0} b(p, v^0) dp - \Delta y$$

$$EV = e(p^0, v^1) - e(p^1, v^1) - (y^0 - y^1)$$

$$= \oint_{p^1}^{p^0} b(p, v^1) dp - \Delta y$$

where $y^0 = e(p^0, v^0)$, $y^1 = e(p^1, v^1)$ and where the first terms of both equations denote the *consumer's surplus*, as defined by the line integral of the Hicksian compensated demand functions $b(p, v^0)$ and $b(p, v^1)$ along any path from p^1 to p^0 (for proof, see, for example, Diamond and McFadden 1974). Hence, if consumer's surplus and the lump-sum tax are taken to reflect "benefits" and "cost," respectively, then CV and EV in this case are both seen to have the classical "benefits minus costs" interpretation.

Figure 10–1(a).   Definition of *CV* and *CI*

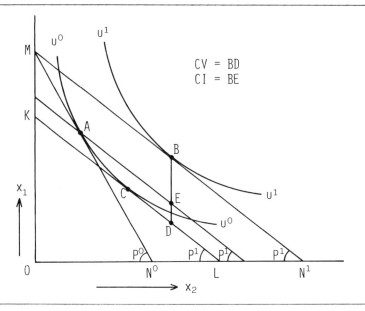

Figure 10–1(b).   Definition of *EV* and *RI*

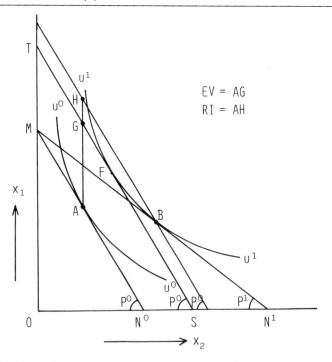

simple indifference map as shown in Figure 10–1. Here we assume that there are only two private goods 1 and 2, where good 1 is a numeraire with price equal to one, and where the price of good 2 has fallen from p^0 to p^1.

In this situation we consider a consumer with constant income OM as in Figure 10–1.[3] The initial price for good 2 is given by the slope of p^0 and falls to p^1. Then for Figures 10–1(a) and 10–1(b), the four measures can be depicted as follows:

compensating variation	$CV = BD$	(Figure 10–1(a))
equivalent variation	$EV = AG$	(Figure 10–1(b))
current income change	$CI = BE$	(Figure 10–1(a))
real income change	$RI = AH$	(Figure 10–1(b)),

where A and B are the equilibrium points for the old and new prices for good 2, respectively, and where u^0 and u^1 are the associated indifference curves. Since C is a tangent point of line with the slope of new price p^1, to the old indifference curve u^0, OK is the amount of income necessary to keep the original utility level u^0 at the new price p^1, which means that OK is the value of expenditure function $e(p^1, v^0)$. Therefore,

$$CV = y^1 - e(p^1, v^0) = OM - OK = MK = BD,$$

or by denoting the combinations of goods at the points B and C as (x_1^1, x_2^1) and (c_1, c_2), respectively,

$$CV = (x_1^1 + P^1 x_2^1) - (c_1 + P^1 c_2)$$

$$= (1, p^1) \begin{pmatrix} x_1^1 - c_1 \\ x_2^1 - c_2 \end{pmatrix}$$

$$= p^1(x^1 - c), \tag{10–8}$$

where

$$p^1 = (1, p^1), \quad x^1 = \begin{pmatrix} x_1^1 \\ x_2^1 \end{pmatrix}, \quad c = \begin{pmatrix} c_1 \\ c_2 \end{pmatrix}.$$

By the same token,

$$EV = e(p^0, v^1) - y^0 = OT - OM = MT = AG,$$

3. It is important to note that while the assumption of constant income simplifies the present illustration, it is in no way necessary for our analysis. Indeed, most relevant projects proposed will involve income changes for one or more of the individuals affected.

and denoting points A and F as (x_1^0, x_2^0) and (f_1, f_2), respectively,

$$EV = (f_1 + p^0 f_2) - (x_1^0 + p^0 x_2^0)$$
$$= p^0 (f - x^0) \qquad (10\text{--}9)$$

where

$$p^0 = (1, p^0), \quad f = \begin{pmatrix} f_1 \\ f_2 \end{pmatrix}, \quad x^0 = \begin{pmatrix} x_1^0 \\ x_2^0 \end{pmatrix},$$

and

$$CI = p^1 (x^1 - x^0) = BE \qquad (10\text{--}10)$$

$$RI = p^0 (x^1 - x^0) = AH. \qquad (10\text{--}11)$$

We may then summarize the proposed criteria for measuring welfare change as follows:

1. the *compensating variation criterion* ΣCV:
   If $\Sigma CV > 0$, then the change should be accepted.
2. the *equivalent variation criterion* ΣEV:
   If $\Sigma EV > 0$, then the change should be accepted.
3. the *current national income criterion CNI*:
   If $CNI > 0$, then the change should be accepted.
4. the *real national income criterion RNI*:
   If $RNI > 0$, then the change should be accepted.

We shall employ the general term *cost benefit criterion* (CB–*criterion*) to refer to any or all of these four criteria.

In order to formalize these ideas to many commodities and individuals, it is convenient to introduce the following definitions. Consider a *society* (economy) I of finitely many individuals $i \in I$. If x_i^0 denotes the optimal consumption and factor-supply vector for each individual $i \in I$ under a given equilibrium price vector p^0, and if we write this collection of optimal consumption levels as $x^0 = (x_i^0 | i \in I)$, then the pair (p^0, x^0) is said to be an *equilibrium state* for society I. By a *proposed social change* for society I, we mean any change which results in the movement from one equilibrium state (p^0, x^0) to another, say (p^1, x^1). Hence each proposed social change may be formally identified with a pair of equilibrium state $[(p^0, x^0), (p^1, x^1)]$. For each individual $i \in I$ with utility function u_i, the sets

$$s_i^0 = \{z_i | u_i(z_i) \geqslant u_i(x_i^0)\}, \quad i \in I \tag{10-12}$$

$$s_i^1 = \{z_i | u_i(z_i) \geqslant u_i(x_i^1)\}, \quad i \in I \tag{10-13}$$

denote the commodity bundles z_i which are at least as preferred as equilibrium bundles x_i^0 and x_i^1, respectively.

In this context, if we consider a given proposed social change $[(p^0, x^0), (p^1, x^1)]$, then for each individual i we may identify a least expensive commodity handle c_i under price system p^1 which would have i as well off as with handle x_i^0. More formally, we now define a *compensated demand bundle* c_i for i to be any bundle $c_i \in s_i^0$ satisfying

$$p^1 c_i = \min_{z_i} \{p^1 z_i | z_i \in s_i^0\} \tag{10-14}$$

Similarly, each commodity bundle $f_i \in s_i^1$ satisfying

$$p^0 f_i = \min_{z_i} \{p^0 z_i | z_i \in s_i^1\} \tag{10-15}$$

is a least expensive bundle under prices p^0 which would leave i as well off as he or she would be with bundle x_i^1. Hence we may designate each such f_i as an *equivalent demand bundle* for i.[4]

Finally, if we define the corresponding aggregate quantities

$$X^0 = \sum_i x_i^0 \tag{10-16}$$

$$X^1 = \sum_i x_i^1 \tag{10-17}$$

$$C = \sum_i c_i \tag{10-18}$$

$$F = \sum_i f_i \tag{10-19}$$

then the positivity conditions defining the four CB criteria can be defined formally as follows:

$$\Sigma CV > 0 \leftrightarrow p^1(X^1 - C) > 0 \tag{10-20}$$

$$\Sigma EV > 0 \leftrightarrow p^0(F - X^0) > 0 \tag{10-21}$$

$$CNI > 0 \leftrightarrow p^1(X^1 - X^0) > 0 \tag{10-22}$$

$$RNI > 0 \leftrightarrow p^0(X^1 - X^0) > 0 \tag{10-23}$$

4. The quantities c_i and f_i are both related to the classical concept of "Hicksian compensated demand."

where prices are in row-vector form and commodities are in column-vector form.

THREE COMPENSATION TESTS

Three relevant compensation tests are as follows (Graaf 1957):

Kaldor Test (KT)

For any proposed social change, if output after the change could be redistributed in lump sum so as to make the modified new situation Pareto-superior to the original, then accept the proposed change (Kaldor 1938).

Hicksian Test (HT)

For any proposed social change, if output before the change could not be redistributed in lump sum so as to make the modified new situation Pareto-superior to the after-change position, then accept the proposed change (Hicks 1940).

Scitovsky Test (ST)

If a proposed social change passes both the Kaldor and Hicksian tests simultaneously, then accept the proposed change (Scitovsky 1941).

These three tests can now be stated formally by introducing the following aggregate notation. Let:

$$S^0 = \left\{ Z = \sum_i z_i \;\middle|\; z_i \in s_i^0, \quad i \in I \right\} \tag{10-24}$$

$$S^1 = \left\{ Z = \sum_i z_i \;\middle|\; z_i \in s_i^1, \quad i \in I \right\} \tag{10-25}$$

denote the vector sums of the collections of sets $\{s_i^0 : i \in I\}$ and $\{s_i^1 : i \in I\}$, respectively. Then S^0 and S^1 denote the sets of aggregate consumption vectors which could be distributed in such a way as to

Figure 10–2.   Three Compensation Tests

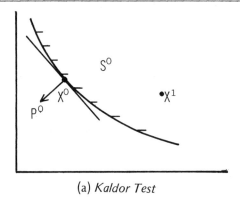

(a) *Kaldor Test*

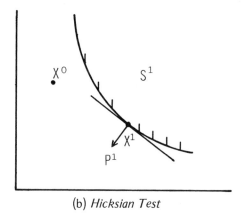

(b) *Hicksian Test*

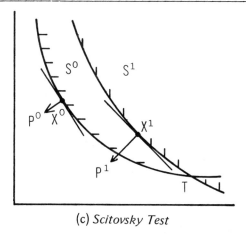

(c) *Scitovsky Test*

be *weakly Pareto-superior* to the individual consumption levels $x^0 = (x_i^0 | i \epsilon I)$ and $x^1 = (x_i^1 | i \epsilon I)$, for society I, respectively. As can be seen from Figure 10–2, these sets consist of all points on or above the *"Scitovsky community indifference curves"* (that is, *Scitovsky contours*) through X^0 and X^1 (which correspond to the associated aggregate consumption vectors for x^0 and x^1, respectively).

Using the concept of S^0 and S^1, three compensation tests can be simply reformulated as follows (see Figure 10–2):

Kaldor Test (KT)

The proposed social change should be accepted *iff $X^1 \epsilon S^0$*.

Hicksian Test (HT)

The proposed social change should be accepted *iff $X^0 \notin S^1$*.

Scitovsky Test (ST)

The proposed social change should be accepted *iff $X^1 \epsilon S^0$* and $X^0 \notin S^1$.

At this moment it might be helpful to interpret the difference between the Kaldor and Hicksian tests.

The former test focuses on whether or not the *gainers could compensate the losers* by redistributing the after-change community bundle X^1 so as to make everyone better off than in X^0. Hence the question here is whether or not X^1 is in the set S^0. *If the gainers could compensate the losers*, that is, if $X^1 \epsilon S^0$, then the change passes the Kaldor test. On the other hand, the latter test focuses on whether or not the *potential loser could bribe the gainers* by redistributing the before-change community bundle X^0 so as to make everyone better off than in X^1. Thus the question here is whether or not X^0 is in the set S^1. *If the potential losers could not bribe the gainers*, that is, if $X^0 \notin S^1$, then the change passes the Hicksian test.

First, note that under the usual convexity assumption regarding

Figure 10–3(a).   Scitovsky Paradoxes: Contradiction of Kaldor Test

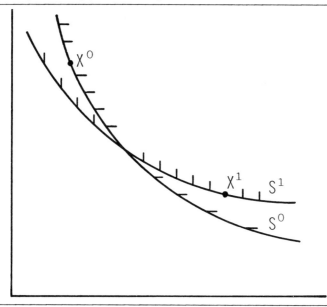

Note. $X^1 \in S^0$ and $X^0 \in S^1$.

Figure 10–3(b).   Scitovsky Paradoxes: Contradiction of Hicksian Test

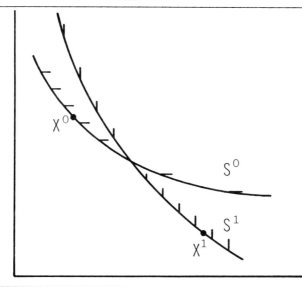

Note. $X^0 \notin S^1$ and $X^1 \notin S^0$.

each individual's preference ordering, the set S of weakly Pareto-superior points must be a convex set bounded below by the Scitovsky contour (since S is a vector sum of convex sets s_i, each bounded below by the relevant indifference curve for individual i).

Second, note that, unlike individual indifference curves, Scitovsky contours can *intersect* one another. For example, the intersection T of the Scitovsky contours for X^0 and X^1 shown in Figure 10–2(c) identifies a combination of goods which can be distributed in such a way that all the members of society can jointly realize the same utility levels as those under some distribution of X^0 or X^1, respectively.

Third, notice that if we adopt either Kaldor or Hicksian test only, we have the possibility of contradiction for such a case as shown in the Figure 10–3. For according to the Kaldor test, $X^1 \in S^0$ implies that the proposed change from X^0 to X^1 should be adopted. Now consider the reverse change from X^1 to X^0. Since $X^0 \in S^1$, it follows that if this change were to be subsequently proposed, then it would be adopted, and one obtains a "cycle" or "contradiction" as shown in Figure 10–3(a). The same type of contradiction is possible for the Hicksian test in the case shown by Figure 10–3(b). The situations in both Figures 10–3(a) and 10–3(b) are designated as *Scitovsky paradoxes* in honor of Scitovsky (1941) who first pointed them out and advocated the test ST (defined earlier) in order to avoid such contradictions. In particular, this test avoids such contradictions by requiring that both $X^1 \in S^0$ and $X^0 \notin S^1$ hold in order that the proposed social change be accepted.

Hence if we now define a given proposed social change $[(p^0, x^0),$ $(p^1, x^1)]$ to be *paradox free* if and only if both $(X^0 \in S^1, X^1 \in S^0)$ and $(X^0 \notin S^1, X^1 \notin S^0)$ fail to hold, then the observations by Scitovsky lead to the following equivalence theorem:

Proposition 1 (Equivalency of Kaldor and Hicksian Tests).   The Kaldor test (KT) and the Hicksian test (HT) are equivalent for a given proposed social change if and only if the proposal change is paradox free.

Proof.   Suppose first that KT and HT are not equivalent for a given proposed social change $[(p^0, x^0), (p^1, x^1)]$. Then the proposed change either satisfies KT and fails to satisfy HT, or vice versa. But in the first case $(X^1 \in S^0, X^0 \in S^1)$ must hold, and in the second case $(X^1 \notin S^0, X^0 \notin S^1)$ must hold. Hence $[(p^0, x^0), (p^1, x^1)]$ cannot be paradox-free. Conversely, if $[(p^0, x^0), (p^1, x^1)]$ is paradox-free, then $HT \rightarrow X^0 \notin S^1 \rightarrow$ not $(X^1 \notin S^0) \rightarrow X^1 \in S^0 \rightarrow KT$, and similarly, $KT \rightarrow X^1 \in S^0 \rightarrow$ not $(X^0 \in S^1) \rightarrow X^0 \notin S^1 \rightarrow HT$, so that KT and HT are equivalent. *End of Proof.*

This fact yields important consequences for the welfare implications of cost-benefit analysis. In particular, if we wish to employ either the Hicksian or Kaldor tests in evaluating projects, then we are obliged to confine ourselves to proposed social changes which are paradox-free. But, within this framework, the Kaldor test is necessarily equivalent to the Hicksian test. Hence, we may as well adopt the Hicksian test whenever this test is easier to carry out than the Kaldor test. Indeed, this is precisely what we shall do here.

COST-BENEFIT CRITERIA AND COMPENSATION TESTS

Sufficiency of Cost-Benefit Criteria

In terms of relationships between the four CBA criteria and three compensation tests above, the main problem to be addressed in this section is the following: are there any CBA criteria which yield sufficient conditions for the Hicksian test? The answer is yes. In fact, both the equivalent variation ΣEV and the current national income CNI criteria yield such sufficient conditions.

Proposition 2 (Sufficiency of Equivalent Variation Criteria).   The equivalent variation criterion is sufficient for the Hicksian test.

Proof.   First recall from (10–15) that by definition, $p^0 f_i \leqslant p^0 z_i$ holds for all consumers i and all $z_i \in s_i^1$: hence for any $Z = \sum_{i=1}^{I} z_i \in S^1$,

$$p^0 Z = \sum_i p^0 z_i \geqslant \sum_i p^0 f_i = p^0 \sum_i f_i = p^0 F. \qquad (10\text{–}26)$$

But if the equivalent variation criterion is satisfying for X^0, p^0, and F, then from (10–21)

$$\Sigma EV > 0 \rightarrow p^0 F > p^0 X^0. \tag{10-27}$$

Thus (10–26) and (10–27) together imply that X^0 cannot be an element of S^1, and hence that HT holds. *End of Proof.*

A second sufficient condition is given by the current national income criterion. While this result has already been established graphically by Mishan (1976), it is instructive to provide an analytical proof of this result which emphasizes the parallels between these two sufficiency conditions.

Proposition 3 (Mishan).   The current national income criterion is sufficient for the Hicksian test.

Proof.   As in the proof of Proposition 2, consider first an arbitrary element $Z = \sum_i z_i \in S^1$ and observe that since $X^1 = \sum_i x_i^1$ is by definition consumer equilibrium at prices p^1, it must be true that $p^1 x_i^1 \leqslant p^1 z_i$ for all consumers i and all $z_i \in s_i^1$ (for otherwise x_i^1 would not be an optimal purchase and factor supply for p^1). Hence we must have

$$p^1 X^1 = \sum_i p^1 x_i^1 \leqslant \sum_i p^1 z_i = p^1 \sum_i z_i = p^1 Z \tag{10-28}$$

for all $Z \in S^1$. But if the current national income criterion is satisfied for p^1, X^1, and X^0, then

$$CNI > 0 \rightarrow p^1 X^1 > p^1 X^0 \tag{10-29}$$

Hence (10–28) and (10–29) again imply that X^0 cannot be an element of S^1, and thus that HT holds. *End of Proof.*

On the other hand, it is well known that both the compensating variation criterion ΣCV and the real national income criterion RNI fail to be sufficient for the Kaldor test (see, for example, Boadway 1974; Foster 1976; Smith and Stephen 1975; and Varian 1978). Hence in even cases where the Kaldor and Hicksian tests are equivalent, that is, even when no Scitovsky paradoxes are present, it follows at once that these criteria also fail to be sufficient for the Hicksian test. Failure of sufficiency in these cases is illustrated by the counterexamples in Figures 10–4(a) and 10–4(b), respectively.

Finally, combining Propositions 1, 2, and 3, we obtain the following immediate consequence:

Figure 10–4(a).   Failure of ΣCV for *HT* Sufficiency

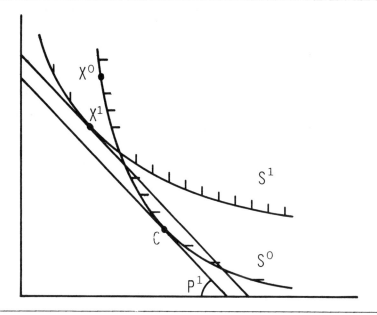

Note. $\Sigma CV = p^1 (X^1 - C) > 0$ but $X^0 \, \epsilon \, S^1$, *HT* fails.

Figure 10–4(b).   Failure of *RNI* for *HT* Sufficiency

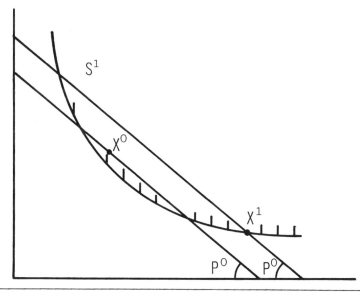

Note. $RNI = p^0 (X^1 - X^0) > 0$ but $X^0 \, \epsilon \, S^1$, *HT* fails.

Proposition 4 (Sufficiency of Equivalent Variation and Current National Income Criteria for Kaldor and Hicksian Tests).   For any proposed social change, which is paradox free, the equivalent variation criterion and the current national income criterion are each sufficient for both the Kaldor and Hicksian tests.

This result represents the major finding of this chapter, and indeed may be said to provide a new welfare foundation for cost-benefit analysis. For this result shows that if social costs and benefits are measured in terms of either the equivalent variation index ΣEV or the current national income index CNI, then any proposed social change which satisfies the resulting cost-benefit criterion is guaranteed to improve social welfare in both the Kaldor and Hicksian sense—whenever these welfare concepts are both well defined. Hence, from a welfare viewpoint, it may be argued that either of these indices is more appropriate for measuring social costs and benefits than the more traditional index of compensating variation ΣCV.

Necessity of CBA Criteria

It is also important to check whether or not any CBA criteria can serve as necessary conditions for compensation tests. For if so, then such criteria provide a partial test of the proposed change: if the given CB index is negative, then the associated compensation test fails. Boadway (1974) and Foster (1976) proved that the ΣCV criterion is a necessary condition for the Kaldor test. Within the present framework, this result can be proved in a simple way as follows:

Proposition 5 (Boadway and Foster).   The ΣCV criterion is necessary for the Kaldor test, that is, $X^1 \in S^0$ implies $\Sigma CV = p^1(X^1 - C) \geqslant 0$.

Proof.   As in the proof of Proposition 2, recall from (10–14) that by the definition of c_i, $p^1 c_i \leqslant p^1 z_i$ holds for all consumers i and all $z_i \in s_i^0$. Hence for any $Z = \sum_{i=1}^I z_i \in S^0$, $p^1 Z = \sum_i p^1 z_i \geqslant \sum_i p^1 c_i = p^1 \sum_i c_i = p^1 C$, so that in particular, $X^1 \in S^0$ implies $p^1 X^1 \geqslant p^1 C$. *End of Proof.*

In a similar manner, the following result of Varian (1978) may also be proved:

Proposition 6 (Varian).   The *RNI* criterion is necessary for the Kaldor Test, that is, $X^1 \in S^0$ implies $RNI = p^0(X^1 - X^0) \geq 0$.

Proof.   Observe that since $X^0 = \sum_i x_i^0$ is by definition consumer equilibrium at price p^0, it must be true that $p^0 x_i^0 \leq p^0 z_i$ for all consumers i and all $z_i \in s_i^0$ (for otherwise x_i^0 would not be an optimal purchase and factor supply for p^0). Hence for any $Z = \sum_i z_i \in S^0$,

$$p^0 X^0 = \sum_i p^0 x_i^0 \leq \sum_i p^0 z_i = p^0 \sum_i z_i = p^0 Z,$$ so that in particular, $X^1 \in S^0$ implies $p^0 X^0 \leq p^0 X^1$. *End of Proof.*

Finally, we may observe from the counterexamples in Figure 10–5 that no other *CB* criteria are necessary for either the Kaldor test or Hicksian test (even if attention is restricted to only paradox-free cases).

A SUFFICIENT CONDITION FOR HICKSIAN SCITOVSKY PARADOXES

In view of Proposition 4, it is clearly desirable to be able to verify that a given proposed social change is paradox-free. Unfortunately, no general test exists. However, for Scitovsky paradoxes of the Hicksian type, that is, of the form $(X^0 \notin S^1, X^1 \notin S^0)$, our results do provide us with several conditions which are sufficient for the presence of such paradoxes. In particular, we have the following result:

Propostion 7 (A Sufficient Condition for Hicksian Scitovsky Paradoxes).   If a given proposed social change $[(p^0, x^0), (p^1, x^1)]$ satisfies either $(\Sigma EV > 0, \Sigma CV < 0)$ or $(ENI > 0, RNI < 0)$, then $(X^1 \notin S^0, X^0 \notin S^1)$.

Proof.   By Propositions 2 and 5, $(\Sigma EV > 0, \Sigma CV < 0) \rightarrow (HT,$ not $KT) \rightarrow (X^0 \in S^1, X^1 \notin S^0)$. Similarly by Propositions 3 and 6, $(CNI > 0, RNI < 0) \rightarrow (HT,$ not $KT) \rightarrow (X^0 \notin S^1, X^1 \notin S^0)$. *End of Proof.*

Figure 10–5(a).   Failure of ΣEV for KT Necessity

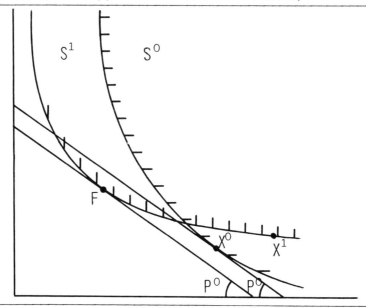

Note. $X^1 \in S^0 KT$ holds but $\Sigma EV = P^0 (F - X^0) < 0.$

Figure 10–5(b).   Failure of CNI for KT Necessity

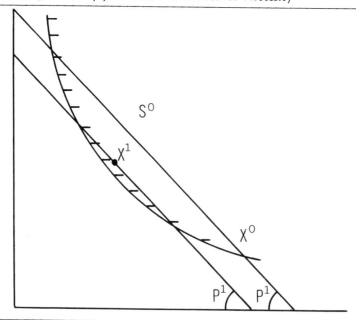

Note. $X^1 \in S^0 KT$ holds but $CNI = P^1 (X^1 - X^0) < 0.$

Figure 10–5(c).   Failure of ΣEV for HT Necessity

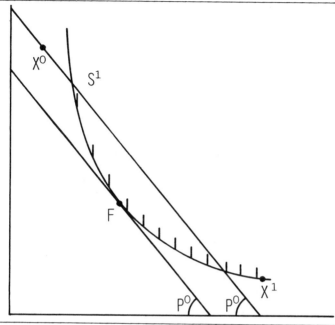

Note. $X^0 \notin S^1 HT$ holds but $\Sigma EV = P^0 (F - X^0) < 0$.

Figure 10–5(d).   Failure of CNI for HT Necessity

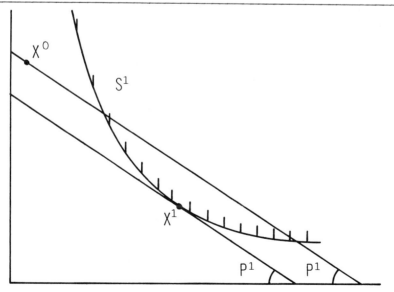

Note. $X^0 \notin S^1 HT$ holds but $CNI = P^1 (X^1 - X^0) < 0$.

Hence, we may conclude that in order for the results of Proposition 4 to be applicable to a given proposed social change, it is necessary that the joint conditions ($\Sigma EV > 0$, $\Sigma CV < 0$) and ($CNI > 0$, $RNI < 0$) both fail to hold.

CONCLUDING REMARKS

As stated in Proposition 4, the main result of this chapter has been to show that the equivalent variation criterion ΣEV and the current national income criterion CNI can each be given a strong welfare interpretation in all cases where the Kaldor and Hicksian tests of welfare improvement are both meaningful. However, a number of important questions remain to be explored.

First one may ask whether it is possible to determine which of these cost-benefit criteria is most appropriate in any given situation. From a theoretical viewpoint, it may be argued that there are strong grounds for preferring ΣEV to CNI in many cases. To see this, observe first that both these evaluation criteria can in general only guarantee that social changes consistent with a *potential* Pareto-superior situation (that is, which passes the Kaldor test) will be adopted. In particular, they do *not* guarantee that the requisite income compensation needed to achieve such Pareto-superior allocations will actually be realized. With this in mind, it is of interest to consider the behavior of cost-benefit indices (CBI) with respect to proposed social changes in which all individuals are actually made better off by the change, and hence in which no reallocations are required. In such cases, it is natural to require that the proposed social change be accepted by any reasonable index. This suggests the following axiom for admissibility of a CBI:

Pareto Axiom

For any given proposed social change $[(p^0, x^0), (p^1, x^1)]$ for society I, if $u_i(x_i^1) > u_i(x_i^0)$ for all $i \in I$, then the change should always be accepted by CBI, that is, $CBI > 0$.

If we adopt this Pareto axiom as a criterion for the admissibility of cost-benefit indices, then there are strong theoretical grounds for preferring ΣEV to CNI. In particular, ΣEV always satisfies

Figure 10–6.   Failure of *CNI* for Pareto Test

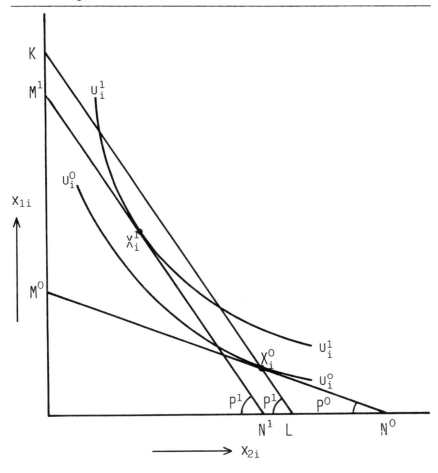

the Pareto axiom, but *CNI* does not. To see this, observe first that by definition, $f_i \epsilon s_i^1 \rightarrow u_i(f_i) \geqslant u_i(x_i^1)$. Hence, if $u_i(x_i^0) < u_i(x_i^1)$ for all $i \epsilon I$, then $u_i(x_i^0) < u_i(x_i^1) \leqslant u_i(f_i) \rightarrow p^0 f_i > p^0 x_i^0 \rightarrow \Sigma EV = p^0 \Sigma_i (f_i - x_i^0) > 0$ and ΣEV is seen to satisfy the Pareto axiom.

On the other hand, consider a proposed social change $[(p^0, x^0), (p^1, x^1)]$ which yields a situation for the individuals of society I as depicted in Figure 10–6. Then each individual i achieves both a utility gain and a loss in current income, that is, $u_i(x_i^1) > u_i(x_i^0)$ and $p^1 x_i^1 < p^1 x_i^0$. This proposed social change is preferred by all $i \in I$, but $CNI = p^1 \sum_i (x_i^1 - x_i^0) < 0$. Thus CNI can fail to satisfy the Pareto axiom.

Aside from the theoretical behavior of these two cost-benefit criteria, it is also important from a practical viewpoint to consider their computational feasibility. For in cases when no clear Pareto dominance exists among alternative social states, and in which CNI is more readily computable than ΣEV, then they are still strong grounds for preferring the CNI index. As one illustration, suppose that a previously adopted social change is to be evaluated *post hoc.* Then since the calculation of $CNI = p^1(X^1 - X^0)$ requires only knowledge of the prior and posterior equilibrium states, this index may often be readily computed in such cases. On the other hand, calculation of the equivalent variation index $\Sigma EV = p^0(F - X^0)$ requires some estimate of *aggregate equivalent demand F*, which in turn depends on some knowledge of individual preferences. Hence the determination of CNI is clearly more feasible than ΣEV in such cases.

However, when proposed social changes are being evaluated *prior* to their adoption—which is, of course, the main objective of cost-benefit analysis—it may be argued that the equivalent variation criterion is in many cases more operational than the current national income criterion. In particular, the calculation of ΣEV requires no knowledge of the posterior equilibrium state (p^1, x^1). In such cases it may be easier to estimate ΣEV directly in terms of its individual components EV_i than to predict the posterior equilibrium state (p^1, x^1). For example, if one is evaluating a proposed public works project, it may be possible (by selected interviews or questionnaires) to determine the income subsidies EV_i which representative households $i \in I$ would be willing to accept in lieu of giving up the proposed project. Hence, in such cases, one may in fact be able to establish ΣEV more directly than CNI. It should be noted, however, that macro-econometric techniques can often yield reasonable (short-run) estimates of predicted prices and aggregate consumption changes which do not require detailed preference information. Hence, CNI may be viable as an alternative of ΣEV when such estimation techniques are available.

In view of this discussion, it is our contention that from among the four cost-benefit criteria considered in this chapter, the equivalent variation criterion is generally the best. However, it should again be emphasized that all such indices are subject to the same limitation of guaranteeing only the *potential* Pareto-superiority of accepted social changes. Moreover, it is equally clear that none of these indices even begins to address the difficult questions of *equitable* social change. Hence a host of fundamental questions still remains to be answered in the search for better methods of cost-benefit analysis.

REFERENCES

Boadway, R.W. 1974. "The Welfare Foundations of Cost-Benefit Analysis." *Economic Journal*, 84: 926–939.

——. 1976. "The Welfare Foundations of Cost-Benefit Analysis—A Reply." *Economic Journal*, 86: 359–361.

Currie, J.M., J.A. Murphy, and A. Schmitz. 1971. "The Concept of Economic Surplus and Its Use in Economic Analysis." *Economic Journal*, 81: 741–799.

de V. Graaf, J. 1957. *The Theoretical Welfare Economics*. Cambridge, England: Cambridge University Press.

Diamond, P.A., and D.L. McFadden. 1974. "Some Uses of the Expenditure Function in Public Finance." *Journal of Public Economics*, 3: 3–21.

Foster, E. 1976. "The Welfare Foundation of Cost-Benefit Analysis—A Comment." *Economic Journal*, 86: 353–358.

Hicks, J.R. 1940. "The Valuation of the Social Income." *Economica* 7: 105–124.

Kaldor, N. 1938. "Welfare Proposition of Economics and Interpersonal Comparisons of Utility." *Economic Journal* 49: 549–552.

Mishan, E.J. 1972. *Cost Benefit Analysis*. London: George Allen and Unwin.

——. 1976. "The Use of Compensating and Equivalent Variations in Cost-Benefit Analysis." *Economica* 43: 185–197.

Scitovsky, T. 1941. "A Note on Welfare Propositions in Economics." *Reveiw of Economic Studies* 9: 77–88.

Smith, B., and F.H. Stephen. 1975. "Cost-Benefit Analysis and Compensation Criteria: A Note." *Economic Journal* 85: 902–905.

Varian, H.R. 1978. *Microeconomic Analysis*. New York: Norton and Company.

11 Efficiency and Equity in Regional Development with Agglomeration Economies*

Masahisa Fujita

The potential conflict between aggregate efficiency and interregional equity is a subject of critical importance to both regional economics and planning, as Richardson (1977) pointed out. At present, the most systematic study of the trade-off relationship between aggregate efficiency and interregional equity can be found in Mera (1975), who begins with the following observation. When conventional neoclassical assumptions[1] are employed, the efficiency—equity trade-off problem between regions rarely arises; and if it does, the competitive market system will resolve it in the long run. The facts, however, are far from what theory indicates, and hence the failure of neoclassical theory can be attributed to faulty assumptions.

Mera (1975) reasons that the assumptions of identical regional

*This material is based upon work supported by the National Science Foundation (USA) under Grant No. SE 80-14257 which is gratefully acknowledged. The author is also grateful to Professors Walter Isard and Yoshimi Nagao for their encouragement in writing this chapter.

1. Briefly speaking, the complete set of assumptions for the Hecksher-Ohlin theorem for factor-price equalization are as follows: a two-region, two-good, two-factor world; perfect competition; full employment of the factors; free trade; no transport costs; no interregional mobility factors; identical production functions for the same good in both regions; constant returns to scale with diminishing returns; no joint production; and no complete specialization. See, for example, Takayama (1972).

187

production functions and the zero transport cost are largely responsible for the inadequacy of conventional theory. Thus, throughout his work, Mera emphasizes differences in regional production functions. He scrutinizes the ways in which production functions figure in the efficiency—equity trade-off problem.

Undoubtedly, regional differences in production functions, overlooked by neoclassical theory, are crucial to the study of the conflict between efficiency and equity in the real world. However, there are other shortcomings to the conventional framework. In particular, the assumption of constant (or decreasing) returns to scale is also unrealistic and must therefore be held partly responsible for the defects in neoclassical thinking. A number of studies (Carlina 1981; Kawashima 1975; and Mera 1975) demonstrate that a significant level of agglomeration economies is observable in regional production functions. For example, both Kawashima (1975) and Carlina (1981) conclude that the "optimal" city size in the United States occurs with a population of about 3 million. Mera (1975: 17) also asserts that in terms of economic efficiency, even the largest metropolitan area in the world is likely to be less than the "optimal" size. The existence of agglomeration economies implies that perfect competition is either impossible or inefficient. And, as will be demonstrated in this chapter, the aggregate efficiency—interregional equity problem cannot be adequately addressed without a thorough consideration of agglomeration economies.

In this chapter, we employ a simple aggregate model of a two-region economy. With this model, we assess how agglomeration economies and diseconomies precipitate the conflict between efficiency and equity; we also investigate conflict resolution. Unlike Mera (1975), we assume here that both regions possess the same production function. This enables us to concentrate on the pure effects of agglomeration economies and diseconomies. In short, the purpose here is to complement the study of Mera (1975) by considering the same problem from a slightly different perspective.

In the second section we consider, first, the efficient allocation of capital between our two-region economy so as to maximize aggregate income. Labor is assumed to be immobile between regions. The model here is static in the sense that the total amount of capital is fixed and only allocation is considered. The efficient allocation of capital depends on the total stock and also on the strength or weakness of agglomeration diseconomies. It is shown that when the total amount of capital is not excessively abundant, efficient development requires a polarized, or uneven, allocation of capital between two regions. It follows that if the interregtional income transfer is politically infeasible, the trade-off between aggregate efficiency and interregional equity must be explicitly considered. To this end, we derive transformation curves, following Mera (1975), between regional incomes. With these, we are then able to obtain efficiency—equity trade-off curves with which we can study the fundamental problem.

Though the results of the second section provide useful insights into efficiency—equity conflict, a definitive account requires a dynamic approach. Hence, in the following section we reconsider the same problem, but this time within a dynamic framework. First we examine efficient investment-allocation processes, whereby maximum aggregate income may be achieved at some target date. Our primary interest is the specification of the *switching function*, which regulates investment allocation between regions. In particular, the switching function determines when to start investing in the less developed region, since the more developed region is usually favored at first. As we will show, the efficient growth process always takes the form of polarized development in the initial stages. Given the efficiency of polarized development, the problem of equity is immediately manifested. Therefore, we next equip our model with political constraint on income transfer, and study the efficiency— equity trade-off problem in a dynamic context.

In order to explicate fully the implication of the efficient growth paths obtained in the third section, we compare them, in the fourth section, with those that would be realized by the competitive market economy. It is shown that the market economy tends to concentrate capital in the more developed region in excess of the optimal amount when agglomeration economies and diseconomies prevail in production.

STATIC ANALYSIS

Let us assume a system which consists of two regions, $l = 1, 2$. Each region produces homogeneous output, which we will call *income*, from two inputs, capital and labor. That is

$$Y_l = F(K_l, L_l), \qquad l = 1, 2, \qquad (11-1)$$

where Y_l is the income, K_l is the capital, and L_l is the labor in region l. The regional production function, F, is assumed to be the same for both regions. Labor is assumed to be immobile and apportioned in equal quantities between regions.

$$L_1 = L_2 = \bar{L}. \tag{11-2}$$

Thus, capital (K_l) is the only input variable, so we have

$$Y_l = F(K_l, \bar{L}),$$

which is simply expressed as follows:[2]

$$Y_l = F(K_l), \tag{11-3}$$

where $F(K_l) \equiv F(K_l, \bar{L})$. We will also call $F(K_l)$ the regional production function.

We assume that because of agglomeration economies and diseconomies present in each region, the regional production function has the property of *variable returns to scale*, namely,

$$F'(K) > 0 \quad \text{for all} \quad K \geq 0, \qquad F''(K) > 0 \quad \text{for} \quad 0 \leq K < K^*,$$

$$F''(K) = 0 \quad \text{for} \quad K = K^*, \qquad F''(K) < 0 \quad \text{for} \quad K > K^*,$$

$$\tag{11-4}$$

where $F'(K) = dF(K)/dK$, $F''(K) = dF'(K)/dK$, and K^* is the *inflection point* of function F. The *marginal productivity curve*, $F'(K)$, is assumed to be continuous for all $K \geq 0$. In addition, $F(0) \geq 0$. The regional production function, $F(K)$, and the marginal productivity curve, $F'(K)$, are depicted in Figure 11-1. We say that a region is in the *increasing phase* or in the *decreasing phase* depending on whether the amount of its capital is less than K^* (that is, $0 \leq K_l < K^*$), or more than or equal to K^* (that is, $K^* \leq K_l$). That is, when a region is in the increasing phase, agglomeration economies dominate agglomeration diseconomies, and hence the regional production function exhibits the character of increasing returns to scale; when a region is in the decreasing phase, the opposite characteristics hold.

---

2. Production function (11-3) can be derived also under the following alternative set of assumptions. Namely, $L_1 \neq L_2$, but labor is abundant in both regions and hence

$$\partial F(K_l, L_l)/\partial L = 0 \quad \text{for} \quad l = 1, 2.$$

Then, the scarce input in regional production is only K_l, and thus we have (11-3).

Figure 11–1.   Production Function (a) and Marginal Productivity Curve (b)

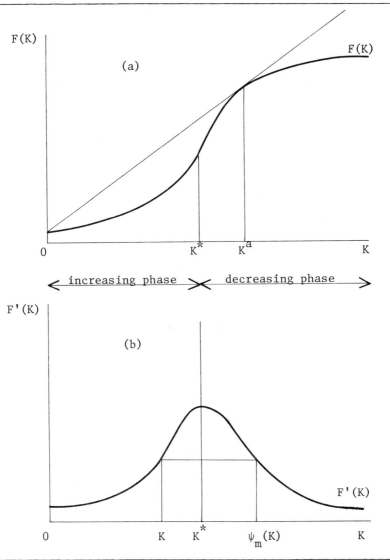

The objective of this section is to examine the effects of the distribution of capital on income for both regions. The model here is static in the sense that the total amount of capital is fixed and only its allocation is considered.

We first examine the problem allocating a given amount of capital, $\bar{K} > 0$, between the two regions so as to maximize the aggregate income. This problem is formulated as follows.

Problem 1.   Maximize $F(K_1) + F(K_2)$

$$\text{subject to} \qquad K_1 + K_2 = \bar{K}, \qquad K_1 \geqslant 0, \qquad K_2 \geqslant 0.$$

Analytically, the following reformulation of the problem is convenient.

$$\text{Maximize} \qquad \int_0^{K_1} F'(K)dK + \int_0^{K_2} F'(K)dK, \qquad (11-5)$$

$$\text{subject to} \qquad K_1 + K_2 = \bar{K}, \qquad K_1 \geqslant 0, \qquad K_2 \geqslant 0.$$

The existence of a solution for Problem 1 is obvious since it is a maximization of a continuous function on a compact set. Since solutions of Problem 1 are symmetric for both regions, we will discuss only those solutions which satisfy the next condition.

$$K_1 \geqslant K_2. \qquad (11-6)$$

The first-order and second-order necessary conditions for optimality are:[3]

$$F'(K_1) = F'(K_2) \quad \text{if} \quad K_1, K_2 > 0, \qquad F'(K_1) \geqslant F'(0)$$

$$\text{if} \quad K_1 = \bar{K} \quad \text{and} \quad K_2 = 0, \qquad (11-7)$$

$$F''(K_1) + F''(K_2) \leqslant 0 \quad \text{if} \quad K_1, K_2 > 0. \qquad (11-8)$$

For convenience, we introduce a function, $\psi_m(K)$, which is defined by

$$F'(\psi_m(K)) = F'(K) \quad \text{where} \quad \psi_m(K) \geqslant K^* \geqslant K. \qquad (11-9)$$

The meaning of function ψ_m is clear from Figure 11–1(b). From (11–4), (11–7) and (11–8), we can conclude as follows.

Lemma 1.   At the solution of Problem 1,
  1. If $K^* > K_1 \geqslant K_2$,   then $K_2 = 0$.
  2. If $K_1 \geqslant K^* \geqslant K_2 > 0$,   then $K_1 = \psi_m(K_2)$.
  3. If $K_1, K_2 \geqslant K^*$,   then $K_1 = K_2$.
From this, the next lemma follows.

---

3. Put $K_2 = \bar{K} - K_1$, and $L(K_1) = F(K_1) + F(\bar{K} - K_1)$. If $K_1 > 0$ and $K_2 = \bar{K} - K_1 > 0$, the first-order condition is, $0 = L'(K_1) = F'(K_1) - F'(\bar{K} - K_1)$; and the second-order condition is, $0 \geqslant L''(K_1) = F''(K_1) + F''(\bar{K} - K_1)$. If $K_1 = \bar{K}$ and $K_2 = 0$, then the first-order condition is, $0 \leqslant L'(K_1) = F'(K_1) - F'(\bar{K} - K_1)$.

Lemma 2. Only the following three patterns are possible for the solution of Problem 1.

Polarized development: $K_1 = \bar{K}, K_2 = 0.$

Uneven development: $K_1 = \psi_m(K_2) > K^* > K_2 > 0,$

where $K_2 + \psi_m(K_2) = \bar{K}.$

Even development: $K_1 = K_2 = \bar{K}/2 \geqslant K^*.$

In polarized development, the entire amount of capital is concentrated in one region. In uneven development, the *more developed region* locates in the decreasing phase, and the *less developed region* locates in the increasing phase so that the marginal productivity of capital is the same in the two regions. Finally, in even development, both regions locate in the decreasing phase with the same amount of capital.

Let us now examine how the solution pattern of Problem 1 changes with the total amount of capital, $\bar{K}$. It immediately follows from Lemma 2 that if $\bar{K} \leqslant K^*$, a polarized development prevails (that is, $K_1 = \bar{K}$, $K_2 = 0$). However, when $\bar{K} > K^*$, the solution pattern of Problem 1 depends on the shape of the marginal productivity curve. Therefore, we consider the following two cases:

Weak agglomeration diseconomies:

$$F''(K) > -F''(\psi_m(K)) \quad \text{for all} \quad K < K^*. \quad (11{-}10)$$

Strong agglomeration diseconomies:

$$F''(K) < -F''(\psi_m(K)) \quad \text{for all} \quad K < K^*. \quad (11{-}11)$$

The marginal productivity curve corresponding to each case is depicted in Figure 11–2. We examine each case separately, and then later show that the *symmetric case*,

$$F''(K) = -F''(\psi_m(K)) \quad \text{for all} \quad K < K^*, \quad (11{-}12)$$

is the boundary case between weak and strong agglomeration diseconomies.[4]

---

4. Many other cases are, of course, conceivable. However, since solutions for other cases can be inferred from those solutions for the three cases, we do not discuss them further here.

Figure 11–2.   Marginal Productivity Curves Corresponding to: (a) Weak Agglomeration Diseconomies and (b) Strong Agglomeration Diseconomies

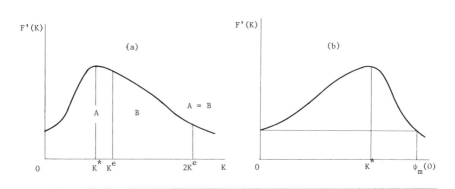

Weak Agglomeration Diseconomies

Under assumption (11–10), if $K_1 = \psi_m(K_2)$, then $F''(K_1) + F''(K_2) > 0$ which violates the second-order condition, (11–8). Hence, in the case of weak agglomeration diseconomies, uneven development is not optimal. Therefore, as long as $\bar{K} < 2K^*$, from Lemma 2, a polarized development must be the solution to Problem 1. To determine when polarized development is replaced by even development, we define the *even point*, K^e, of the marginal pro-ductivity curve by

$$\int_0^{K^e} F'(K)dK = \int_{K^e}^{2K^e} F'(K)dK. \qquad (11-13)$$

We can easily show that, under assumption (11–10), K^e uniquely exists and the following relation is satisfied.

$$K^* < K^e < K^a < 2K^e < \psi_m(0), \qquad (11-14)$$

where K^a is the *point of maximum average productivity* of additional capital which is defined by the maximum of function, $(F(K) - F(0))/K$ (refer to Figure 11–1(a)). By using (11–10) and (11–13), we can also confirm without difficulty that:

$$\int_0^{\bar{K}} F'(K)dK \gtrless 2\int_0^{\bar{K}/2} F'(K)dK \quad \text{as} \quad \bar{K} \lessgtr 2K^e,$$

which implies that, whenever $\bar{K} < 2K^e$ ($\bar{K} > 2K^e$), the polarized development (even development) maximizes the aggregate income. In summary, we have:

Theorem 1. In the case of weak agglomeration diseconomies given by (11—10):
 1. If $\bar{K} < 2K^e$, aggregate income is maximized by polarized development (that is, $K_1 = \bar{K}$, $K_2 = 0$).
 2. If $\bar{K} > 2K^e$, aggregate income is maximized by even development (that is, $K_1 = K_2 = \bar{K}/2$).

Strong Agglomeration Diseconomies

Under assumption (11—11), we can easily observe the following:
 1. $K + \psi_m(K) > \psi_m(0)$ for all $K \leq K^*$.
 2. $\psi_m(0) < 2K^*$.
 3. $K + \psi_m(K) < 2K^*$ for all $K < K^*$.
And, using (11—7), we can see that:
 4. When $\bar{K} > \psi_m(0)$, polarized development is not the solution for Problem 1.

Combining these observations with Lemma 2, we can obtain the next result without difficulty.

Theorem 2. In the case of strong agglomeration diseconomies given by (11—11),
 1. If $\bar{K} \leq \psi_m(0)$, aggregate income is maximized by polarized development (that is, $K_1 = \bar{K}$, $K_2 = 0$).
 2. If $\psi_m(0) < \bar{K} < 2K^*$, the aggregate income is maximized by uneven development (that is, $K_1 = \psi_m(K_2)$ where $K_2 + \psi_m(K_2) = \bar{K}$).
 3. If $\bar{K} \geq 2K^*$, aggregate income is maximized by even development (that is, $K_1 = K_2 = \bar{K}/2$).

From Theorems 1 and 2, for each case, the distributional pattern of capital corresponding to the maximum aggregate income changes as follows with the increase in the total amount of capital, $\bar{K}$.

Weak agglomeration diseconomies: polarized → even

Strong agglomeration diseconomies: polarized → uneven → even.

From this analysis we can conclude that when the total amount of the capital is not excessively abundant, efficient development requires either a polarized or uneven allocation of capital between the two regions. In a sense, this is a surprising property, since it says that the efficient spatial development requires *unequal treatment of equals*. But this is a reasonable result if we notice that efficiency under the existence of scale economies requires a concentration of activities.

Having studied the capital allocation for maximum aggregate income, we next discuss the relative merits of alternative distributional states. For this purpose, we first obtain *transformation curves* between regional production incomes, Y_1 and Y_2. Let $K = G(Y)$ be the inverse function of $Y = F(K)$, which represents the required capital as a function of income. The transformation curve under a total amount of capital, $\bar{K}$, is a set of points, (Y_1, Y_2), which satisfy the following constraint.

$$G(Y_1) + G(Y_2) = \bar{K}. \tag{11-15}$$

From total differentiation of (11−15),

$$\frac{dY_2}{dY_1} = -\frac{F'(K_2)}{F'(K_1)}, \frac{d^2Y_2}{dY_1^2} = \frac{F'(K_1)F'(K_2)}{F_1'(K_1)^2}\left(\frac{F''(K_1)}{F'(K_1)} - \frac{F''(K_2)}{F'(K_2)}\right),$$

$$\tag{11-16}$$

where $Y_1 = F(K_1)$, $Y_2 = F(K_2)$. Using (11−10), (11−16), and Theorem 1, we obtain income transformation curves in the case of weak agglomeration diseconomies, which are depicted in Figure 11−3(a). Similarly, using (11−11), (11−16), and Theorem 2, we obtain Figure 11−3(b) which depicts income transformation curves in the case of strong agglomeration diseconomies.[5] In Figure 11−3(a), all transformation curves are concave in the northeast of point D, they are convex in the rest of area. The maximum aggregate income is realized on broken lines, OA and BC, which are discontinuous at the point of total income where $\bar{K} = 2K^e$. Each point on line OA (BC) corresponds to a polarized (even) development. In Figure 11−3(b), all transformation curves are convex in the southwest of point B; they are concave elsewhere.

---

5. In Figure 11−3(a) and (b), it is assumed that $F(0) = 0$. If $F(0) > 0$, these figures, of course, must be modified.

Figure 11–3.   Income Transformation Curves under (a) Weak and
(b) Strong Agglomeration Diseconomies

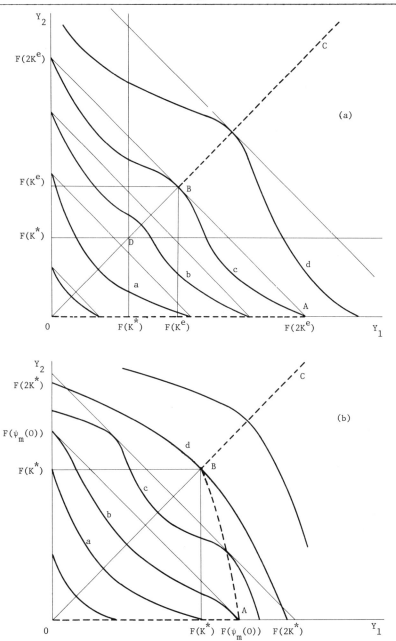

The maximum aggregate income is achieved on broken lines, OA, AB, and BC. Each point on line OA (AB, BC) corresponds to a polarized (uneven, even) development.

Note that in both cases, when the optimal capital allocation moves from point A to point B in Figure 11–3(a) or (b), the amount of capital in the more developed region decreases, and it is transferred to the less developed region. In the case of weak agglomeration diseconomies, this movement from point A to point B is discontinuously achieved. Note also that the symmetric case, (11–12), is the boundary between the two cases above. Namely, we can easily confirm that, under assumption (11–12), the range of $\bar{K}$ for uneven development shrinks to one point; that is, uneven development occurs only when $\bar{K} = 2K^*$.[6]

Following Mera (1975; Ch. 5), let us assume here that only the redistribution of capital is politically feasible, but income is not.[7] Then the income acquired by a region is equal to the income produced in the region, Y_i. Under this assumption, we introduce the following indices (Mera 1975) in order to evaluate alternative states of the system.

$$Efficiency\ index: \quad E = (Y_1 + Y_2)/\hat{Y},$$

$$Equity\ index:^8 \quad Q = Y_2/Y_1,$$

where $\hat{Y}$ is the maximum aggregate income achievable under each $\bar{K}$ (that is, $\hat{Y}$ corresponds to the solution of Problem 1). By definition, $0 \leqslant E \leqslant 1$, and under conditions (11–6), $0 \leqslant Q \leqslant 1$. The maximum efficiency, $E = 1$, is achieved on lines OA and BC in Figure 11–3(a), on line $OA–AB–BC$ in Figure 11–3(b); while in both figures, the maximum equity, $Q = 1$, is realized on the $45°$

---

6. It is not difficult to see that actually, when $\bar{K} = 2K^*$, any allocation of $\bar{K}$ between the two regions is a solution of Problem 1 under (11–12), that is, any allocation gives the same aggregate income.

7. If perfect income transfer were feasible politically, then in the present context of static analysis, no problem of trade-off between efficiency and equity would arise. However, in the real world, the political feasibility of regional income transfer is often very limited. Hence, we here consider this extreme case as an example. In the third section, the possibility of income transfer is treated more generally.

8. Note that, because of the assumption, $L_1 = L_2$,

$$Q = Y_2/Y_1 = (Y_2/L_2)/(Y_1/L_1)$$

which represents the ratio between regional per capita incomes.

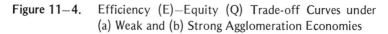

Figure 11–4.   Efficiency (E)–Equity (Q) Trade-off Curves under (a) Weak and (b) Strong Agglomeration Economies

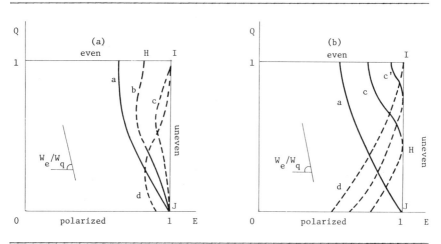

line OBC. If the system is so abundant in capital that $\bar{K} \geqslant 2K^e$ in (a) or $\bar{K} \geqslant 2K^*$ in (b), then there is no problem of trade-off between efficiency and equity; both maximum efficiency and maximum equity can be achieved by even development. On the other hand, if the system is relatively scarce in capital so that $\bar{K} < 2K^e$ in (a) or $\bar{K} < 2K^*$ in (b), then the problem of trade-off between efficiency and equity arises.

In order to analyze this trade-off problem, we draw *trade-off curves* between E and Q in Figure 11–4, which are obtained from the transformation curves in Figure 11–3. Shapes of $E–Q$ trade-off curves (measured by the horizontal difference from line IJ) in Figure 11–4 are essentially the same as shapes of $Y_1–Y_2$ transformation curves (measured by the difference from downward-sloped $45°$ lines) in Figure 11–3. Curves a, b, c, and d in Figure 11–4(a) correspond to curves a, b, c, and d in Figure 11–3(a), respectively; curves a, c, d in 11–4(b) correspond to curves a, c, d in 11–3(b). Curve c' in 11–4(b) corresponds to a curve in 11–3(b) which lies between curves c and d. Each side of the square in 11–4(a) and 11–4(b) corresponds to even, uneven, and polarized development. By definition,

$$\frac{dE}{dQ} = \frac{Y_1}{\hat{Y}} \frac{1 + dY_2/dY_1}{dY_2/dY_1 - Y_2/Y_1}.$$

Since $dY_2/dY_1 < 0$,

$$\frac{dE}{dQ} \gtreqless 0 \leftrightarrow \frac{dY_2}{dY_1} \lesseqgtr -1.$$

That is, $E-Q$ curve is negatively (positively) sloped if and only if the corresponding Y_1-Y_2 curve is less steep (steeper) than -1. In Figure 11−4, the part of each curve depicted by the broken line represents states which are dominated by (that is, Pareto-inferior to) some point on the curve. For example, in 11−4(a), the broken-line part of curve b is dominated by point H; the whole part of each curve starting from point I is dominated by that point. Hence, in the case of weak agglomeration diseconomies (that is, in Figure 11−4(a)), we see that the closer $\bar{K}$ is to $2K^e$, the larger the part of $E-Q$ curve dominated by even development. Alternatively, in the case of strong agglomeration diseconomies (that is, in Figure 11−4(b)), the closer $\bar{K}$ is to $\psi_m(0)$, the larger the part of $E-Q$ curve dominated by uneven development (that is, by a point on IJ line).

Suppose that some central planning authority chooses the optimal point on each $E-Q$ curve by the following rule:

$$\text{maximize} \quad w_e E + w_q Q,$$

where w_e and w_q are (positive) weights attached to efficiency and equity. Then, in the case of weak agglomeration diseconomies, we see from Figure 11−4(a) that either an even development or a polarized development is chosen. For example, if the ratio, w_e/w_q, is the one depicted in 11−4(a), polarized development is chosen for small $\bar{K}$; as $\bar{K}$ approaches $2K^e$, even development tends to be preferred. If $\bar{K} \geqslant 2K^e$, even development is chosen. In the case of strong agglomeration diseconomies, an uneven development which is close to side IJ might possibly be chosen. For example, under w_e/w_q depicted in 11−4(b), a polarized development is chosen for small $\bar{K}$; as $\bar{K}$ approaches $2K^*$, an uneven development tends to be chosen.

In the real world, polarized developments would not be politically acceptable. Given this condition, a more sensible approach to solving the efficiency−equity problem may be described as:

$$\text{maximize} \quad w_e E + w_q Q,$$
$$\text{subject to} \quad Q \geqslant Q_0.$$

That is, the minimum equity level (Q_o) tolerable to the system is fixed from the very start as a constraint. The optimal point on the part of $E-Q$ curve which satisfies the equity constraint is then determined by appropriately choosing weights w_e and w_q. According to this rule, uneven development, which is not most efficient, is chosen for small $\bar{K}$; for large $\bar{K}$, even development is chosen.

DYNAMIC ANALYSIS

The static model of the previous section sheds light on the relative merits of alternative distributional states at some future target date. However, as suggested by Mera (1975: Ch. 7), this static approach to an essentially dynamic problem is incomplete in the following aspects. First, though the choice of target date crucially affects the solution of the problem, a method for choosing an appropriate target date is not established. Second, the dynamic process whereby the desired state is achieved at the target date is left unspecified. Thus, the *regional investment process* which achieves each target state must be explicitly ascertained by theory. Furthermore, performance during both intermediate and post-target date must be taken into account. Considering these inherent short-comings to the static analysis, we present in this section a dynamic model for the study of regional efficiency and equity. The main analytical problem faced here is determining the regional investment process that achieves the desired state.

We keep the same modeling framework developed in the previous section. That is, we assume a system of two regions with identical production functions, given by equation (11–1). In order to focus on the process of regional capital accumulation, we also retain assumption (11–2), which implies that population in each region is constant over time. Production function (11–3) is now expressed as follows:

$$Y_l(t) = F(K_l(t)), \qquad l = 1, 2, \qquad (11\text{--}17)$$

where, $F(K_l(t)) = F(K_l(t), \bar{L})$, and $Y_l(t)$ and $K_l(t)$ are the production income and amount of capital stock of region l at time t. Function F satisfies the set of conditions in (11–4). We first address the problem of finding the mose efficient allocation of investments between regions in order to achieve the maximum growth of the system by a given target date, T. The political feasibility of the process and the equity aspect are considered later.

Suppose that the saving ratio, s, for the entire system is positive and, for simplicity of notation, is constant over time.[9] Then the total investment fund available for the system at time t will be equal to $s(Y_1(t) + Y_2(t))$. In addition, assume that capital stock is not transferable between regions, but that new investment is. Then, if $\theta_l(t)$, termed the *investment ratio*, is the proportion of investment allocated to region l ($= 1$ or 2) at time t, we have

$$\dot{K}_l(t) = \theta_l(t)s(Y_1(t) + Y_2(t)) = \theta_l(t)s(F(K_1(t)) + F(K_2(t))),$$

$$l = 1, 2,$$

where $\dot{K}_l(t) = dK_l(t)/dt$. Here, for simplicity, the depreciation of capital is neglected. The problem is to choose investment ratios, $\theta_l(t)$, $l = 1$, 2, at each time so as to maximize the total income, $Y_1(T) + Y_2(T) = F(K_1(T)) + F(K_2(T))$, at the target date, T. We can summarize this as follows.

Problem 2.   Choose investment ratios, $\theta_l(t)$, $l = 1$, 2, for each time t so as to maximize the total income at the target date,

$$F(K_1(T)) + F(K_2(T)), \tag{11-18}$$

subject to,

$$\dot{K}_l(t) = \theta_l(t)s(F(K_1(t)) + F(K_2(t))), \qquad l = 1, 2 \tag{11-19}$$

$$\theta_1(t) + \theta_2(t) = 1, \qquad \theta_1(t) \geqslant 0, \qquad \theta_2(t) \geqslant 0, \tag{11-20}$$

$$K_l(0) = K_l^o, \qquad l = 1, 2,$$

where K_l^o is the amount of capital in region l at the initial time, $t = 0$. It is assumed that $K_1^o + K_2^o > 0$ and $s > 0$.

Recall that in the previous section, one of the primary undertakings was determining the effect of parameter $\bar{K}$ (total amount of capital at the target date) on the solution of Problem 1. However, in Problem 2, $K_1(t)$ and $K_2(t)$ are functions of time, and so the

9. The reader can use $s(t)$ instead of s in the following analysis and see that all the results hold to be true when s is replaced by $s(t)$. It is not necessary to consider that ratio s reflects the "natural propensity to save" in the system. s can be the target saving ratio planned by the central authority, and this level can be enforced, for example, by taxation policy. For the study of the problem where the saving ratio is also a control variable, see Appendix F of Fujita (1978).

primary interest here involves assessing the effect of parameter T (the length of plan period) on the solution of Problem 2. It will be shown later that as long as T is greater than a minimum length, the solution of Problem 2 is essentially independent of T.

In order to obtain the necessary conditions for optimality in Problem 2, we introduce auxiliary variables, $P_l(t)$, $l = 1$, 2, and define the Hamiltonian function H by

$$H = P_1(t)\dot{K}_1 + P_2(t)\dot{K}_2$$
$$= (\theta_1 P_1(t) + \theta_2 P_2(t))s(F(K_1(t)) + F(K_2(t))).$$

Then, from the Maximum Principle in optimal control theory,[10] we must choose allocation ratios θ_1 and θ_2 at each time so as to maximize H. This implies that

$$\text{if} \quad P_1(t) > P_2(t), \quad \text{then} \quad \theta_1(t) = 1 \quad \text{and} \quad \theta_2(t) = 0,$$

$$\text{if} \quad P_1(t) < P_2(t), \quad \text{then} \quad \theta_1(t) = 0 \quad \text{and} \quad \theta_2(t) = 1,$$

$$\text{if} \quad P_1(t) = P_2(t), \quad \text{then} \quad 0 \leqslant \theta_l(t) \leqslant 1, \quad l = 1, 2,$$

$$\text{and} \quad \theta_1(t) + \theta_2(t) = 1. \tag{11-21}$$

From optimal control theory we know that the auxiliary variable, $P_l(t)$, represents the *incremental amount of final income* (11–18) which is obtained by exogenously increasing the stock of capital in region l by one unit at time t on the optimal growth path. Namely, $P_l(t)$ represents the shadow price (discounted back to time 0) of a unit of capital in region l at time t in terms of the final aggregate income. We simply call $P_l(t)$ the *price of capital* in region l at time t. From the Maximum Principle, the rate of price change, $\dot{P}_l(t) \equiv dP_l(t)/dt$, is given by $\dot{P}_l(t) = -\partial H/\partial K_l$. Hence, considering (11–21), we have

$$\dot{P}_l(t) = -\max(P_1(t), P_2(t))sF'(K_l(t)), \quad l = 1, 2. \tag{11-22}$$

Finally, from the terminal condition of the Maximum Principle, we have

$$P_l(T) = F'(K_l(T)), \quad l = 1, 2. \tag{11-23}$$

Using conditions (11–21), (11–22), and (11–23), we next examine some basic properties of the optimal growth path.[11] In the following

10. For the Maximum Principle, see Pontryagin and others (1962).

11. For the rigorous proofs of Lemmas 3, 4, and 5, and Theorem 3, see Appendix E of Fujita (1978). For simplicity here, we give only intuitive explanations of the lemmas and theorem.

as in the previous section, we examine only the case in which

$$K_1^o \geqslant K_2^o. \tag{11-24}$$

When both regions are in the decreasing phase (recall Figure 11–1), the marginal productivity of capital is always higher in the less developed region (that is, in the region with the smaller amount of capital stock); moreover, the marginal productivity continues to decrease in both regions as the capital increases in the future. Hence, the price of capital should be higher in the less developed region. That is,

Lemma 3.   On the optimal growth parth for Problem 2,
    1. If $K_1(t) > K_2(t) \geqslant K^*$, then $P_1(t) < P_2(t)$; hence $\theta_1(t) = 0$ and $\theta_2(t) = 1$.
    2. If $K_1(t) = K_2(t) \geqslant K^*$, then $P_1(t) = P_2(t)$; hence $\theta_1(t) = \theta_2(t) = 1/2$.
Namely, when both regions are in the decreasing phase, all of the investment should be allocated to the less developed region until both regions come to have the same amount of capital. After that, the investment should be equally divided between the regions.

On the other hand, when both regions are in the increasing phase, the marginal productivity of capital is greater in the more developed region (that is, the region with the larger amount of capital stock). Hence the price of capital should be higher in the more developed region. That is,

Lemma 4.   On the optimal growth path for Problem 2,
    1. If $K^* > K_1(t) > K_2(t)$, then $P_1(t) > P_2(t)$; hence if $K^* > K_1^o > K_2^o$, the whole investment should be allocated to region 1 at least until it goes out of the increasing phase.
    2. If $K^* > K_1(t) = K_2(t)$, then $P_1(t) > P_2(t)$ or $P_1(t) < P_2(t)$, and the choice of one relation among the two is arbitrary; hence if $K^* > K_1^o = K_2^o$, we must arbitrarily choose one of the two regions at the initial time, and all of the investment should be allocated to that region at least until it leaves the increasing phase.
The second part of this lemma presents another example of *unequal treatment of equals*. Namely, it says that even though the two regions are economically indistinguishable ($K_1^o = K_2^o$), the central authority must choose one as a favored region. To enable the central

Figure 11–5.   Relation among Functions ψ_a, ψ_s and ψ_m

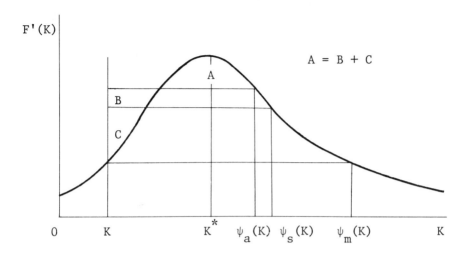

authority to make this "asymmetric choice," initial values of capital prices should have the "asymmetric relation" as described in the second part of Lemma 4.

Let us now turn to the investigation of relations between the capital prices when the two regions locate on opposite sides of the inflection point, K^*. Suppose first we have $K^* > K_2(t)$ and $K_1(t) > \psi_m(K_2(t))$, where function ψ_m is defined in (11–9). Then, the marginal productivity of capital is always greater in region 2 until it catches up to region 1 (refer to Figure 11–5). Even if $K_1(t) = \psi_m(K_2(t))$, that is, even if both regions have the same marginal productivity of capital at present (that is, at time t), the marginal productivity is going to increase in region 2 and decrease in region 1. Hence we should have

Lemma 5.   On the optimal growth path for Problem 2, if $K^* > K_2(t)$ and $K_1(t) \geqslant \psi_m(K_2(t))$, then $P_1(t) < P_2(t)$, where $t < T$.

From the first part of Lemma 3 and from Lemma 5, we see that if $K^* > K_2^o$ and $K_1^o \geqslant \psi_m(K_2^o)$, all of the investment should be allocated to region 2 until it catches up to region 1. Furthermore, Lemma 5 suggests that when the rest of planning period, $T = t$, is long enough, $P_1(t)$ is possibly equal to $P_2(t)$ only when $K_1(t)$ is *considerably* smaller than $\psi_m (K_2(t))$. That is, even if the marginal productivity of capital in region 2 is slightly less than that in region 1 at the present time, we should prefer region 2 because of its future. Therefore, a question of interest is: what is the lower limit of the range for $P_1(t) < P_2(t)$? That is, given $K_2(t) < K^*$, what is the value of $K_1(t)$ under which $P_1(t)$ becomes equal to $P_2(t)$? We denote such a value of $K_1(t)$ by $\psi_s(K_2(t))$. Namely, function ψ_s is defined by the condition:

$$P_1(t) = P_2(t) \quad \text{when} \quad K_1(t) = \psi_s(K_2(t)),$$

$$\text{where} \quad K_1(t) > K^* > K_2(t). \tag{11-25}$$

We call function ψ_s the *switching function* since, as we will see later, it tells us when the allocation of investment should be switched from the more to the less developed region. We can show that, given $K_2(t)$, if the rest of the plan period, $T - t$, is not less than a certain length, $T_{min}(K_2(t))$, then function $\psi_s(K_2(t))$ is independent of time t. Both the switching function $\psi_s(K)$ and the minimum planned period $T_{min}(K)$ can be determined by the next theorem. (For the derivation of this theorem, see Appendix A.)

Theorem 3. For each $K \leqslant K^*$, define the number, $\psi_s(K)$, by the solution of the following equation:

$$\int_K^{\psi_s(K)} \frac{F'(K_2) - F'(\psi_s(K))}{(F(\psi_s(K)) + F(K_2))^2} \, dK_2 = 0$$

$$\text{where} \quad \psi_s(K) \geqslant K^* \geqslant K. \tag{11-26}$$

And define function $T_{min}(K)$ by

$$T_{min}(K) = \int_K^{\psi_s(K)} \frac{1}{s(F(\psi_s(K)) + F(K_2))} \, dK_2. \tag{11-27}$$

Then, on the optimal growth path for Problem 2, if

$$T - t \geqslant T_{min}(K_2(t)),$$

then the relation

$$P_1(t) = P_2(t) \quad \text{and} \quad K_1(t) \geqslant K^* \geqslant K_2(t)$$

holds to be true if and only if $K_1(t) = \psi_s(K_2(t))$. Function $\psi_s(K)$, called the switching function, is uniquely defined on the domain, $0 \leqslant K \leqslant K^*$.

From definition (11–26), the following properties of the switching function can be immediately obtained.

Corollary 1. Switching function $\psi_s(K)$ defined by (11–26) has the following properties.

1. It is independent of time parameter t.
2. It is independent of the saving ratio s (or $s(t)$).
3. It is symmetric with respect to K_1 and K_2; if $K_1 = \psi_s(K_2)$ is the switching function under condition $K_1 \geqslant K^* \geqslant K_2$, then $K_2 = \psi_s(K_1)$ is the switching function under condition $K_2 \geqslant K^* \geqslant K_1$.
4. $\psi_s(K^*) = K^*$, and $d\,\psi_s(K)/dK < 0$.
5. $\psi_m(K) > \psi_s(K) > \psi_a(K)$ for each $0 \leqslant K < K^*$.

In the last property, function $\psi_a(K)$ is defined by

$$F'(\psi_a(K)) = \frac{F(\psi_a(K)) - F(K)}{\psi_a(K) - K}, \qquad \psi_a(K) \geqslant K^* \geqslant K.$$
$$(11-28)$$

Namely, $\psi_a(K)$ represents the *point of maximum average productivity of additional capital*. Observe that function $\psi_a(K)$ is equivalently defined by the following equation:

$$\int_K^{\psi_s(K)} (F'(K_2) - F'(\psi_a(K)))\, dK_2 = 0, \qquad \psi_a(K) \geqslant K^* \geqslant K.$$
$$(11-29)$$

Relationships among the three functions, ψ_a, ψ_m, and ψ_s are depicted in Figure 11–5.

Using Theorem 3 and Corollary 1, the *optimal switching curve*, $K_1 = \psi_s(K_2)$ $(K_1 \geqslant K^* \geqslant K_2)$ and $K_2 = \psi_s(K_1)$ $(K_2 \geqslant K^* \geqslant K_1)$ can be depicted as in Figure 11–6. From the fourth part of Corollary 1, $\psi_s(K_2)$ is a downward sloping curve of K_2. The *equal marginal productivity curve* ψ_m and the *maximum average productivity curve* ψ_a are also depicted in the figure.

Now suppose the plan period, T, is sufficiently long. Then, through an application of Lemma 3 and 4, together with Theorem 3 and Corollary 1, optimal growth paths for Problem 2 can be depicted as in Figure 11–6. For example, when the initial capital stock (K_1^o, K_2^o) is located at point b in the figure, the optimal capital-stock path is given by a curve, $b \to c \to e \to f$. On the other hand,

Figure 11–6.   Investment Switching Curve $\psi_s(K)$ and Optimal
Growth Paths for Problem 2

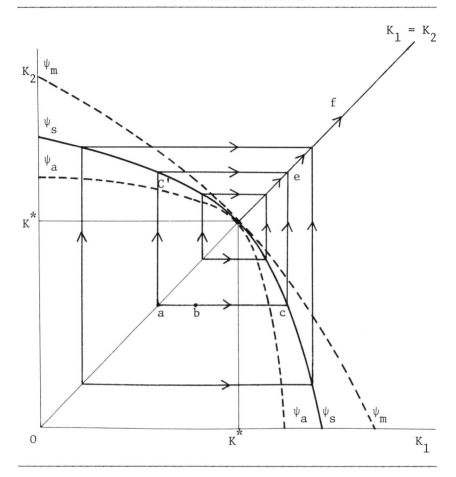

when the initial capital stock (K_1^o, K_2^o) is located, for example, at
point a in the figure, we must choose one region as our favorite
region. If we choose region 1, the optimal capital-stock path is
given by a curve, $a \rightarrow c \rightarrow e \rightarrow f$; but if we choose region 2, the
optimal path is given by $a \rightarrow c' \rightarrow e \rightarrow f$. Whenever the initial
position is below the switching curve, ψ_s, each optimal growth
path follows the next unique pattern.

$$polarized\ growth \rightarrow catching\ up \rightarrow even\ growth. \qquad (11\text{–}30)$$

We can show that the optimal switching curve ψ_s is generally not very close to curve ψ_a or curve ψ_m. This implies that on each optimal growth path for Problem 2, the investment allocation should be switched from the more developed region to the less developed region *considerably after* the average productivity of the total investment in the more developed region becomes maximum, but *long before* the marginal productivity of capital become the same in the two regions.

It is interesting to observe the following difference in the solutions of the static and dynamic allocation problems. Recall that in each case of static optimal allocation of capital stock, the optimal allocation pattern changed in two different ways depending on whether agglomeration diseconomies were strong or weak. However, in the case of dynamic investment allocation here, the optimal growth path follows a unique pattern given by (11−30). This difference arises from the following reason. In the case of static optimal allocation represented in Figure 11−3, the movement from point A to point B (in Figure 11−3(a) or (b)) requires a shift of capital stock from the more developed region to the less developed region, and a decrease in capital stock occurs in the more developed region. However, in the case of dynamic analysis, capital stock cannot be shifted between regions, by assumption, the capital stock cannot decrease in any region (because of no capital depreciation). Hence, in the case of dynamic analysis, a change like that from A to B in Figure 11−3 cannot occur. We therefore have a unique growth pattern.[12]

In Figure 11−6 it is assumed that the plan period T is so long that when each capital-stock path reaches the switching line $K_1 = \psi_s(K_2)$, the rest of the plan period is no less than $T_{min}(K_2)$ which is given by (11−27). Under this condition, optimal growth paths are independent of the length of plan period T. On the other hand, when the plan period T is not sufficiently long, the (short-run) optimal switching time of capital from the more developed region to the less developed regions depends on the plan length T.[13] A

12. If we introduce capital depreciation in Problem 2 and if the rate of capital depreciation is sufficiently large, two different growth patterns will emerge depending on whether agglomeration diseconomies are strong or weak.

13. Since in this section we are mainly concerned with the case in which the plan period is sufficiently long, we note only the following conclusion. When the plan period T is not sufficiently long, the (short-run) optimal switching curve lies between the two curves (ψ_a and ψ_m), and it converges to the (long-run) optimal switching curve, ψ_s, as T becomes larger.

repetition of such short-run optimal plans loses efficiency in the long run. Therefore, in order to achieve long-run efficiency in the growth of the system, given an intial capital stock (K_1^o, K_2^o), the plan length T must be sufficiently long so that

$$T \geqslant T_{min}(K_2^o). \tag{11-31}$$

So far, we have completely neglected the problem of equity, and how, via political constraints, it affects the optimal growth path. Now we shall modify the previous analysis in order to examine explicitly the efficiency—equity trade-off problem.

At each time t, the *production income* in each region is given by $Y_i(t) = F(K_i(t))$. Suppose that $Y_1(t) \geqslant Y_2(t)$. Then, under the political constraint on income transfer, the most equitable distribution of *disposable income*, $(Y_1^*(t), Y_2^*(t))$, is given by

$$Y_1^*(t) = Y_1(t) - \frac{\alpha}{2}(Y_1(t) - Y_2(t)),$$

$$Y_2^*(t) = Y_2(t) + \frac{\alpha}{2}(Y_1(t) - Y_2(t)), \tag{11-32}$$

where α is the index which represents the degree of the political feasibility for income transfer $(0 \leqslant \alpha \leqslant 1)$. $\alpha = 1$ means the perfect transferability of income, and $\alpha = 0$ means that no income transfer is feasible. Given the representation of disposable income as in (11–32), regional consumption $C_i(t)$ can be written as,

$$C_1(t) = (1 - s) Y_1^*(t),$$

$$C_2(t) = (1 - s) Y_2^*(t),$$

and the total investment fund as

$$sY_1^*(t) + sY_2^*(t) = s(Y_1(t) + Y_2(t)) = s(F(K_1(t)) + F(K_2(t))).$$

We now introduce an equity constraint on regional consumption. This is given by,

$$\frac{C_2(t)}{C_1(t)} \equiv \frac{Y_2^*(t)}{Y_1^*(t)} \geqslant Q, \tag{11-33}$$

where Q represents the lower limit on consumption equity and $0 \leqslant Q \leqslant 1$. Substituting (11–17) and (11–32) into (11–33), we have

$$F(K_2(t)) \left(1 - \frac{\alpha}{2} - \frac{\alpha Q}{2}\right) \geqslant F(K_1(t)) \left(Q - \frac{\alpha}{2} - \frac{\alpha Q}{2}\right).$$

Or, equivalently,

$$F(K_2(t)) \geqslant \beta F(K_1(t)),$$

where

$$\beta = \left(Q - \frac{\alpha}{2} - \frac{\alpha Q}{2}\right) \Big/ \left(1 - \frac{\alpha}{2} - \frac{\alpha Q}{2}\right). \tag{11-34}$$

Adding this constraint to Problem 2, a new problem of regional development with an equity constraint can be described as follows.

Problem 3. Choose investment ratios, $\theta_l(t)$, $l = 1$, 2, at each time so as to maximize the total income at the target date,

$$F(K_1(T)) + F(K_2(T)),$$

subject to

$$\dot{K}_l(t) = \theta_l(t) \, s(F(K_1(t)) + F(K_2(t))), \qquad l = 1, 2,$$

$$F(K_2(t)) \geqslant \beta F(K_1(t)), \qquad F(K_1(t)) \geqslant \beta F(K_2(t)),$$

$$\theta_1(t) + \theta_2(t) = 1, \qquad \theta_1(t) \geqslant 0, \qquad \theta_2(t) \geqslant 0,$$

$$K_l(0) = K_l^o, \qquad l = 1, 2 \tag{11-35}$$

where $K_1^o + K_2^o > 0$, $F(K_2^o) \geqslant \beta F(K_1^o)$, $F(K_1^o) \geqslant \beta F(K_2^o)$, $s > 0$, $0 \leqslant \beta \leqslant 1$.

Note that constraint (11–35) is binding only when $\beta > 0$. Namely, from (11–34), the solution of Problem 3 can be different from the solution of Problem 2 only if

$$Q > \frac{\alpha}{2 - \alpha}. \tag{11-36}$$

Let us assume that relation (11–36) holds true, and also that the plan period T is sufficiently long. Then, the optimal growth paths for Problem 3 can be obtained by applying the results of Problem 2 (see Appendix B), and they can be depicted as in Figure 11–7. In this figure, ψ_s is the same (switching) curve as in Figure 11–6. In the following discussion, we consider only the case in which $K_1^o \geqslant K_2^o$.

Figure 11–7.   Optimal Growth Paths for Problem 3

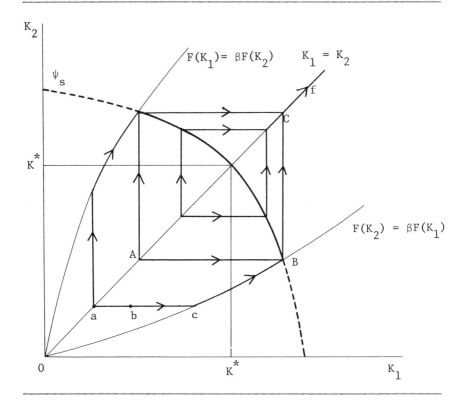

If the initial capital stock (K_1^o, K_2^o) is given at a point above the line AB and curve $F(K_2) = \beta F(K_1)$ in Figure 11–7 (that is, if both regions are well developed from the beginning), then the optimal growth path for Problem 3 is the same as that for Problem 2. In this case, the equity constraint (11–35) does not bind the optimal growth path. On the other hand, if the initial position is given at point b in Figure 11–7, the optimal growth path is given by $b \rightarrow c \rightarrow B \rightarrow C \rightarrow f$. Namely, if initial condition lies below line AB, the whole investment should first be allocated to the more developed region until the capital-stock path reaches the equity constraint line, $F(K_2) = \beta F(K_1)$. From here, the system grows along the equity constraint line until it reaches point B; then, the whole investment is allocated to the less developed region until it catches up to the more developed region; at which point, the two regions grow

Figure 11–8. Parameter Area Binding Problem 3

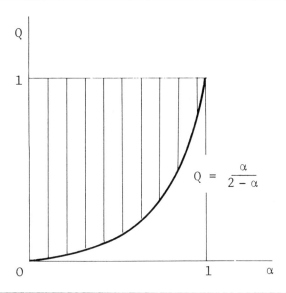

$$Q = \frac{\alpha}{2 - \alpha}$$

together. In short, if the system starts from a point below line AB (that is, the two regions are not both well developed at the beginning), the optimal growth path follows the next pattern:

polarized	*uneven*		*even*	
	$\rightarrow$	$\rightarrow$ *catching up* $\rightarrow$		. $\quad$ (11–37)
growth	*growth*		*growth*	

Let us now examine the impacts of parameters α and Q on the solution of Problem 3. As noted before, equity constraint (11–35) is binding only when relation (11–36) holds true. That is, parameter set (α, Q) is binding only when point (α, Q) falls within the shaded area in Figure 11–8. Therefore, if $\alpha = 1$ (that is, if income transfer is perfectly feasible), the maximum aggregate efficiency can be attained while satisfying any equity constraint. On the other hand, if $\alpha = 0$ (that is, if no income transfer is feasible), there is always a trade-off between aggregate efficiency and the equity constraint. To examine this trade-off, let us define

efficiency index: $E = (Y_1(T) + Y_2(T))/(\hat{Y}_1(T) + \hat{Y}_2(T))$

$$(11-38)$$

Figure 11–9.   Trade-off Curves between E and Q

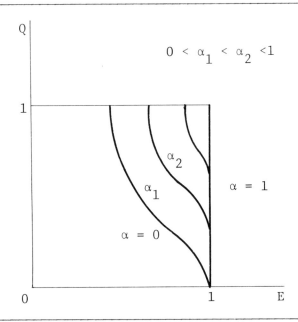

where $\hat{Y}_1(T) + \hat{Y}_2(T)$ is the maximum aggregate income obtained by the solution of Problem 2 at the final period T.

The trade-off curves between E (aggregate efficiency) and Q (equity constraint index) can be depicted as in Figure 11–9.[14] We observe from this figure that the problem of trade-off between efficiency and equity is more easily solved as α gets larger (that is, as income transfer grows easier). Given α (the degree of political feasibility for income transfer), the central authority must choose an appropriate point on the trade-off curve corresponding to α.

MARKET VERSUS PLANNING

In the previous section, we obtained optimal growth paths both with and without an equity constraint. Let us now briefly examine

14. Note that although the shapes of the trade-off curves in Figure 11–9 change with the length of plan period T, their ordering for different values of α and the interceptions between each curve and the vertical line, $E = 1$, do not change with T as long as T is sufficiently long.

whether these paths can be achieved by a competitive market mechanism. We will assume that the agglomeration economies and diseconomies under consideration are *Marshallian external economies*. That is, the production function of firm i in region l ($l = 1, 2$) can be described as follows:

$$Y_i = g(K_l, L_l)f(K_i, L_i)$$
$$= g(K_l, \bar{L})f(K_i, L_i)$$
$$= g(K_l)f(K_i, L_i) \tag{11-39}$$

where Y_i is the rate of output by firm i, K_i is the amount of capital, and L_i is the amount of labor used by firm i. K_l and L_l represent the total amount of capital and labor employed by all firms in region l. Here, $g(K_l, \bar{L}) \equiv g(K_l)$ represents the agglomeration economies (or diseconomies) which are experienced by each firm in region l as a function of the magnitude of the production activities in that region. Function g represents the so-called Marshallian economies which are external to each firm but internal to the region.

To make the economy consistent with the assumption of perfect competition, let us assume that $f(K, L)$ is linearly homogeneous, and concave with respect to K and L,

$$\partial f(K, L)/\partial K > 0, \qquad \partial f(K, L)/\partial L > 0. \tag{11-40}$$

Let us also assume that each firm takes the size of the regional economy as given and chooses the best combination of input factors. Then, at the equilibrium at each time t, we have

$$\sum_i Y_i(t) = g(K_l)f(K_l(t), \bar{L}), \qquad l = 1, 2. \tag{11-41}$$

Putting $f(K, \bar{L}) \equiv f(K)$, and defining

$$F(K) = g(K)f(K), \tag{11-42}$$

we have

$$\sum_i Y_i(t) = F(K_l(t)), \qquad l = 1, 2$$

which is the regional production function previously defined by (11-3). At equilibrium, the capital rent, $R_l(t)$, in each region at time t is given by

$$R_l(t) = g(K_l(t))f'(K_l(t)), \qquad l = 1, 2.$$

Figure 11–10.   Relation between $F'(K)$ and $R(K)$ Curves

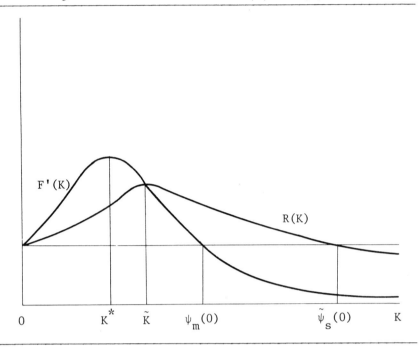

Hence, if we define

$$R(K) = g(K)f'(K), \qquad (11-43)$$

we get

$$R_l(t) = R(K_l(t)), \qquad l = 1, 2. \qquad (11-44)$$

From (11–42) and (11–43), we also have

$$F'(K) - R(K) = g'(K)f(K), \qquad (11-45)$$

so,

$$F'(K_l(t)) - R_l(t) = g'(K_l(t))f(K_l(t)), \qquad l = 1, 2. \qquad (11-46)$$

Let us further assume that the *agglomeration function*, $g(K)$, has the following property: $g(K)$ is continuous, $g(K) > 0$ for all K, and there exists $\tilde{K}(\tilde{K} \geqslant K^*)$ such that

$$g'(K) > 0 \quad \text{for} \quad K < \tilde{K}, \quad \text{and} \quad g'(K) < 0 \quad \text{for} \quad K > \tilde{K}.$$

$$(11-47)$$

That is, agglomeration economies are dominant for small regional

Figure 11–11.   Comparison of Optimal Switching Curve ψ_s and Market Switching Curve $\tilde{\psi}_s$

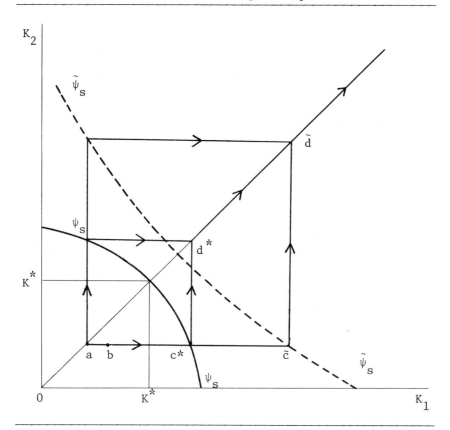

economies, while agglomeration diseconomies are dominant for large regional economies, which endure considerable congestion effects. From (11–4), (11–46), and (11–47), the relation between $F'(K)$ and $R(K)$ can be depicted as in Figure 11–10.[15]

Investment behavior in a dynamic economy with the presence of agglomeration economies is not easy to specify. To simplify the analysis, let us presume here that investors are *myopic* in their decisions. This means they follow the signal of the rental price of capital at each time. That is, the investment allocation ratios, $\tilde{\theta}_1(t)$ and $\tilde{\theta}_2(t)$, determined by the market, have the following property:

15. In Figure 11–10, it is assumed for graphical convenience that $f(0) = 0$. But this is not necessary for the following analysis.

$$\tilde{\theta}_1(t) = 1 \quad \text{and} \quad \tilde{\theta}_2(t) = 0 \quad \text{if} \quad R_1(t) > R_2(t),$$
$$\tilde{\theta}_1(t) = 0 \quad \text{and} \quad \tilde{\theta}_2(t) = 1 \quad \text{if} \quad R_1(t) < R_2(t).$$
(11−48)

Let us define a function $\tilde{\psi}_s(K)$ by

$$R(K) = R(\tilde{\psi}_s(K)) \quad \text{where} \quad K \leqslant \tilde{K} \leqslant \tilde{\psi}_s(K). \qquad (11-49)$$

We call curve $\tilde{\psi}_s(K)$ the *market switching curve* since it represents the line on which the market switches investment from the more developed region to the less developed region.

Both the optimal switching curve ψ_s (defined by (11−26)) and the market switching curve $\tilde{\psi}_s$ are depicted in Figure 11−11. From Corollary 1 of Theorem 3 and from Figure 11−10,

$$\psi_s(K) < \psi_m(K) < \tilde{\psi}_s(K). \qquad (11-50)$$

Therefore, the market switching curve $\tilde{\psi}_s$ is above the optimal switching curve ψ_s. By using this figure, we can compare optional growth paths (without an equity constraint) and market growth paths. For example, suppose the initial position of the economy is given at point b in Figure 11−11. Then the optimal growth path and the market growth path are described, respectively, as follows:

$$\text{the optimal:} \quad b \to c^* \to d^* \to \ldots,$$

$$\text{the market:} \quad b \to \tilde{c} \to \tilde{d} \to \ldots.$$

If we consider the equity constraint given by (11−35), the investment may be switched to region 2 before reaching point c^*.

Therefore, we can conclude that if the market economy follows the myopic capital allocation described by (11−49), an amount of capital in excess of the social optimum tends to be accumulated in the more developed region. The market growth path is inefficient since it cannot correctly account for the future agglomeration economies and diseconomies nor the effects of external economies and diseconomies at present. Hence, when investment occurs within a competitive economy, allocation will be switched from the more developed region to the less developed region only after the more developed region becomes so congested that agglomeration economies accumulated in the initial stages are completely outweighed by agglomeration diseconomies accumulated in the later stages. In order to achieve the socially desired growth path, the control of regional investment allocation by the central authority is necessary.

This might be accomplished, for example, by a congestion tax on investment.

CONCLUDING REMARKS

In this chapter, we have analyzed the efficiency—equity trade-off problem, given the presence of agglomeration economies and diseconomies in regional production. Though we have obtained some useful results, they are based on a number of simplifying assumptions. This means that several extensions are needed to deepen the theory and make it more comprehensive. In particular, we must generalize the analysis by considering the case when regions possess different production functions. We must also consider mobile factors of production, especially labor migration. In order to study interregional trade and investment simultaneously, the hypothetical economy of the models must be broadened to include a field of multiple commodities. Representing production by a single, homogeneous income is unrealistic. As a final extension, it would be valuable to reformulate the problem in a game theoretic context for applications in which no central authority is present to make binding decisions. It is hoped that this chapter has laid a foundation from which these important extensions might be effectively pursued.

APPENDIX A: DERIVATION OF SWITCHING FUNCTION $\psi_s(K)$

We here derive the equation of switching function, (11–26), from an intuitive argument based on Figure 11–5. Suppose that at some time, say $t = t'$, we have

$$P_1(t') = P_2(t'), \quad \text{and} \quad K_1(t') \equiv K_1' > K^* > K_2(t') \equiv K_2'.$$
$$(A11-1)$$

For example, $K_1' = \psi_s(K)$ and $K_2' = K$ in Figure 11–5. Then, since the marginal productivity of capital is going to increase in region 2 with the increase in the amount of capital, and it is going to decrease in region 1,

$$\left.\begin{array}{l} \theta_1(t) = 0, \quad \theta_2(t) = 1 \\ P_2(t) > P_1(t) \end{array}\right\} \quad \begin{array}{l} \text{for all } t > t' \text{ until region 2} \\ \text{catches up region 1.} \end{array} \qquad \text{(A11–2)}$$

Now suppose that at a time $t(>t')$, $K_2(t) = K_2$ while $K_1(t) = K_1'$, where $K_2' < K_2 < K_1'$. Then the value of the contribution of one unit of capital in region l per unit of time at time t (to the increase of the final income of the economy) is given by

$$P_2 s F'(K_l) = \text{(the value of one unit of the investment fund in the economy)}$$
$$\times \text{(the saving ratio of the economy)} \times \text{(the marginal product}$$
$$\text{of one unit of capital in region } l), l = 1, 2,$$

where $P_2 = P_2(t)$. Note that, in the above calculation, the value of one unit of the investment fund in the economy should be measured by the price of capital in region 2 at that time since it is higher in region 2 as long as $K_2' < K_2 < K_1'$. Hence, the difference in the contributions of one unit of capital in the two regions per unit of time is given by

$$P_2 s F'(K_2) - P_2 s F'(K_1').$$

Hence, for the time interval dt, the difference is

$$s(F'(K_2) - F'(K_1')) P_2 dt.$$

Since all investment is allocated to region 2, that is, $\theta_2(t) = 1$, when $K_2' < K_2 < K_1'$, from (11–19) we have $dK_2/dt = s(F(K_1') + F(K_2))$, and hence $dt = dK_2/s(F(K_1') + F(K_2))$. Therefore, the above difference can be rewritten as

$$\frac{F'(K_2) - F'(K_1')}{F(K_1') + F(K_2)} P_2 dK_2.$$

This difference is negative when $K_2' \leqslant K_2 < \psi_m^{-1}(K_1')$, and positive when $\psi_m^{-1}(K_1') < K_2 < K_1'$. Hence, for "the losses" and "the gains" to cancel out each other while K_2 moves from K_2' to K_1', the next relation should hold.

$$\int_{K_2'}^{K_1'} \frac{F'(K_2) - F'(K_1')}{F(K_1') + F(K_2)} P_2 dK_2 = 0. \qquad \text{(A11–3)}$$

Next, since $dt = dK_2/s(F(K_1') + F(K_2))$, from (11–22) we have

$$\frac{dP_2}{dK_2} = \frac{-P_2 F'(K_2)}{F(K_1') + F(K_2)} \quad \text{for} \quad K_2' \leqslant K_2 \leqslant K_1'.$$

Solving this differential equation, we have

$$P_2(K_2) = P_2(K_2 = K_1') \exp\left(\int_{K_2}^{K_1'} \frac{F'(K)}{F(K_1') + F(K)} dK\right)$$

$$= P_2(K_2 = K_1') \frac{2F(K_1')}{F(K_1') + F(K_2)}. \qquad (A11-4)$$

Substituting (A11−4) into (A11−3) and neglecting constant terms, we have

$$\int_{K_2'}^{K_1'} \frac{F'(K_2) - F'(K_1')}{(F(K_1') + F(K_2))^2} dK_2 = 0.$$

Replacing $K_2' = K$ and $K_1' = \psi_s(K)$, we obtain (11−26).

APPENDIX B: OPTIMAL GROWTH PATHS FOR PROBLEM 3

Here we consider the case in which the plan period, T, is sufficiently long so that the optimal growth path reaches a point on the $K_1 = K_2$ line (above ψ_s curve) by the end of plan period. Only a brief sketch of the proof is given. It is obvious that if the initial point occurs above line AB and curve $F(K_2) = \beta F(K_1)$ in Figure 11−7, then the optimal growth path for Problem 3 is identical to that of Problem 2. In this case, the equity constraint is not binding the optimal growth path. To obtain the optimal growth path originating from a point below line AB in Figure 11−7, we define the Hamiltonian H by

$$H = P_1\dot{K}_1 + P_2\dot{K}_2 + q(F'(K_2)\dot{K}_2 - \beta F'(K_1)\dot{K}_1)$$

$$= [\theta_1(P_1 - \beta qF'(K_1)) + \theta_2(P_2 + qF'(K_2))] s(F(K_1) + F(K_2))$$

where P_1, P_2, and q are auxiliary variables. From the Maximum Principle (Pontryagin and others 1962, and Hestenes 1966), we know that at each time t, $\theta_1(t)$ and $\theta_2(t)$ must be chosen so as to maximize function H. And, at each time,

$$\dot{P}_1 = -\partial H/\partial K_1, \qquad \dot{P}_2 = -\partial H/\partial K_2,$$

$$\dot{q} \leqslant 0, \qquad (F(K_2) - \beta F(K_1))\dot{q}(t) = 0,$$

where

$$P_1(T) = F'(K_1(T)), \qquad P_2(T) = F'(K_2(T)), \qquad q(T) = 0.$$

Suppose that the initial capital stock, (K_1^o, K_2^o), is given at point b in Figure 11–7. Consider a feasible growth path which is not the one depicted in Figure 11–7 ($b \to c \to B \to C \to f$). For example, consider the growth path, $b \to x \to z \to B \to$. . . in Figure 11–B1. Note that the optimal path starting from point b never crosses or goes above line AB before reaching point B, and that, in the area above line AB, the optimal growth path is time-invariant. Consider the alternative growth path, $b \to x \to y \to z \to B$, depicted in Figure 11–B1. By using the optimality conditions given above and by employing a method similar to that used for the proof of Lemma 6.4 in Fujita (1978), we can show that this alternative is better than the path, $b \to x \to z \to B$. Thus, we can conclude that the optimal growth path must follow the line, $b \to c \to B$.

Figure 11–B1.   Alternative Growth Paths

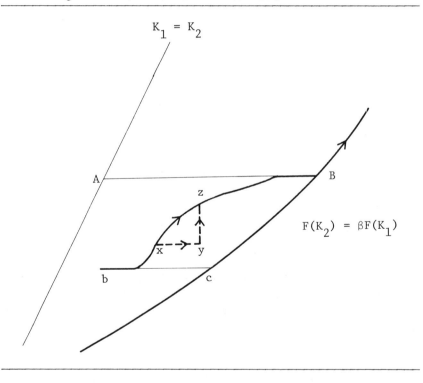

REFERENCES

Carlina, G.A. 1981. "Manufacturing Agglomeration Economies as Returns to Scale: A Production Function Approach." Paper presented at the Regional Science Association Meetings, Montreal, November 15.

Fujita, M. 1978. *Spatial Development Planning*. Amsterdam: North-Holland.

Hestenes, M.R. 1966. *Calculus of Variations and Optimal Control Theory*. New York: Wiley.

Kawashima, T. 1975. "Urban Agglomeration Economies in Manufacturing Industries." *Regional Science Association Papers* 34: 157–175.

Mera, K. 1975. *Income Distribution and Regional Development*. Tokyo: University of Tokyo Press.

Pontryagin, L.S., V.G. Boltyanskii, R.V. Gamkrelidze, and E.F. Mishenko. 1962. *Mathematical Theory of Optimal Process* (English translation). New York: Interscience.

Richardson, H.W. 1977. "Aggregate Efficiency and Interregional Equity." In *Spatial Inequalities and Regional Development* edited by H. Folmer and J. Oosterhaven. The Hague, Netherlands: Martinus Nijhoff Publishing.

Takayama, A. 1972. *International Trade*. New York: Holt, Rinehart & Winston.

Author Index

225

Subject Index

About the Editors

Walter Isard is professor of economics at Cornell University. He received his Ph.D. in economics from Harvard University and has subsequently been awarded honorary doctorates from Poznan Academy of Economics (Poland), Erasmus University of Rotterdam (Netherlands), University of Karlsruhe (West Germany), Umea University (Sweden), and University of Illinois. Dr. Isard has been active in peace research for many years and was a founding member of the Peace Science Society (International). He has authored or co-authored numerous articles and books, including *Methods of Regional Analysis* (MIT Press, 1960), *General Theory: Social, Political, Economic and Regional* (MIT Press, 1969), and *Spatial Dynamics and Optimal Space-Time Development* (North Holland, 1979).

Yoshimi Nagao is professor of transportation engineering at Kyoto University, Japan. He received his Ph.D in engineering from Kyoto University in 1961. From 1945–1965, he was engaged in transportation planning and management at the Ministry of Transport of Japan, and has been a professor at Kyoto University since 1965.

He was the Chairman of the Committee of Planning of Civil Engineering Systems and has been the Chairman of Kansai Branch of Japan Association for Planning Administration since 1980. He has served on many governmental committees, having been awarded a decoration by the Minister of Transport in 1982 for his contribution to the development of port and harbours of Japan.

He has authored the well-known books *Port and Harbour Engineering* (1968) and *Introductory Treatise on Planning of Public Works* (1973) and many other items.

List of Contributors

Ulrich Blum is at the Institute of Economic Policy and Research, University of Karlsruhe, Germany.

Bruce Burton is in the Fields of Regional Science and Peace Science, Cornell University, Ithaca, New York.

Hajime Eto is at the University of Tsukuba's Institute of Socio-Technology, Sakura, Ibaraki, Japan.

Masahisa Fujita is in the Department of Regional Science, University of Pennsylvania, Philadelphia.

Rolf H. Funck is at the Institute of Economic Policy and Research, University of Karlsruhe, Germany.

Walter Isard is in the Fields of Economics and Peace Science, Cornell University, Ithaca, New York.

Katsuhiko Kuroda is in the Department of Transportation Engineering, Kyoto University, Japan.

Yee Leung is in the Department of Geography, The Chinese University of Hong Kong, Shatin, Hong Kong.

Kyoko Makino is in the Department of Mathematics, Chuo University, Kasuga, Bunkyo-ku, Tokyo, Japan.

Hisayoshi Morisugi is in the Civil Engineering Department, Gifu University, Gifu, Japan. He is presently visiting lecturer in the Regional Science Department, University of Pennsylvania, Philadelphia.

Yoshimi Nagao is in the Department of Transportation Engineering, Kyoto University, Japan.

Peter Nijkamp is in the Department of Economics, The Free University, Amsterdam, The Netherlands.

Jean H.P. Paelinck is in the Rotterdam Institute for Multi- and Interdisciplinary Research, Erasmus University, Rotterdam.

Noboru Sakashita is in the Institute of Socio-Economic Planning, University of Tsukuba.

Christine Smith is in the Department of Economics, University of Queensland, Australia.

Paulus H. Vossen is in the Rotterdam Institute for Multi- and Interdisciplinary Research, Erasmus University, Rotterdam.

Ikujiro Wakai is in the Department of Transportation Engineering, Kyoto University, Japan.